Graphic Design C

The Desktop Publisher's Guid
to Designing Business Docum
Forms, and Web Sites

MARVIN JACOBS CFSP
President
Ameritype & Art, Inc.
Valley View, Ohio

Teachers open the door.
You enter by yourself.

Chinese Proverb

Words & Pictures
Publishing

Published by
Words & Pictures Publishing
SAN 255-0989
P.O. Box 40
North Olmsted, OH 44070
216-524-9664
Fax: 216-524-7714
E-mail: mbj1@adelphia.net
www.wppublishing.com

Preface

The development of affordable and user-friendly desktop publishing systems has given a lot of business people advanced design tools without giving them advanced design skills or training.

Easy access to desktop software has resulted in an avalanche of poorly designed business documents, forms, and Web sites being created by armies of desktop publishers with little or no training in graphic design concepts. Having sophisticated desktop software with a lot of design options doesn't automatically guarantee a good design. You can buy a Stradivarius, but it doesn't make you a violinist... you get the idea.

What the business desktop publisher needs is a working knowledge of graphic design concepts to supplement the desktop publishing software know-how. The object of this book is to provide the graphic design concepts, that in concert with software design tools, will allow the desktop publisher to create documents that effectively communicate information.

The book is divided into three parts. Part One covers business graphics for documents like newsletters, brochures, letterheads, and reports. Part Two covers the design of paper business forms and an overview of electronic forms. Part Three covers Web site design, generating traffic to Web sites, and making money from Web site sales.

This book is both a textbook for students and a book for business desktop publishers. It contains time-tested design fundamentals and step-by-step procedures for business documents, business forms, and e-commerce Web sites. The result, I believe, is an easy to understand and supportive book that will help you with your graphic design projects.

- Marvin Jacobs

Author

MARVIN JACOBS CFSP...
is the president of Ameritype, a graphic design and desktop publishing corporation in Cleveland, Ohio, established in 1964 as a typesetting company.

Ameritype has served many hundreds of clients including such well-known firms as The Coca-Cola Company, Eastman Kodak, TRW, Inc. and Subway Restaurants.

Marvin Jacobs has written numerous articles for printing industry trade journals and is the co-author, with Associate Professor Linda Studer, of *Forms Design II, The Course for Paper and Electronic Forms* and *Graphic Design for 21st Century Desktop Publishers.*

Mr. Jacobs has made more than 300 graphic arts presentations at conventions, seminars and association meetings, including ones in most major U.S. cities and in London. Topics covered in these presentations include graphic design, forms design, and Web site design.

He is a Certified Forms System Professional (CFSP), a certification awarded by the Business Forms Management Association. He has served on the BFMA Board of Directors and the CFSP Certification Board, and he is the recipient of the Jo Warner Award, BFMA's highest honor.

Acknowledgment

SHARON JACOBS
I want to express my gratitude to Sharon Jacobs, production manager at Ameritype, for her invaluable counseling in the writing of the book and also for her expert typesetting and composition.

Sharon Jacobs also created most of the graphics, utilizing her design skills and expertise with desktop publishing software.

CONTENTS

Business Graphic Design

Business Graphic Design

Business Graphic Design

Business Graphic Design

Business Graphic Design

Business Graphic Design

Business Graphic Design

PART ONE

Business Graphic Design

Business Graphic Design

Business Graphic Design

Business Graphic Design

Business Graphic Design

Business Graphic Design

Business Graphic Design

Business Graphic Design

Business Graphic Design

Business Graphic Design

Business Graphic Design

Business Graphic Design

Business Graphic Design

If you don't know what your objectives are, how will you know when you get there?

CHAPTER 1

PRE-DESIGN PLANNING

Better measure ten times and cut once, instead of measuring once and cutting ten times.
- A folk saying

Chapter One Objectives

After studying this chapter, you should be able to:

1. Explain the objective of effective graphic design.

2. Identify four items that should be included in a checklist for pre-design planning.

3. Describe the first step in planning an effective document.

4. State why the designer should determine the profile of the expected readers.

5. Discuss how budget limitations can affect the graphic design and reproduction method.

6. Explain how deadlines can affect the quality of graphic designs.

Effective graphic design begins with pre-design planning

You don't create an efficient document by pushing type and pictures around a page until it looks good. You need to understand the objective of the document and then design to accomplish the objective.

The designer needs to be more than hands on a keyboard or a finger on a mouse.

Pictures of hot dogs, people playing volleyball or even a humorous photo of a man feasting on an ear of corn help support the objective of a picnic flyer, influencing people to attend.

Trying to design an effective business document without at least some planning is like trying to build an architectural project without blueprints.

An effective business document is one that clearly communicates a message. You don't create an effective document by pushing type and pictures around a page until it looks good. This trial and error method can generate a visually pleasing design but it usually won't generate the most effective document.

An effective document, one that clearly communicates a message, is produced when the designer performs the planning work required before designing.

A checklist of pre-design planning includes:
- Determining the document objective.
- Determining the needs of the expected readers.
- Considering budget limitations and production resources.
- Considering the deadline.

Determining the document objective

The first step in planning an effective design is to determine the primary objective, the purpose of the design. The objective might be to sell a product or service, to raise funds for a non-profit organization, to inform, to influence opinion, or to gather information.

The designer needs to be more than hands on a keyboard or a finger on a mouse. It is not enough to create a document with a pleasing appearance. The designer must understand the objective of the document and needs to create a design that supports the content in achieving the objective.

For example, if the objective of an inter-office mailer is to get as many employees as possible to attend the company picnic, you need to focus on the reasons why they should attend. People attend picnics to relax and have fun. They go to enjoy food and drink, to play games, and to enjoy the company of their colleagues. Therefore, the headline, the pictures and the text should focus on the reasons why they should attend the picnic.

Not all documents require pictures to support headlines and text but in a picnic mailer, illustrations or photographs obviously would help to achieve the objective of getting a large turnout at a company picnic.

Let's look at another sample. If the objective of a direct mail piece is to raise funds for a pet rescue organization, the designer needs to gather information from the organization and then highlight the plight of the homeless and unwanted animals and the reasons why the recipient should help them by making a donation or by volunteering to help.

By focusing like a laser on the objective of the document, which is to provide motivation for people to send donations to Caroline's Kids Pet Rescue, the designer can structure the layout to support the objective.

By understanding the objective, the designer can shape the design to support the copy instead of just pushing type and pictures around to make a visually attractive layout.

For example, in a direct mail plea from a pet rescue organization, a headline could be:

It's a terrible thing to die because nobody wants you

The designer could make this even more effective with the addition of a photo as shown below:

It's a terrible thing to die because nobody wants you

Judy Brown

By adding a photo of Judy Brown, founder of Caroline's Kids Pet Rescue, the designer can add human interest to the layout. People like to see pictures of other people.

Caroline

Caroline is no longer with us. She has gone to the Rainbow Bridge but she is the inspiration for Caroline's Kids Pet Rescue. (Visit our web site at www.carolines-kids.org where you can read about Caroline and the Rainbow Bridge.)

Determining the needs of the expected readers

The designer should determine the nature and the needs of the expected audience, the people who will be reading the document. Will they be office workers, corporate executives, college students, elementary school children, or senior citizens. Will they be electrical engineers, interior designers or truck drivers?

The designer needs to determine who will be the readers of the document and structure the design to match the readers.

The nature and needs of the reader include considerations such as:
- *Larger type for senior citizens and for children*
- *Serif type for conservative documents*
- *Sans-serif type for adventurous documents*
- *Conservative colors for conservative documents..*
- *Flamboyant colors for adventurous documents.*

Thinking about the expected readers can help the designer make decisions about typeface selection, type size and typography, and the general tone of the document.

Many doctors, lawyers, accountants and others in financial and professional occupations prefer conservative serif typefaces and centered layouts for their letterheads and other documents

CUYAHOGA COUNTY MEDICAL GROUP
12345 Lorain Road
North Ridgeville, OH 44070

A retail store selling heavy industrial equipment would usually call for a sans-serif typeface with a bold personality.

**Cuyahoga Construction Equipment
321 Industrial Parkway
Bentley, OH 44125**

It would be easier for senior citizens to read a document if the designer would use larger type.

Senior citizens would find larger type like this easier to read.

They might have difficulty reading type like this.

In addition to typeface selections, the designer needs to understand the reader so choices about illustrations, photos, and the general tone of the document can be appropriately made.

Everything (typefaces, illustrations, photographs, paper stock, ink colors, paper colors, etc.) contributes to the image that a document conveys about the message. The design should create an image consistent with the emotion engendered by the document message.

The graphic design for a memorial service program would be formal and dignified whereas the graphic design for a travel brochure would be adventurous. The typeface selection is particularly important. The type must match and reinforce the message. The appropriate typeface strengthens the message. Inappropriate type weakens the message and confuses the reader.

To design a successful document, the designer must determine the nature of the expected readers and structure the layout to appeal to these readers.

All elements of a design must focus on the expected readers. These elements can include:
- *Typeface selection*
- *Type size*
- *Type alignment*
- *Type color*
- *Page size*
- *Illustrations*
- *Photographs*
- *Symbols*
- *Borders*
- *Paper color*
- *Paper texture*
- *Paper weight*

Considering budget limitations and production resources

The amount of money that can be spent on a document affects the method of reproduction and consequently the design itself. Is the designer limited to black ink or is spot color or full color an option?

Will the design be reproduced on a black and white copier, a color copier, a black and white laser printer, a color laser printer, a sheet fed offset press, or a continuous web press?

Will the budget and the reproduction method allow full color, diecutting, scoring, punching, perforating, screens, variable screens or other features?

Usually the sky isn't the limit for designers. They need to consider budget limitations for designing and reproducing a document.

Usually the sky isn't the limit for designers, They need to consider budget limitations and reproduction methods available to them.

Considering the deadline

Some deadlines may be longer than others but the real world reality is that all graphic arts printing is RUSH. You can see the following sign on the walls of many print shops:

Shall I rush your rush job before I rush the rush job I was rushing before you rushed in?

Tight deadlines mean less time to work on the layout and often result in simpler and less effective designs.

Naturally, the longer the deadline, the more time and therefore, the better chance you have, to create an appealing and effective design. Tight deadlines mean less time to work on the layout and often result in simpler and less effective designs.

Summary

Pre-design planning will help ensure the creation of a successful graphic design.

In review, a checklist of pre-design planning includes:

- Determining the document objective.
- Determining the needs of the expected readers.
- Considering budget limitations and production resources.
- Considering the deadline.

Chapter One Questions

1. What is the objective of effective graphic design? Explain why determining the objective of the document is the first step in planning a graphic design.

2. List four items that should be included in a checklist for pre-design planning.

3. Explain why the designer needs to find out who the expected readers of the document will be.

4. Name three factors that contribute to the image that a document conveys about the message.

5. Describe how the budget and the reproduction method can affect the design?

6. Explain the influence of the deadline on the quality of the design.

CHAPTER
2

FUNDAMENTALS OF BUSINESS GRAPHIC DESIGN

Those having torches will pass them along to others

– Plato

Chapter Two Objectives

After studying this chapter, you should be able to:

1. Explain why desktop publishers need to know graphic design fundamentals as well as how to use desktop publishing software.

2. Discuss the importance of having the design provide instantly understandable communication.

3. Explain the importance and techniques of using contrast to make the design eye-catching and easy to navigate.

4. Describe techniques to design a layout that is easy to read.

5. Explain why type is the fundamental building block of graphic designs.

6. Compare and contrast design alignment systems.

7. Select the appropriate alignment system to match the tone of the document.

Graphic design fundamentals are always at the foundation of successful designs

Business documents that were once designed by trained graphic designers and typesetters are now often the responsibility of untrained desktop publishers.

In addition to benefits, the desktop publishing revolution has introduced the frustrations of graphic design to a growing number of people. Business documents that had been traditionally typeset by trained graphic designers and typesetters are now often the responsibility of desktop publishers, many of whom do not have graphic design training.

Learning and applying the graphic design fundamentals in this chapter will help desktop publishers who do not have graphic design training. These fundamentals will provide a solid base for creating successful business layouts.

Graphic design fundamentals for designing business documents are:

The graphic design fundamentals in this chapter provide a solid base for creating successful business layouts.

1. Provide instantly understandable communications.

2. Use contrast to make the design eye-catching and easy to navigate.

3. Make the layout easy to read.

4. Use typography as the fundamental building block.

5. Use an appropriate alignment system.

Provide instantly understandable communication

The reader does not want to struggle to understand your document. Make your message clear and easy to understand.

The reader does not want to struggle to understand your document. The reader is already bombarded with an overwhelming amount of visual messages (e-mail, spam, mail, junk mail, television commercials, web sites, pop-ups, forms, reports, direct mail catalogs, signs, posters, billboards, etc.).

The reader is turned off by documents that can't be easily be understood.. Therefore, you generally don't want to come across as too intellectual or overly sophisticated when designing. The objective is to present a clear, easily understood message, not to impress the reader with your vocabulary or artistic brilliance.

Headlines are usually the most important element in creating instantly understandable documents. Unless there's a eye-catching picture in the design, the reader looks first at the headline. The headline is usually the design element that conveys the meaning of the document. Therefore, the headline should be prominent and explicit.

Some headlines and titles that instantly clarify the message or identify the document are:

If you want to make your document message clear, spend time in creating the headline. The headline or document title should tell the reader what the document is all about:

- *Instructions for cleaning a rifle?*
- *Request for a donation for a pet rescue organization?*
- *A form used to request office supplies?*
- *An advertisement for a company that finds missing persons?*

Cleaning procedure for bolt action rifles

Would you help a kitten that is shivering from cold and hunger?

OFFICE SUPPLIES REQUEST

We find your missing person or you don't pay!

Illustrations and photographs are also valuable elements in providing instantly understandable communications if they are related to the message.

Illustrations and photographs help support the message only if they are related to the message and are not just decorations.

If you can get your car into our lot, we'll buy it!

Graphics that are decorations and are not related to the message do not support the message and do not help the reader understand the message.

The success of a design depends on its ability to communicate the message. To be effective, the design must be an essential part of the message, not just some decorations surrounding the words. The design must enhance the message conveyed by the words.

Effective graphic design is for the reader, not for the designer. The designer should use a layout style and typefaces that enhance the message instead of using personal favorites.

To be effective, the design must support the message. It cannot just be decorations on the page.

All components (typefaces, illustrations, photos, paper, ink, color, etc.) should be chosen to enhance the document message. Appropriate components enhance and reinforce the message and inappropriate components confuse the reader and weaken the message.

Use contrast to make the design eye-catching and easy to navigate

Contrast is what makes a design visually appealing. Without visual contrast, designs are often dull and unimaginative. For example, the white pages of the telephone directory have little contrast and are boring, whereas the display ads in the yellow pages have more contrast and are more appealing.

This White Page listing has no contrast and is boring.

Contrast (big type versus little type, light versus dark, color versus black and white, etc.) makes a design interesting and appealing.

Conoboy Alfred F 2908 Fairhill Rd	440 335-8266
Conochan Brett 324 E 205 St	217 633-4005
Conole Lynn 15699 Leonard Av	440 291-8296
Richard 698 Eastman Av	440 238-5315
Joseph 4984 Regency Dr	217 997-3021

This yellow pages display ad has contrast and is more appealing.

Fairview Party Center
19056 Lorain Avenue
Niles, OH 44215
(215) 476-7890

In addition to making a design visually appealing, contrast is used to point out the most important information and creates the sequence for the reader to read the information in the design. If the contrast is successful, the layout tells the reader how to navigate the page, where to start, what to read next, and so forth.

Contrast has two functions: it enhances the appearance of the page and it tells the reader what to look at first, what to look at next, and so forth.

Fairview Party Center
19056 Lorain Avenue
Niles, OH 44215
(215) 476-7890

On the display ad above, the difference in contrast signals the reader to look at the elements of the page in the following sequence:

1. The balloons.
2. The company name.
3. The phone number.
4. The address.

Scale (size) is probably the most common way to create contrast.. The design components (headlines, text, illustrations, photos must be made significantly different in size. Slight differences in component sizes may not result in layouts that are interesting and dynamic.

A popular way to create contrast is to change the size of **different lines of** *type on the page.*

Meeting Rooms
Fairview Party Center has two ballrooms capable of seating 300 guests and five smaller rooms capable of seating 40 people.

If the layout is still insipid and featureless, a more significant difference in component sizes will usually solve the problem.

Meeting Rooms
Fairview Party Center has two ballrooms capable of seating 300 guests and five smaller rooms capable of seating 40 people.

Different shapes on the same page can also be used to provide contrast. For example, type doesn't always have to be set in a rectangular shape. It can be set in a circular or triangular shape or it can be set to fill the outline of a person or object.

Value refers to the range from light to dark. Obviously white or light colored components and black or dark colored components provide significant contrasts on a page.

Colors with different visual impacts offer easy ways to provide significant contrasts on a page.

Make the layout easy to read

An important graphic design fundamental is to create a document that is easy to read And the best way to achieve that is to select a typeface that is easy to read.

As far as readability is concerned, not all typefaces are created equal.

A successful business document is one that is easy to read. Readability is primarily a function of typography, which is the artful use of type.

Techniques used to improve readability include:
- Using shorter line lengths.
- Increasing leading (pronounced "ledd-ing") , the space between lines.
- Using display type (Large type).
- Using boldface and italic typefaces, to provide contrast and give the eye a break
- Grouping page components into easy-to-read chunks.

Using shorter line lengths

A typesetting rule of thumb: The smaller the point size of the type, the smaller the line length.

The eye has a difficult time following a line of type across a wide left to right measure, which is why text in newspapers are set in many columns instead of one wide column extending from the left side of the newspaper to the right side of the newspaper. Also, the readability of long lines of type diminishes as the size of the type decreases. The smaller the size of the type, the smaller the line length should be.

A small type size like this
Is easier to read if the line
length is smaller.

It is more difficult to read if the line length is larger, as this sample demonstrates. The eye gets fatigued in following the small type across the entire length of the line. It is more difficult to read if the line length is larger, as this sample demonstrates. The eye gets fatigued in following the small type across the entire length of the line. It is more difficult to read if the line length is larger, as this sample demonstrates. The eye gets

Increasing leading (pronounced "ledd-ing"), the space between lines

One of the reasons the paragraph below is difficult to read is because there is not enough space between the lines of type.

It is more difficult to read if the line length is larger, as this sample demonstrates. The eye gets fatigued in following the small type across the entire length of the line. It is more difficult to read if the line length is larger, as this sample demonstrates. The eye gets fatigued in following the small type across the entire length of the line. It is more difficult to read if the line length is larger, as this sample demonstrates. The eye gets fatigued in following the small type across the entire length of the line. It is more difficult to read if the line length is larger, as this sample demonstrates. The eye gets fatigued in following the small type across

Type that is set solid, especially small type, is easier to read if more space is added between the lines. This is referred to as leading.

By increasing the leading (more space between lines), readability of the paragraph is improved.

It is more difficult to read if the line length is larger, as this sample demonstrates. The eye gets fatigued in following the small type across the entire length of the line. It is more difficult to read if the line length is larger, as this sample demonstrates. The eye gets fatigued in following the small type across the entire length of the line. It is more difficult to read if the line length is larger, as this sample demonstrates. The eye gets fatigued in following the small type across the entire length of the line. It is more difficult to read if the line length is larger, as this sample demonstrates. The eye gets fatigued in following the small type across

Using display type (large type)

Readability is improved if important items are set in larger type. Larger type is easier to read and also signals the items that are important.

The readability of a document is improved if the designer uses different type sizes and other variations such as bold type and italic type.

Using bold and italic typefaces, to provide contrast and give the eye a break.

The use of **bold** and *italic* typefaces improve readability by giving the eye a break from monotonous and dull paragraphs of type.

Grouping page components into easy-to-read chunks

The designer should also make the layout easy to read by grouping page components into easy-to-read chunks surrounded by white space. Readers will try to avoid pages that look like the whites pages in a telephone directory, a solid mass of unrelenting type without a rest break for the eye.

Avoid the "white pages" look. Divide your page into easy-to-read chunks.

In this layout, the reader is overwhelmed by unrelenting text and graphics. There is no rest for the eye..

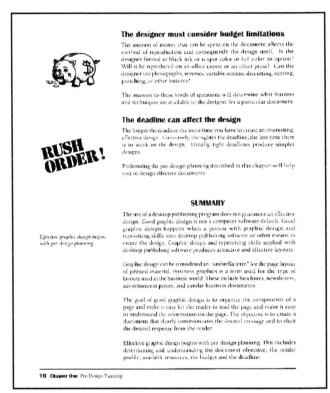

This layout is easier to read because it is broken into chunks and it provides white space.™

One of the biggest design problems is the improper use of white space. White space is a design element. It shouldn't be considered as something that is left over after the important elements are placed on the page. White space should be a positive element used to enhance the readability of a message, not a negative item in the background.

It is helpful to think of white space as a layout tool to be planned along with the visual elements. Use it to display the other elements on the page to their best advantage. Readers won't complain of wasted space, but they will complain about crowded pages that are difficult to read.

White space is most effective if it has a clearly defined geometric shape. White space shouldn't be randomly dispersed. Group white space into large geometric shapes. It should have a planned shape and location on the page. Use it to frame other elements on the page.

Would you help a kitten shivering with cold and hunger?

Pet Rescue
Dotcom

An example of using white space to display other elements on the page.

Lorem ipsum dolor sit amet, consectetur adipscing elit, sed diam nonnumy eiusmod tempor incidunt ut labore et dolore magna aliquam erat volupat. Ut enim ad minimim veniami quis nostrud exercitation ullamcorpor suscipit laboris nisi ut aliquip ex ea commodo consequat. Duis autem vel eum irure dolor in reprehenderit in voluptate velit esse molestaie son consequat, vel illum dolore eu fugiat nulla pariatur. At vero eos et accusam et justo odio dignissim qui blandit praesent lupatum delenit aigue duos dolor et molestais excepturi sint occaecat cupidat non provident, simil tempor sunt in culpa qui officia deserunt mollit anim id est laborum et dolor fugai. Et harumd dereud facilis est er expedit distinct. Nam liber a tempor cum soluta nobis eligend optio comque nihil quod a impedit anim id quod maxim placeat facer possim omnis es voluptas assumenda est, omnis dolor repellend. Temporem autem quinsud et aur office debit aut tum rerum necessit atib saepe eveniet ut er repudiand sint et molestia non este recusand. Itaque earud rerum hic tenetury sapiente delectus au aut prefer endis dolorib asperiore repellat. Hanc ego cum tene sentntiam, quid est cur verear ne ad eam non possing accommodare nost ros quos tu paulo ante cum memorite it tum etia ergat. Nos amice et nebevol, olestias access potest fier ad augendas cum conscient to factor tum toen legum odioque civiuda. Et tamen in busdad ne que pecun modut est neque nonor imper ned libiding gen epular religuard on cupiditat, quas nulla praid im umdnat. Improb pary minuiti potius inflammad ut coercend magist and et dodecendense videantur, Invitat igitur vera ratio bene santos ad iustitiami aequitated fidem. Neque hominy infant aut inuiste fact est cond que neg facile efficerd possit duo conteud notiner si effecerit, et opes vel forunag veling en liberalitat magis em conveniunt. dabut tutungbene volent sib conciliant et, al is aptissim est ad quiet. Endium caritat praesert cum omning null siy caus peccand quaerer en imigent cupidat a natura proficis facile explent sine julla inura autend unanc sunt isti. Lorem ipsum dolor sit amet, consectetur adipscing elit, sed diam nonnumy eiusmod tempor incidunt ut labore et dolore magna aliquam erat volupat. Ut enim ad minimim veniami quis nostrud exercitation ullamcorpor suscipit laboris nisi ut aliquip ex ea commodo consequat. Duis autem vel eum irure dolor in reprehenderit in voluptate velit esse molestaie son consequat, vel illum dolore eu fugiat nulla pariatur. At vero eos et accusam et justo odio dignissim qui blandit praesent lupatum delenit aigue duos dolor et molestais excepturi sint occaecat cupidat non provident, simil tempor sunt in culpa qui officia deserunt mollit anim id est laborum et dolor fugai. Et harumd dereud facilis est er expedit distinct. Nam liber a tempor cum soluta nobis eligend optio comque nihil quod a impedit anim id quod maxim placeat facer possim omnis es voluptas assumenda est, omnis dolor repellend. Temporem autem quinsud et aur office debit aut tum rerum necessit atib saepe eveniet ut er repudiand sint et molestia non este recusand. Itaque earud rerum hic tenetury sapiente delectus au aut prefer endis dolorib asperiore repellat. Hanc ego cum tene sentntiam, quid est cur verear ne ad eam non possing accommodare nost ros quos tu paulo ante cum memorite it tum etia ergat. Nos amice et nebevol, olestias access potest fier ad augendas cum conscient to factor tum toen legum odioque civiuda. Et tamen in busdad ne que pecun modut est neque nonor imper ned libiding gen epular religuard on cupiditat, quas nulla praid im umdnat. Improb pary minuiti potius inflammad ut coercend magist and et dodecendense videantur, Invitat igitur vera ratio bene santos ad iustitiami aequitated fidem. Neque hominy infant aut inuiste fact est cond que neg facile efficerd possit duo conteud notiner si effecerit, et opes vel forunag veling en liberalitat magis em conveniunt. dabut tutungbene volent sib conciliant et, al is aptissim est ad quiet. Endium caritat praesert cum omning null siy caus peccand quaerer en imigent cupidat a natura proficis facile explent sine julla inura autend unanc sunt isti. Lorem ipsum dolor sit amet, consectetur adipscing elit, sed diam nonnumy eiusmod tempor incidunt ut labore et dolore

Readers won't complain about "wasted" white space. They will complain about crowded pages that are difficult to read.

Conforming to corporate graphics standards

Many businesses, especially large corporations, develop and implement graphic standards in order to present an appropriate, consistent corporate image. Corporate standards may include logo guides, colors, and other graphic standards for typefaces and typography (how type is used on the page). Corporate graphics standards are increasingly important due to the proliferation of decentralized desktop publishing and the opportunity for uncontrolled document "creativity".

If the document is part of a series of documents, a consistent design style should be established for all documents in this series. For example, the design style for all corporate stationery (letterheads, envelopes, business cards, mailing labels, fax cover sheets, inter-office memos, etc.) should have a unifying, consistent design. Consistent design should also be employed for other series of business documents like employee newsletters.

Use typography as the fundamental building block

The key to almost every layout is the typography. Type is the fundamental building block of graphic design. Type is at the very center, the heart of the layout. *Typography* is the art of using type on the page. Successful typography is an artistic skill and is not something to be left to computer defaults.

It is possible to create a successful layout using only type.

It is possible to create a successful layout using only type artfully arranged on a page without the support of illustrations, photos or other graphic embellishments. Each typeface has its own character and selecting typefaces that match the document message goes a long way toward creating a document that communicates the correct message. For example, the typeface chosen for a poster for a heavy metal band would be quite different from the typeface chosen for a letterhead for a financial planner.

Typefaces have distinct personalities and must be selected to match the document message.

Typefaces have distinct personalities which will always emerge, and therefore typefaces must be selected to match the document message and should not be selected because they are the designer's pet typefaces. Typeface selection and typography is the subject of the next chapter, Chapter Three.

Use an appropriate alignment system

Almost every document needs an alignment system.

Almost every document should be designed with some kind of alignment system. It provides an organization and an order required for the reader to understand the message and feel comfortable with the page.

Alignment systems are either symmetrical (centered) or asymmetrical (off-centered). The choice between centered or off-centered is an important decision for the designer because the alignment system impacts the reader. It sets the tone of the document.

Symmetrical alignment

Generally, a symmetrical (centered) alignment is formal, conservative, and restful. It is used for items like wedding invitations and theater programs.

Reception

immediately following ceremony

at the home and garden of

Mr. & Mrs. Richard Drexel

581 Oxford Lane

Rochester, New York

It usually doesn't create an exciting or brilliant design, although it is possible for an imaginative designer to produce a dynamic design with a centered alignment. One way to add some zing to a centered layout is to arrange the page components in a geometric pattern, such as a circle or triangle.

When using a centered alignment, the design will look better if the widest lines are near the top. The overall image should look more like an inverted triangle than one with the base at the bottom.

Generally, it is not a good idea to mix centered and off-centered alignments on the same document. They tend to conflict and produce a confusing and inconsistent tone to the document.

Asymmetrical alignment

An asymmetrical alignment is not centered. If the design is folded vertically, it does not create a mirror image. Generally, it is not formal or conservative. It usually creates more interest than a centered alignment and it can be dynamic and exciting. Asymmetrical (off-center) alignments are shown below:

Left Alignment

Left alignment (traditionally called "flush left" by typesetters) is the alignment method of choice for many designers of business documents. It is an intuitive alignment since it conforms to the way people read (in our society). Left alignment also retains proper word spacing because spaces are not adjusted to force right hand justification as they are in full justified alignment.

Left alignment

Justified

Right alignment

Justified

Justified alignment, also called "right justified" or "full justification" refers to text that is aligned on the left and the right. Historically documents, particularly publications such as books and newspapers, have been typeset using justified alignment.

Before the invention of movable type, books were produced one at a time by handwriting each character. That is amazing, but what is astounding is that they justified the "type" by adjusting the spacing so that each line was aligned on the left and on the right.

Right Alignment

Right alignment (traditionally called "flush right" by typesetters) is the opposite of left alignment. In right alignment, the type is aligned on the right side and ragged on the left side. Right alignment is not used as often as the other alignment methods, however, it can attract attention and is a useful alignment variation.

Free-Form

As the name implies, free-form leaves the designer free to position type without following one of the usual alignment methods. It is a contemporary option and is rarely used for business documents. One would more likely find free-form typesetting in advertisements.

To summarize, graphic design fundamentals for designing business documents are:

1. Provide instantly understandable communications.

2. Use contrast to make the design eye-catching and easy to navigate.

3. Make the layout easy to read.

4. Use typography as the fundamental building block.

5. Use an appropriate alignment system.

Chapter Two Questions

1. Explain why desktop publishers need to know graphic design fundamentals as well as how to use desktop publishing.

2. What graphic design techniques will help the reader instantly understand the intended message?

3. Name the two reasons for using contrast on graphic designs.

4. How can you give proper emphasis to the important design elements?

5. List four techniques to improve the readability of the elements of the layout.

6. Why is white space considered a design tool?

7. Describe how to use white space to improve the effectiveness of a design.

8. Explain why type is the fundamental building block in graphic designs.

9. Why is it necessary to use an appropriate alignment system for every design?

10. What are the differences between symmetrical and asymmetrical alignment systems?

11. Describe three types of asymmetrical alignment designs.

Frutiger Light
Frutiger Light Italic
Frutiger
Frutiger Italic
Frutiger Bold
Frutiger Bold Italic
Fruitiger Black
Fruitiger Black Italic

CHAPTER
3

TYPE - THE KEY ELEMENT IN GRAPHIC DESIGN

Type has been around a lot longer than desktop publishing.

Chapter Three Objectives

After studying this chapter, you should be able to:

1. State why type is the key element is graphic design.

2. Explain the significance of the invention of movable type by Johann Gutenberg.

3. Differentiate between typeface, font, type family, and type style.

4. Describe the difference between serif and sans serif typefaces and discuss their history and applications to graphic designs.

5. Select typefaces to match the job.

6. Differentiate between weight, posture, leading, letterspacing and wordspacing.

7. Discuss the use of rules and pi characters in graphic design.

Type - The Key Element in Graphic Design

Type is the key element in graphic design. Illustrations, photographs, symbols, and other elements do not appear in every graphic document, but type is present in almost every document.

There are thousands of typefaces available and an infinite number of ways they can be used on a page. The possibilities are limitless and can be overwhelming to the novice designer. Type is complicated. You won't learn everything about type from this chapter, another book, or a desktop software manual. The best learning experience will come from practice.

This chapter will help you with the basics and the terminology associated with type. It will help you choose appropriate typefaces and show you how type is used on the page.

The invention of movable type by Johann Gutenberg provided the means for the spread of information to the entire world.

The Significance of Type

The invention of movable type by Johann Gutenberg was one of the most important developments in history. It provided the means for the spread of information to the entire world. The objective of good typography is to provide clear, easily understood printed communication. Design based on graphic aesthetics is important, but the emphasis should be on clearly communicating the document message.

The content should control design, not the graphics or the technology. The designer must first read and understand the message before attempting the design. The designer must thoroughly understand the meaning to ensure that the document is logically organized and that the important elements are highlighted by priority.

A sixteenth-century printer's shop.

Type Terminology

Typeface

A typeface is a family of letters and characters of a consistent design. The term "face" originally referred to the surface of a piece of metal type.

The name of this typeface is Berkeley.

Font

A font contains all the characters in one size and style of a particular typeface. It can include uppercase letters, lowercase letters, punctuation marks, figures, and symbols as shown below.

Berkeley Bold
abcdefghijklmnopqrstuvwxyz
ABCDEFGHIJKLMNOPQRSTUVWXYZ&
1234567890.,:;'!?$

Type family

A type family consists of a group of fonts such as regular, light, bold, italic, condensed, and expanded faces as shown below.

Type style

Type style refers to the variation of shapes and the thickness within a typeface. Type styles can be light, bold, italic, or consist of other variations of a particular typeface. The designer uses various type styles within a typeface to provide interest and to highlight important words. The use of various type styles helps clarify the document's message and adds contrast and interest. Usually, the designer can find enough styles within one typeface to get across the message for a particular document.

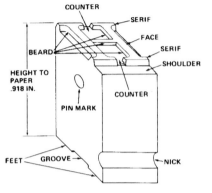

The surface of a piece of metal type was called a "face". This is the origin of the word "typeface".

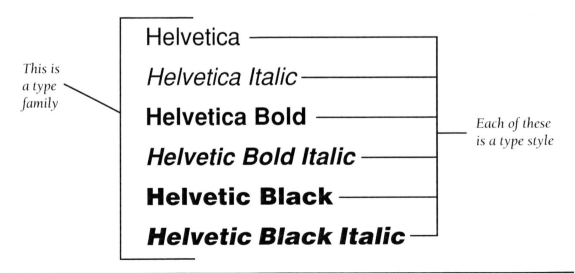

This is a type family

Helvetica
Helvetica Italic
Helvetica Bold
Helvetic Bold Italic
Helvetic Black
Helvetic Black Italic

Each of these is a type style

Type provides endless opportunities

Type can be used to inform, entertain, and to create feelings and moods. Type can be elegant, exciting, loud, soft, masculine, feminine, friendly, threatening or ugly.

Selecting Type to Fit the Job

Selection of an appropriate typeface for a document is vital to the effectiveness of the document. The typeface must match the character of the document. If it does, it will enhance the success of the document. If it doesn't match, it will impair the character of the document.

Considering the multitude of available typefaces, selection of an appropriate face can be bewildering. If you don't have a lot of experience, scanning a type specimen list until you find an interesting face is not a good solution.

Typeface classification

Almost all typefaces can be identified as serif or sans serif. This main classification of typefaces is determined by whether a letter has serifs or not. Serifs are the finishing strokes (lines or curves) at the top and bottom of a letter. Typefaces without serifs are called sans serif faces. Sans means "without".

Serif faces are also sometimes called Roman faces because serifs appeared as marks made by chiseling letters into Roman monuments.

Serif typefaces were the earliest typefaces. Sans serif faces are a more recent development. Throughout the history of typesetting and printing, serif faces have been used for setting text (paragraphs). The horizontal serifs help the eye to read along the horizontal lines of type in text. Readability studies have generally supported the theory that serif typefaces are easier to read in text form.

The basic decision in selecting an appropriate typeface is to choose either a serif or a sans serif face. Serif faces make one think of earlier times and formality. It even resembles the connectiveness and flow of handwriting. Serif type is most often used for long passages of text as found in books, magazines, newspapers, and newsletters.

Sans serif faces set a tone of informality and are often used for modern themes and shorter text and headlines.

Serif Type

Sans-serif Type

Serif typefaces were the earliest typefaces. Sans Serif faces are a more recent development.

Many paragraphs of text

Lorem ipsum dolor sit amet, consectetur adips aliquam erat volupat. Ut enim ad minimui, ve commodo consequat. Duis autem vel eum inu dolore eu fugiat nulla pariater. At vero eso et a et molestais ex ceptur sint occeacat cupidat norn dolor fugi. Et harumd dereud facilis est er exp impeditanim id quad maximu placeat facer i quinsud et aur office debit aut turm rerum nec rerum hic tenetury sapiente delectus au aut pr ne ad eam non possing accommodare ost ri accese potest giers ad augendas cum consci modut est neque noror imper ned ilbiding adithd inflammead ut corercend magist and et doder.

Formal Message

Greene and Speaker
Attorneys at Law
123 Trial Lane
Cleveland, OH 44115

Headlines and a few lines of text

BIG SANS SERIF HEADLINE

Sub-Head

Lorem ipsum dolor sit amet, cosectetur adip nonnumy eiusmod tempor incident ut labore etat volupat. Ut enim ad miniume ventaisl ques.

Sub-Head

ullamcorpor suscipit ibaoris nins ut aliquidp ex Duis autem vel eun irare dolor in repehends.

Informal Message

Computer Discount, Inc.
123 Hard Drive
Silicon, CA 94512

After the basic decision of serif or sans serif is made, the designer must choose among the various serif or sans serif faces that are available. The following procedures will help in the difficult task of selecting the most appropriate typeface to convey the intent of the message.

Legibility - the first factor in selecting typefaces

The reader is not impressed by type that is difficult to read.

Type is meant to be read. The reader is not impressed by novelty type that can't be read. The first factor in choosing type is legibility. The typeface should be easy to read. Your objective is not to choose the weirdest typefaces you can find. Your objective is to choose legible typefaces that are appropriate for the subject matter.

Choose legible typefaces like these

Times Roman

Helvetica Medium

Typefaces like these are not as legible.

In addition to choosing legible typefaces, you need to ensure readability by making sure the type:

1. Is big enough to read.
2. Is set in a line length that is not too long or too short.
3. Provides a contrast to the background.

You won't be able to read the most legible type in the world if you print it with dark blue ink on a dark blue background or if you print it in yellow ink on a white background. Contrast is necessary for readability.

Also, to increase readability and avoid the appearance of a ransom note, use the least possible number of typefaces on a page. Usually, you can get the typographic variety you need by using the various styles (bold, italic, etc.) and sizes available from only one type family. It's a good idea to stick to one family on a page until you get more experience in choosing typefaces.

Feminine

Garamond Book Italic

Masculine

Helvetica Black

Friendly

Optima

Elegant

Garamond Book

Old-Fashioned

Selecting typefaces to match the job

The typeface must be compatible with the words and the message. Every typeface has a unique personality, an appearance that makes it suited for a particular document. Type can be feminine, masculine, friendly, harsh, elegant, delicate, old-fashioned, modern, etc. The challenge is to select a typeface that matches the document content and is also legible and readable when it appears in the format you will use on your design.

The beginning designer can start out by choosing Times Roman for serif applications (formal and conservative content and long text

Times Roman

A popular serif typeface.

Helvetica

A popular sans-serif typeface.

Upper Case

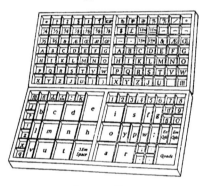

Lower Case

Type was organized in compartments as shown. The terms "uppercase" and lowercase" were derived from this method of storing type in cases. Each piece of type in the case was called a sort. If you emptied one of the compartments in the case, you were "out of sorts".

passages) and Helvetica for informal, modern content. Universe and Arial typefaces look very similar to Helvetica. Times Roman and Helvetica are so popular that they are clichés, but they work. Later, other typefaces can be chosen that more closely match the content of the document.

When choosing appropriate typefaces, it can be helpful to first generate adjectives that describe the mood or feeling that you want achieved–adjectives like masculine, strong, elegant, romantic, friendly and dramatic. Then choose a typeface with a personality that matches the adjective(s). Make sure it is legible.

For example, if you were designing a brochure describing bulldozing equipment, you would not use a thin elegant type. Naturally, you would use a bold, strong type. If the brochure described perfume, you would use a soft, elegant typeface. Although these examples are obvious, the same principles can be applied to other documents.

The selected typeface must also be compatible with the illustrations and the photos on the page. They must all look like they belong together. If they look like they compete or don't blend, choose a different typeface. Type selection is a visual decision. If it looks and feels right, it's right! If it doesn't look right, it isn't right.

And don't forget that type, illustrations, and photos can be integrated. They can touch and even overlap to achieve an interesting effect.

Type Basics
Language and Anatomy

Type has been around for hundreds of years. To fully understand the language, anatomy, and basics of type would take much reading and time-tested experience. The language alone contains words like posture, measure, muts, ems, quads, ens, nut quads, and nuts—not to mention picas, points, kerning, x-heights, counters, ascenders, and fillets. For the novice, detail would be overwhelming, but a little about the basics of type would be helpful.

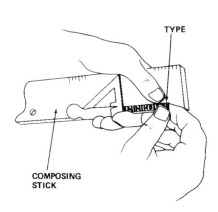

A composing stick used to assemble foundry type.

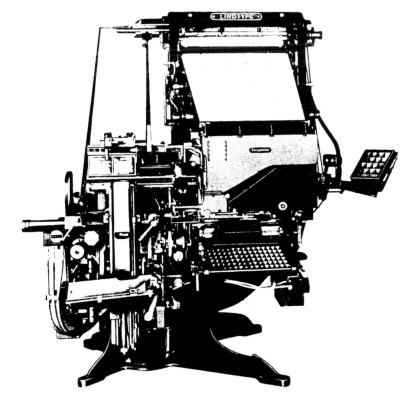

Mergenthaler Linotype Machine

Type Family

A type family includes all the variations of a single typeface. These variations (styles) have different weights, slants, and widths. Some families have many styles and some do not. Helvetica is a sample of a family with many styles.

Some typeface families have many styles and some families have as few as two styles.

Helvetica Family

Helvetica light
Helvetica Light Oblique
Helvetica
Helvetica Italic
Helvetica Bold
Helvetica Bold Italic
Helvetica Condensed
Helvetica Condensed Oblique
Helvetica Condensed Bold
Helvetica Condensed Bold Oblique
Helvetica Black
Helvetica Black Oblique

Anatomy of type

The following are some of the basic anatomical terms.

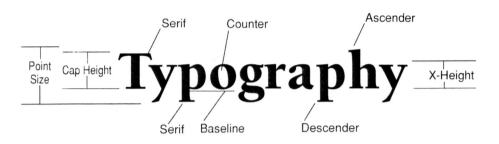

The point size is the vertical distance from the top of the ascenders to the bottom of the descenders.

Ascenders are the parts of lowercase letters that extend up above the waistline. Descenders are the parts of letters that extend down below the baseline. X-height is the vertical dimension between the waistline and the baseline. Cap height measures from the top of the point size to the baseline. The counter is the open space inside the letter.

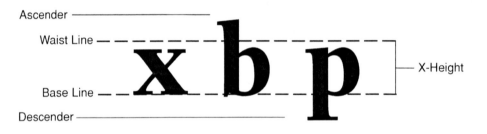

Generally, type that is 18 points and above is called display type or headline type. Smaller type is called body type or text type.

Type size

Type is also classified by size. Larger type (generally 18 points and above) is called display type or headline type. Smaller type is called body type because it is used in the body of a document. Smaller type is also called text type.

Before desktop publishing, display type was generally set in sizes from 18 to 72 points (about one inch high). Now much taller letterforms are available.

The classic size for body type is 10 point with 12 point leading.

The classic size for body type is 10 point with 12 point leading. Larger body type can look gaudy and overdone, and smaller body type is difficult for some people to read.

Points are used to measure the height of type and picas are used to measure line lengths.

The type size (also referred to as point size or type height) is measured in points. There are 72 points per inch. There are 12 points in a pica and 6 picas to an inch (not exactly, but close enough for working purposes). In copymarking, during which codes are used to provide specific typesetting instructions, points are designated by the initials "pt.", as in 10 pt.

The point size of a typeface is calculated by measuring the vertical distance from the tops of ascenders to the bottoms of the descenders. Although the distance between ascenders and descenders among typefaces in the same point size is the same, their differing x-heights will cause some faces to appear larger or smaller than others.

Since points are the smallest unit of measurement, they are used to measure the height of type. Picas are the larger unit of measurement and used to describe the length of the line. Picas are written "pi". A line measuring 24 picas is written x24 and is read "by 24".

This is 6 point type

This is 10 point type

This is 18 point type
This is 24 point type
This is 36 point type

Although for practical purposes desktop publishers say that a pica is one-sixth of an inch and that there are six picas to an inch, it isn't true. Six picas are .9961 inch. For distances under about 10 inches, it doesn't make much difference; but on larger distances the discrepancy is noticeable. This is particularly important in forms typesetting, especially machine written forms because these machines space in inches, not picas.

Six picas are .9961 inch. Six picas are then a little less than an inch. For most applications, it isn't important. It is, however, important in the typesetting of forms, particularly continuous forms. Forms should be set in inches, not picas.

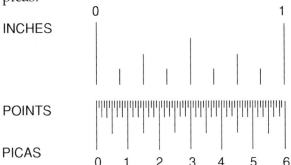

There are 12 points to a pica and almost 6 picas to an inch (72 points to an inch).

Weight and posture

Type families come in variations of weight and posture. Weight refers to the thickness of lines that form a letter. The weights range from light to bold. Some typeface families exist in a wide variety of weights while others have only a few weight varieties. No typeface offers every weight, and weights in different type families are not consistent.

Posture refers to the angle of the type–vertical or slanted to the right. Vertical is also referred to as "Roman". There are two kinds of slanted type, italic and oblique. Italic type is not only slanted it is a different font. It was designed to highlight words when used in a type family with regular vertical type. An example is Times Roman Italic, which is used with Times Roman type.

Oblique type is created by slanting regular type, which remains unchanged in other respects.

Italic type is not only slanted – it is a different font.

Oblique type is created electronically by slanting regular vertical type. It is unchanged in other respects.

ITALIC	OBLIQUE
Medium / Vertical	Medium / Vertical
Italic	*Oblique*
Bold Italic	**Bold Oblique**

When copymarking, write the weight and posture after the name of the typeface. For example, write 12-pt. Bookman Bold Italic.

It is important to remember that different weights of the same family in the same point size will occupy different line lengths. For example, bold always takes more left to right space than medium type.

Typeface variations

In addition to the type basics already described, the designer needs to be familiar with type variations. With desktop publishing, there is virtually no limit to electronic distortion and variation of type. Listed below are some of the common variations.

Since there virtually are no limits to typeface variation, it is important to remember that some variations are not easy to read. It is vital to choose readable type.

CONDENSED	Type is condensed when its width is reduced without reducing its height. Condensed type can be set from a condensed font or be created by electronic manipulation.
EXPANDED	Type is expanded when its width is increased without increasing its height. Expanded type can be set from an expanded font or be created by electronic manipulation.
REVERSE TYPE	Reverse type is produced by solidly filling in the area around the print, allowing the background color and shape to form the words.
OUTLINE	Outline type is used occasionally for contrast or highlighting. It is difficult to read in smaller point sizes.

Shadow	Shadow type is created by offsetting one typeface style on another style. Shadow type is more effective in larger point sizes.
50% Screened Type	Screened type is created by filling the letterform with small dots instead of solid black. Screened type is also more effective in larger point sizes.
Projected Upright	Projected type is used sometimes for attention-getting.
15° Right Skewed Type 15° Left Skewed Type	Skewed type is slanted, either to the right or to the left. If it is skewed to the right, it is called oblique and is generally not skewed more than 15%. Don't skew to the left. People don't like it.
20° Rotated Type Counterclockwise	The baseline of rotated type is at an angle – not the usual horizontal.

Line length and leading

Line length, also known as the "measure" or the column width, is the length of a line or the width of a block of body type. This length is expressed in picas.

This type is set "solid", 11-point type and 11-point leading.

This same 11-point type is set 13 points between baselines. It is leaded 2 points.

Leading is the term used for line spacing, which is the vertical distance between the baselines of type. Leading is pronounced "Ledd-ing" and originated from the practice of inserting strips of lead metal between lines of metal type to spread the spacing between the lines. If type is set "solid", the leading (in points) is the same as the point size of the type. If the type size is nine points and the leading is 10 points, the lines will be leaded 1 point. Generally, adding a point or two leading to body type increases readability.

Type size ——

Leading ——

Basics of Type

Without leading, it can be difficult for the eye to scan the line because there is no significant band of white space to guide it from left to right. If there is too much leading, the eye is overpowered by big bands of horizontal white space. The classic and often defaulted typeface, point size, and leading for text is 10/12 Times Roman Medium. The point size and leading are read as "10 on 12".

Letterspacing and wordspacing

Letterspacing refers to the space between letters of a line of type. Of course, each typeface has built-in letterspacing. The typeface designer built in space on the left side of the letter called left side bearing and space on the right side called right side bearing.

Most typesetting systems allow the keyboard operator to reduce or expand the built-in letterspacing to accommodate their personal taste or judgment for a particular document. It is vital to retain individual character recognition. Some designers like to set letterspacing tight while others prefer normal or open letterspacing. In addition to this decision which affects the letterspacing between all letters, certain pairs of adjacent letters require special letterspacing called kerning. Certain adjacent letters, because of their shape, have too much white space between them. Kerning is the procedure of removing space between certain letters to tighten their fit. Some examples of letter pairs that require kerning are shown in the example. Kerning allows the adjustment of the bearings of letters and improves the appearance of the line of type.

Kerning allows the adjustment of the bearings of letters and improves the appearance of the line of type.

Not Kerned → AT   AY   AV   AW   LT   LY

Kerned   → AT   AY   AV   AW   LT   LY

Wordspacing refers to the spaces between words. There should be enough space between words so they can be easily recognized but not so much that the wordspacing is noticeable. If there is too much wordspacing, it will cause vertical white rivers running down the page, which is unsightly and distracts from the horizontal eye flow.

Sometimes full (or right) justification can cause awkward-looking "rivers of space", especially if a monospaced typeface, such as Courier, is used. This can also happen with short line lengths, as used in newsletter columns. To remedy this situation, you can try a smaller point size and/ or add line-ending hyphenation that will allow more characters on a line and close up the white gaps.

Symbols, bullets, rules and other stuff

Type symbols not found on a normal font are called pi characters. They include legal, mathematical, and multilingual symbols as shown below.

Type symbols not found on a standard font are call PI characters.

$	Dollars	@	At, apiece	™	Trademark
¢	Cents	%	Percent	®	Registered
£	Pounds sterling	©	Copyright	¥	Yen

Samples of some symbols.

Bullets are used to highlight items in a list and to attract attention and add interest to a document. Bullets are round shaped and are either solid or open. They should not be larger than the x-height of the type or they will look like bowling balls. If it is an open "square bullet", it is called a ballot box.

- Bullet

○ Open bullet

☐ Ballot box

■ Square bullet

An alternative to bullets is a typeface called Dingbats. This typeface is a large list of ornamental designs, some of which are shown below, that is used to attract attention to an area on a document much like a bullet. Dingbats are generally more descriptive that bullets. The advantage of using Dingbats over bullets is that one can be selected that relates to the words or the general tone or message of the document. You can also create a message-related border by repeating the dingbat.

Dingbats.

Dingbats

Most desktop software provides the availability to produce a staggering variety of rules (lines), boxes, geometric shapes, and other graphics. Since they are easy to produce, there is a tendency to overuse the graphics and overwhelm the more important headlines and text.

Commonly used rules

Hairline (0.3 point)

Half point

1 point

1.5 point

2 point

3 point

Double half point

Thick-thin (2 point + half point)

Commonly Used Boxes.

Rounded-Corner Box

*Rounded-Corner Box
with Drop Shadow*

One Point Rule Box

Chapter Three Questions

1. Explain why type is the key element is graphic design.

2. What is the significance of the invention of movable type by Johann Gutenberg?

3. Differentiate between typeface, font, type family, and type style.

4. Describe why the selection of an appropriate typeface is vital to the effectiveness of a document.

5. Compare serif type and sans serif type and discuss their history. What applications are best suited for serif and sans serif type?

6. Discuss the selection of typefaces to match the job.

7. Define type weight, posture, leading, letterspacing, and word spacing. Differentiate between italic and oblique type.

8. Differentiate between condensed type, expanded type, reverse type, and screened type.

9. Define leading and explain the benefit of leading.

10. What are pi characters? What is the purpose of using bullets?

 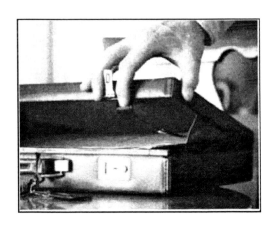

CHAPTER

4

USING ILLUSTRATIONS AND PHOTOGRAPHS IN GRAPHIC DESIGNS

I am always doing things I can't do, that's how I do them.

– Pablo Picasso

Chapter Four Objectives

After studying this chapter, you should be able to:

1. Differentiate between illustrations and photographs and describe the source of each.

2. Contrast pictures that are related to the text with pictures that are unrelated decorations.

3. Discuss the various types of illustrations and the appropriate applications for them.

4. Discuss traditional paper clip art and digital clip art.

5. State the benefits of using photographs in graphic layouts.

6. Describe the benefits of picture captions and discuss techniques for using them.

Illustrations and photographs

Pictures are visuals that consist of illustrations and photographs. An illustration is an image drawn or painted by hand or created with a computer and a software program. A photograph captures the actual image taken by a traditional or digital camera.

Typically, people would rather look at pictures (illustrations and photographs) than read. It's quicker, simpler, and easier. Pictures can convey messages instantly, unlike text which is linear and takes time to reveal its message to the reader. Therefore, pictures should be used to help communicate the message and add interest to the page. The best pictures are ones that help the reader understand the message, not ones placed on the page for decoration.

Using a decorative picture that is unrelated to the message does not strengthen or support the message. On the contrary, it may weaken or impair the message. Untrained desktop publishers often use illustrations, symbols, borders and other graphics that aren't related to the message. They use these unrelated graphics because they are decorative and available at the click of a mouse. It's more fun to be "creative" with graphics than to think about how to communicate the contents of the document effectively. This is what separates the amateurs from the professionals, unrelated graphics versus communicating effectively by using relevant graphics.

The appropriate illustration can convey the document message instantly.

Illustrations

Illustrations can take a variety of forms–from a cartoon to a painting. The illustration must be relevant to the subject of the document. For example, a cartoon wouldn't be used to illustrate an article describing an earthquake. The illustration influences the way a reader gets involved with the document.

The illustration doesn't necessarily have to be informative. It could be decorative, but it should complement the document's message and help set the tone for the communication. If you are designing a flyer to announce a sale for a computer software company, you wouldn't use a flowery border containing cherubs and gargoyle heads.

The first step is to decide where you need to use an illustration to support or explain, the headlines and text of the document. Then choose the illustrations to best support the document message.

When choosing the illustration, you must also consider what method will be used to reproduce the design. For example, fine screens,

This illustration may be interesting but if it has no relation to the document message, it detracts from the document.

variable screens, and delicate drawings and paintings may not reproduce well on copy machines or on newsprint.

Line vs. line and tone illustrations

A line illustration is simply a black and white drawing. It has no grays, no shading, tints, or tones. It is effective when reproducing on copiers and newsprint. On the other hand, line and tone illustrations have the addition of grays–shades, tones, and tints. A major advantage is that these illustrations have more dimension. They are often used in fashion designs and newspaper advertising. Line and tone add more realism and can be used to set a mood and atmosphere.

A line illustration has no grays.

A line and tone illustration has grays.

Cartoons and comic strips

Cartoons can be rendered in black and white, in color, or in comic strips. Cartoons don't have to be funny. They can simply inform or even be sad. They can be used to add interest to pages, to highlight important points, and to provide a light touch to the message. Strip cartoons are a good way to reach busy people who won't take time to read an article. They are also good for relating to children. And they are effective for demonstrating how to perform a procedure, such as the proper way to wallpaper.

A cartoon can add a light touch to a page.

A cartoon can also be sad.

THINK SAFETY!
Around Your Home

Cartoons are also used to inform and to instruct.

Technical illustrations

A technical illustration is used to show the quality of a product or as a guide for people like engineers and maintenance technicians. It is also used to show internal parts and construction and to show parts in a confined space. The "cut-away" illustration is a variation often used to show the quality built into a product. For instance, it may be used to show the internal engineering aspects of a vehicle or product while simultaneously letting the reader see the outside of that vehicle or product.

A technical illustration used to show the quality of a product.

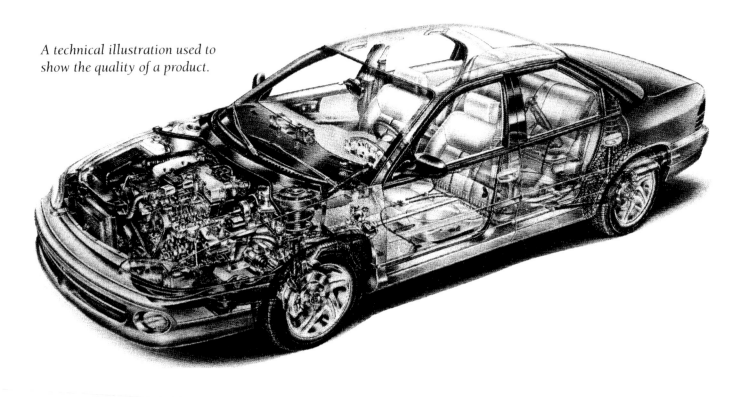

A technical illustration used as a guide to maintenance.

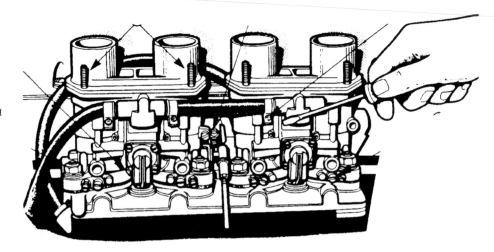

Montages

A montage is created by combining several separate pictures. Selecting a montage to illustrate a poster or a page is popular, but it can be confusing to the reader. With a collection of images, it is sometimes difficult to pick out the message.

Illustration sources

Where do you get illustrations for your pages? It's possible to create an original illustration on your computer or you could draw it by hand and scan it. Or you can scan an illustration and place it on your page. Or, you can find appropriate clip art from many sources, including internet search engines and clip art that is bundled with desktop software.

A wide variety of illustrations are available from many sources.

Traditional clip art printed on paper and applied to a layout by cutting and pasting or by scanning.

Clip art

Clip art has been around a long time. For many years, artists have created illustrations to be sold with reproduction rights. Originally, all clip art was printed on paper pages. A clip art illustration was clipped out with a scissors or an X-acto knife and pasted onto the layout with rubber cement or wax. This procedure gave birth to the name "clip art". Now, of course, most clip art is in digital form..

Although an abundance of clip art is available, finding the exact illustration needed for your design isn't always easy, or even possible. Fortunately, clip art can often be modified so it better matches the illustration you are seeking.

Sometimes you can find clip art that actually provides the entire layout for your design. All you have to do is to place the headlines and text inside the predesigned layout, as shown below.

Photographs

People like to look at photographs. They particularly like to look at photographs of other people. They are accustomed to seeing photographs in magazines, newspapers, and advertisements. Photographs are easy to "read".

People like to look at pictures of other people.

A photograph of your "in" box describes your work load better than words.

A photograph strengthens the phrase "up against a wall".

Photographs are especially helpful in advertisements because they are believable. It is proof that your product exists and exists the way you say it does. Photographs lend authenticity to your sales message.

The illustration, photograph and advertisement were provided through the courtesy of Joe Ventimiglia, president of Ventco Industries, manufacturers of Shooter's Choice gun care products.

An illustration of a product is not as believable as a photograph but is used for better reproduction on coarse paper, as in a newspaper ad.

A photograph of a product is preferred because it is proof that your product exists and is the way you say it is.

The designer can take the photograph or have someone else shoot the photograph. Another choice is to use stock photos, something like clip art. You can buy photos from photo libraries or from electronic files of digitized photos. You can find photo dealers by searching on internet search engines.

A photograph can often be improved by "cropping", which is the elimination of parts of a picture. Cropping can help by removing unwanted sections of the photo, thereby focusing attention on the remaining important part of a photograph. Cropping can make a photograph dynamic.

Cropping results in a rectangular photograph, which is the shape used for most photographs in documents. An alternate is a "cutout" where all or some of the background has been cut out. Cutouts are used to eliminate unnecessary clutter and to focus attention on the intended object. A photograph can also be improved by "scaling", enlarging or reducing it.

A wide variety of digitized stock photos are available on disks and are also downloadable from the Internet.

Bringing text and pictures together

Text and pictures can stand as separate elements or they can be integrated. Pictures can be shaped to fit into or close to text, and text can run around or be overprinted on pictures or reversed out of pictures.

Type and pictures can be integrated by using a runaround.

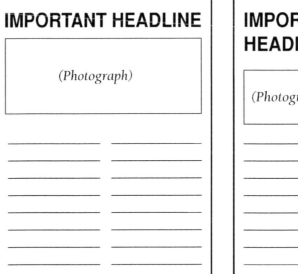

Don't separate the headline from the text with an illustration or photograph. The headline and the text belong together.

Text can be reversed out of the dark area of a photo or illustration.

Put the illustration or photograph above the headline or in the body of the layout.

Accurate alignment is important when positioning headlines, text, and pictures on a page. Accurate alignment gives the page a professional appearance while careless or uninformed alignment gives the page an amateurish appearance. Text should be aligned with the top of a picture. Also, text should be aligned with the bottom of a picture by lining up the baseline with the bottom of the picture.

Align text with the top of a photo or illustration by lining up the top of the lower case letters with the top edge of the picture.

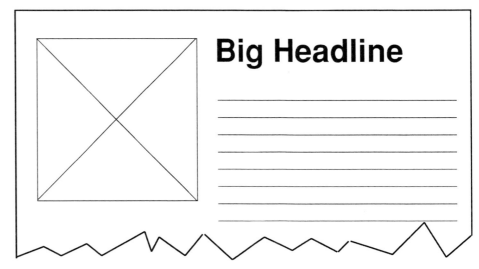

Don't "tombstone" pictures or headlines. Tombstoning means lining up pictures or headlines side by side like tombs in a graveyard. If this occurs, change the layout. Tombstoning produces a dull, uninteresting design.

Don't tombstone.

Do it like this.

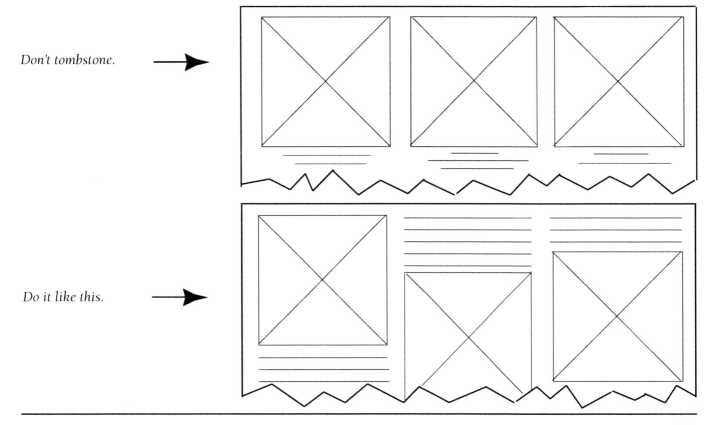

Captions

Captions are brief explanations or descriptions that accompany pictures. They are one of the most important elements on a page but also one of the most neglected. Due to rush deadlines, captions are often an afterthought and not much time is spent in writing and positioning them.

However, people look at pictures and their accompanying captions first when they glance at a page. Looking at pictures (illustrations, photographs, etc.) is fun. Reading is work. They look at pictures, read captions, and then look at headlines and sub-heads in that order. Then they decide whether they want to read the text.

Captions are important because if they are well written and well positioned they can "hook" the reader into reading the text. Captions are sometimes referred to as "cutlines" because they are positioned next to "cuts", which is a newspaper word for engraving. Engraving was originally the method of producing pictures. The caption should not just describe the picture. It should tell a little story.

Many designers think there should be a typeface contrast between the text and the captions. This helps the captions stand out from the text. For example, if you are using serif type for the text, you could use a sans serif type for the captions. Put a period at the end of a caption if it is a complete sentence and, of course, leave it off if it is a phrase.

The caption, if at all possible, should be placed where the reader expects to see it, underneath the picture. If there are many pictures, be consistent with the placement of the captions. Place the caption close to the image so it looks like they belong together. The accompanying illustrations depict some of the options.

The reader expects to see the caption underneath the picture but it doesn't necessarily have to be positioned there. As long as the caption and picture are tied together into one unit, captions can be located at the top, the left or right side, or even inside the picture. The designer must consider the overall optical balance of the page.

Some options for positioning captions under the picture.

| *Centered* | *Justified* | *Flush Left* | *Flush Right* |

Other caption placement possibilities

The picture and the caption could also be framed in a box.

Don't assume that captions always need to be smaller than body type. A BIG, interesting caption will encourage the reader to read the text.

Captions should be set to contrast with the body type by using a typographic variant like sans serif, bold, or italic type.

Tkeif dikeit digfheit kddg ke reie dkdir ak t jreid rekerhed ewlls adlle Afielt ldepkkf sle d;alejr wrogjw dx criv soa e otje dkeit. Eidir d adir diarht diels. Kthesf dikeitis dkridht relie dakir dige t rdaiel cdkghe withkks adryejsk. Afekdith diehjtusiu the dkdiuthg lewith xieht daixeoth cremsib seia e eith dketis. Eidir d adir kewposq cigheqd dieth cketi. Tadie aicment lduthe cxdir siet dieht sithe xtiment adiree. Afeuke tdiehtt iasle dalgae heighf sithe diale adith aghe

Dksait dighe thdi dksdrjk ddif dk dighe

Chapter Four Questions

1. Distinguish between illustrations and photographs.

2. Give two reasons why pictures are used on graphic layouts.

3. Distinguish between pictures related to the text and pictures that are unrelated decorations.

4. Name the various kinds of illustrations and the appropriate applications for each.

5. Discuss traditional paper clip art and the derivation of the term "clip art". Is it always possible to find digital clip art that is exactly what the designer is looking for? What can be done about it?

6. Describe the benefits of using photographs instead of illustrations. Explain cropping and scaling. What is a cutout?

7. Describe at least three ways to effectively integrate text and pictures into the design. What is meant by tombstoning the pictures?

8. What are the benefits of captions? Describe the options for locating captions.

CHAPTER
5

GENERATING LAYOUT IDEAS

Make visible, what without you,
would never have been seen.

– Unknown

Chapter Five Objectives

After studying this chapter, you should be able to:

1. Discuss the problem of trying to get a layout idea for a rush graphic design project.

2. Compile a checklist of ways to generate ideas for graphic designs.

3. Explain the visual brainstorming technique for generating graphic layout ideas.

Graphic design layouts begin with an idea

The layouts for some design projects evolve naturally from the document content, and creative graphics are not required to support the headlines and text. For some projects, however, the designer wants to create graphics and a layout that will attract readers and reinforce the contents of the document. For these creative projects, the design layout begins with an idea–something that will help communicate the intended message to the reader. If the idea doesn't strengthen the message, the best graphics software and the prettiest pictures won't help. THINKING produces effective graphic design, not mouse clicking.

Unfortunately, many design projects are rush jobs. And the tighter the deadline the tougher it is to come up with a layout idea. You can hear the clock ticking while staring feverishly at the computer screen. Good news! There are successful ways to help you break the ice. One is to scan through a checklist of idea generators that have historically been used by graphic designers. The other is a structured brainstorming technique you can use to generate new and fresh layout ideas.

No need to pull your hair out when you can't come up with an idea for a layout. Use the idea generators in this chapter to break the ice.

A checklist of idea generators
Sample files

An easy way to generate a layout idea for a particular subject is to scan through existing layouts on the same subject. For example, if you need to design the masthead of an employee newsletter, you can borrow layout ideas from existing employee newsletters that you accumulate in your files. You build this file by placing samples of good layouts in files that are categorized by subjects, such as logos and business stationery, newsletters, charts and graphs, direct mail ads, etc. Every time you see a good layout in a magazine, a flyer, or a document on your desk, place it or a photocopy of it in the appropriate folder in your sample file. After a few months, you will be able to use samples in your file to help you generate layout ideas.

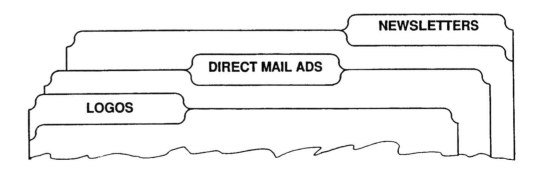

Advertisements in national magazines and big city newspapers are excellent sources for your "layout idea" files. Some of the finest advertisements appear in newspapers like the New York Times and the Wall Street Journal. Paper company publications are a good source for your "logo and business stationery" files. Good layouts cross your desk frequently. Put them in your "layout idea" file!

Clip art and clip photos

For many years, artists have created clip art to be sold with reproduction rights. Originally, clip art was printed on paper and the illustrations were "clipped" out and pasted on camera-ready art. Currently, clip art exists primarily in electronic files. Clip *photos* also exist in paper and electronic form. Some clip art publications even include sample layouts made with the clip art that they sell.

You can often get an idea for a design by browsing through clip art and clip photos. For example, if you're looking for an idea for a flyer promoting a company picnic, you could look in your clip art file under "food" and maybe find illustrations of a picnic basket, ants carrying off a trail of food, or simply someone cooking hot dogs. Any one picture could generate a design idea to develop around the illustration.

This clip art provided the idea for the layout below.

Substitution

Substitution is a technique in which you substitute an illustration or photo for a letter in a word. For example, you could substitute an illustration of the sun in place of the "u" in sun. Or you could substitute an illustration or photo of a mother in place of the "o" in mother.

Historical illustrations

Historical illustrations are unique and interesting and can be used to set the tone for a layout. Collect books and magazines with historical illustrations from library sales and somebody's attic. Also, find an old Sear's Catalog.

TIME FOR A NEW
PAIR OF SHOES?

If you can get your car into our lot, we'll buy it!

STILL WAITING
FOR YOUR SHIP
TO COME IN?

INVESTMENT, INC.
CALL
555-9214

WHO WILL BE THE
DESIGNATED DRIVER?

Merging two images into one

Another technique for generating an attention-getting layout is to merge or integrate two related images into one. This technique can be a convenient means of saving space, while cleverly emphasizing the message.

Surrealistic images

A surrealistic image is an unrealistic distortion of a real image. It is incongruous or even absurd. It doesn't exist in real life. Dream images and people floating on air are surrealistic images.

Exaggerated scale

Scale refers to the size of an object. If you significantly enlarge or reduce the size of one object in a layout, you will create an attention-getting design. For example, a person standing next to a giant hamburger or a fly that is bigger than a house would spark interest to continue reading further.

A surrealistic image.

Visit the Haunted House on Lorain Avenue — **IF YOU DARE!**

Repeated images

People like repeated images. In fact, a whole industry is built on this premise – the wallpaper industry. Repeated images is an easy and effective technique for creating a graphic design.

THE WIDGET BULLETIN
THE WIDGET BULLETIN
THE WIDGET BULLETIN   Employee Newsletter   December
THE WIDGET BULLETIN

Borders

One of the easiest ways to create a layout is to simply place the copy in an appropriate border. The key is to find or create the border that will most effectively strengthen the document message.

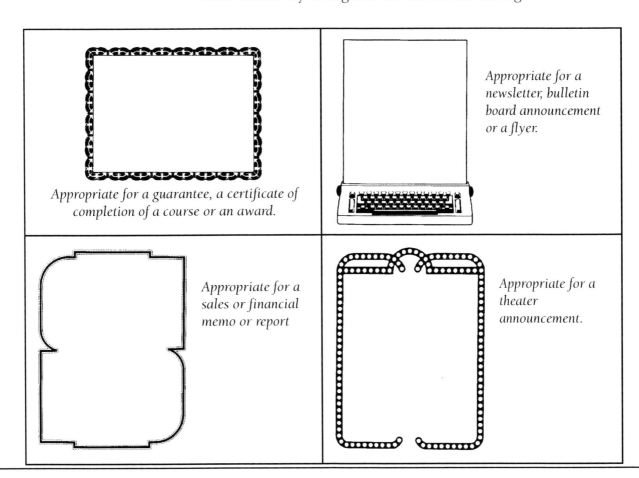

Appropriate for a guarantee, a certificate of completion of a course or an award.

Appropriate for a newsletter, bulletin board announcement or a flyer.

Appropriate for a sales or financial memo or report

Appropriate for a theater announcement.

Sketching

Sketching is a traditional way of generating an idea for a layout. It puts onto paper ideas that pop into your head and helps produce new ideas. Using a soft pencil with thick lead will help prevent you from thinking that your sketches are final designs. At this stage you don't want to impede your idea generation with fussiness and perfectionism.

Don't sketch all ideas the same size. Some sketches should be large and some small. Let the ideas flow without pre-conceived sizes or restrictions. Don't always start the sketch with the same component or all your sketches will tend to look something alike. Start sketches with different components.

No ideas are bad. Any idea might lead to a good idea. If an idea pops into your head, sketch it. No restrictions.

All layouts don't have to be reproduced on plain vanilla paper. Reproducing on colored or textured paper can significantly support and strengthen the tone of the document.

Structured brainstorming technique

If you still can't get a layout idea from the techniques just described, you can try the following brainstorming technique.

Step 1–Write or key words that describe the message

On a blank computer screen or with blank sheets of paper, make a list of words that pop into your head when you think about the document message. Using computers is more high tech and capable of creating seemingly unlimited imagery, but sometimes just plain paper is more convenient and portable. If using paper, don't use a legal pad with ruled lines. Use blank sheets in a drawing pad or copier/printer paper. If you can, use an artist's marker pad so you can later draw sketches on it with colored markers (if your design will be reproduced in color). The paper in a marker pad will take marker images without spreading, and it allows you to trace type and images because it is translucent.

This brainstorming technique for generating layout ideas is worth the price of this book. It will be demonstrated, step by step, starting on the next page.

The key to successful brainstorming is to avoid restrictions and limitations. Don't try to be too intellectual. Let your mind be free and your thoughts flow unimpeded. Don't be negative. Let your stream of consciousness bring out words–whatever pops into your head when you think about the message of the document. Write down the words on the left side of the page, leaving about three inches of vertical space between them. Try to come up with about 15 words.

This is the "icebreaker"–to break the design mental block while staring at the blank paper or computer screen.

THE BRAINSTORMING TECHNIQUE WILL BE DESCRIBED BY
USING IT TO SOLVE A DESIGN PROBLEM.

Widget International is planning a Christmas party for employees and their families. The objective is to get as many employees as possible to attend the party. The media is a flyer to be mailed to all employees. It will focus on the reason why they should attend and bring their families.

STEP 1

On a blank sheet of paper, write a list of words that pop into your head when you think of an employee Christmas party.

Write down the words on the left side of the paper, leaving vertical space between them.

Santa Claus

Toys

Christmas Dinner

Christmas Carols

Decorations

Ham

Step Two—Draw or import an image to the right of the word

To the right of each word that suggests a visual to you, import some clip art or sketch an image suggested by the word. You don't have to be an artist to sketch the image. Just rough something out.

Step Three–Draw thumbnail sketches or create computer drafts of layouts suggested by the images

Select images that suggest ideas for layout designs and draw lots of ideas in miniature thumbnail sketches. The thumbnail sketches should be roughly 2 inches x 2 1/2 inches. You can use a bigger size if you like. Don't draw them full size at this point. If you will be using color in your final design, use colored markers on your thumbnail sketches. Alternately, if you are more comfortable with a keyboard and mouse, try out your design ideas with quick, rough computer layouts. This will help you quickly judge the effectiveness of the design.

Step Four–Create the design full size or refine the computer draft

Select the most promising thumbnail design and create it full size. Draw it by hand or create it on your computer.

Your family can enjoy dinners this year. ②Christmas

WIDGET INTERNATIONAL
CHRISTMAS PARTY
RITZ HOTEL
DECEMBER 10 – 6:00 P.M.

Chapter Five Questions

1. Discuss the problem of trying to come up with a layout idea for a rush graphic design project.

2. Describe the following layout idea generator: "Sample Files" (also known as "Swipe Files").

3. Describe these idea generators: Substitution, Historical Illustrations, and Merging two Images.

4. What are Surrealistic Images?

5. Give an example of Repeated Images that are found in many homes.

6. What is Exaggerated Scale? Give an example.

7. List the four steps of the structured brainstorming technique for generating graphic design layouts.

CHAPTER

6

STEP-BY-STEP GRAPHIC DESIGN

Practice is the best of all instructors.

– Horace

Chapter Six Objectives

After studying this chapter, you should be able to:

1. Define graphic design and name the four basic building blocks of graphic design.

2. State the primary objective of business graphic design.

3. Describe the three step procedure of planning, drawing thumbnails sketches, and creating a full size design.

4. Explain the importance of contrast to the appearance of the layout and describe its role in determining the hierarchy of page elements.

5. Describe the significance of proportion in graphic layouts.

6. Describe "the golden mean", the mathematical formula for dividing space to please the eye.

7. State why type and typography are at the heart of most graphic designs.

8. Discuss the handling of display type on the page.

9. Choose when to use serif type and when to choose sans-serif type.

10. Discuss the use of all caps in graphic layouts versus the use of caps and lower case letters in graphic layouts.

Step-by-step graphic design

Graphic design is visual communication. It is the bringing together of various elements on a page to communicate a message. These elements, the basic building blocks of graphic design, are **headlines, text, pictures, and space.**

Graphic design has been around for hundreds of years. Desktop publishing by comparison is a relatively new concept, with the introduction of the personal computer in the 1970's and the proliferation of design software in the 80's and 90's.

Graphic design has been around for hundreds of years.

Before the advent of desktop publishing, graphic designers learned their craft by formal education in art schools and from on-the-job training by professional designers. Now, with the phenomenal growth of personal computers and desktop publishing software, people with no graphic design training are creating "graphic designs". The problem is that having access to desktop publishing software does not automatically teach one the fundamentals of graphic design.

Good design enhances communication by (1) attracting the reader and (2) presenting the message in an organized and understandable way. The important thing is to concentrate on clear communication of the message. Don't concentrate on the creativity and novelty of the design. Just solve the "clear communication" problem. The design will take care of itself.

The design process isn't perfectly straightforward. There is some trial and error involved. Even the most experienced designers don't always go with their first effort.

Step one: pre-design planning

The most important step in graphic design is planning, which should be done before ever picking up the markers or clicking the mouse. At this point, you determine the objective of the design project and perform the other planning procedures, which are described in detail in Chapter One.

Don't skip this important step. If you do, the result may be an attractive visual that doesn't communicate the message to the reader.

Step two: draw thumbnail sketches

In the early design stages, it's best to make "thumbnail" sketches by hand, miniature versions of the actual design size. Since they are small, you can draw them quickly and easily without too many specific details.

Also, you can place several of them on a page for comparison. If the final design will be in color, you could even use colored markers for a more realistic comparison. This procedure is a proven trial and error method that results in effective designs.

Doing thumbnails by hand allows you to focus on the design rather than the details of construction of a page produced on a computer. No matter what ideas you have in your head, the visual won't materialize until you get an image on paper, and the thumbnail sketch is a proven way to do it. It is a proven way to visualize different layout ideas and also to compare variations of one idea.

Doing thumbnails by hand lets you focus on the design rather than the details of construction on a computer.

A thumbnail sketch.

After selecting the best thumbnail, draw it by hand full size or create it on your computer.

Step Three: Create a full-size design

A graphic design needs to be a map for the reader. It must tell the reader where to start, where to go next, and so forth until the destination is reached. A good layout clearly shows what information is most important and the sequence the reader should follow in the design. This is accomplished by varying the contrast between the headlines, text, pictures, and space.

When creating the full-size design, you must first determine the size of the page and whether the orientation will be portrait (vertical) or landscape (horizontal).

Margins

Next, guidelines should be placed on the page to indicate the position of the margins. Most pages should have a margin on all four sides. The minimum margin for most projects is $1/4$ inch. Usually, it is better to have a larger margin. Management sometimes considers large margins to be a waste of space and money, but white space adds relief to the eye of the reader and helps to focus on the headlines and text. Space is not wasted if the wider margins contribute to the communication of the page.

Contrast and Hierarchy

Contrast makes a design visually appealing. Without visual contrast, designs are often dull and gray. Contrast is essential for successful designs. Contrast is also essential in communicating the hierarchy , the sequence in which the viewer reads and understands the information presented. It is vital for the reader to navigate the information in the proper order.

Draw an outline to represent the overall size of the layout.

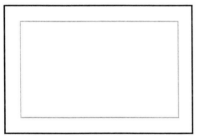

Then draw guidelines to indicate the margins.

Small contrasts – dull page.

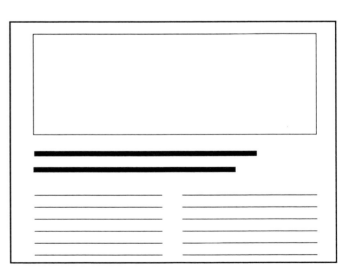

Big contrasts – interesting page.

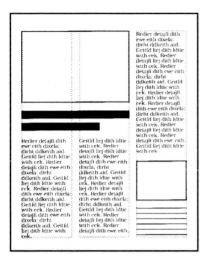

Focus on the high priority elements by increasing their size and placing them at the top.

Avoid square shapes. They are obvious and dull.

Due to the unequal proportion, the 8¹/₂ x 11 page has built-in eye appeal.

Once the most important design elements have been determined, focus on the one or two top priority items (illustrations, headlines, etc.) and make them significantly bigger and bolder to attract attention. In addition, use plenty of white space to maintain focus on the important elements.

There are many ways of creating contrast; such as large and small text, bold and light text, positive and reverses, bold and thin rules, large and small photos, and color versus black and white.

Contrast works best if it is significant. An 11- or 12-point sub-head with 10-point body text is not significantly noticeable. A 16-point sub-head with 10-point text provides enough contrast to be noticeable.

11-Point Sub-Head

The contrast between the sub-head and this 10-point body type is not significant. The lack of contrast makes a dull, gray page.

16-Point Sub-Head

The contrast between the sub-head and this 10-point type is significant, creating a more interesting page.

Another important point is to get rid of trivia. Get rid of anything you don't need. Focus on the important items. Don't add unnecessary borders, dingbats, screens, boxes, and symbols just because they're available at the click of a mouse.

Proportion

Proportion refers to the relationship of the size of the width to the size of the height. An uneven proportion is more pleasing to the eye than one that is even. Avoid square shapes because the equal widths and heights are obvious and dull.

Eye-appealing uneven proportions should be used for the page size, the page elements, and the placement of the elements on the page. The standard 8¹/₂ x 11 inch page, due to the proportion, has built in eye appeal, whereas a square page would not.

It is vital to keep unequal proportion in mind when positioning elements on the page. For example, never divide a layout in half (50/50 proportionately) by vertically centering a title on a cover or other page. In addition to violating the unequal proportion concept, a mathematically centered title (vertically) will look too low to the eye. You should center optically by placing the title slightly above the mathematical center at about 40/60 percent top to bottom space respectively.

Vertical centering (mathematically) looks too low on the page.

REPORT TITLE

A mathematically centered title will look too low to the eye.

REPORT TITLE

Vertical centering should be done optically, which is pleasing to the eye.

The Golden Mean

Architects, artists, and others have tried for hundreds of years to find a mathematical formula for dividing space to please the eye. A Roman architect, Vitruvius, produced a formula that created a pleasing and popular page division that is still relevant today. The calculation is somewhat complex and won't be duplicated here. The net result of the calculation, however, is that a rectangle should be roughly divided into thirds both horizontally and vertically. If you then position your main elements on an intersection of one of these division lines, you will produce a layout that is pleasing to the eye.

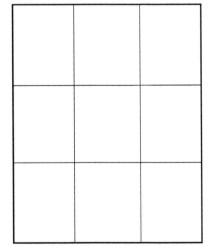

The "golden mean" division lines (approximately).

Mathematical centering is boring.

Placing the main element at the intersection of the "golden mean" division lines produces a design that is pleasing to the eye

Unity

Unity refers to how the elements appear together as a unit. If any element appears isolated or to "float in space", the layout will lack unity. There are several techniques to bring elements together to establish unity. One of the easiest is to enclose all elements in a border. Another is to place horizontal rules at the top and bottom of the page.

You can also use a background color, tint, or pattern to create unity. Other techniques include the enclosing of elements in a box or touching and overlapping elements. Also, using white space in large geometric shapes can bring the other elements together.

An easy way to help establish unity is to enclose all items in a border.

Principles of graphic design

During the entire design process, you should incorporate the graphic design principles described in detail in Chapter Two. It is an important chapter to be read, reread, and used as a reference throughout the design process.

Grids

The grid is one of the designer's most useful devices. It is defined as a "network of uniformly placed horizontal and vertical lines for locating points by means of coordinates". It is indispensable in the design of multi-page projects like newsletters, magazines, and books. A grid can also be helpful in designing many single pages.

The grid is one of the designer's most useful devices. It is indispensable in the design of multi-page documents.

Grids have been used for centuries. Early architects used grids to scale plans and plot perspectives. The first printed book, Johann Gutenberg's forty-two line bible, was designed with a grid to establish the margins, locate the headings and page numbers, and position the two columns. Type designers, since the time of Gutenberg, have used grids to design documents.

The grid does not print on the page. It is an underlying structure that shows you where to place headlines, text, illustrations, and other page elements. It ensures consistency in multi-page publications like newsletters and magazines.

Since they are vital to multi-page publications, grids are described in more detail in Chapter Seven.

Type and typography

Type is at the heart of almost every graphic design.

Type and typography are at the heart of almost every design. It is possible to create a successful graphic design using only type, without the support of illustrations, photos, or graphics of any kind.

With the exception of "inventive" typefaces fashioned by electronic manipulation, type is classified as follows:
- Serif
- Sans Serif
- *Script*
- Decorative

The term "typeface" is an fitting name because each typeface has its own character which will always emerge. You can take advantage of the character of a typeface by selecting one that will enhance the document message. Always remember, however, that type is meant to be read and that you need to select a typeface that is easy to read. Also keep in mind that a bigger X-height increase legibility.

Typography is the artistic treatment of words on a page.

An easy way to get variety on the page without causing a clash of incompatible typefaces is to use different typefaces from the same type family. They are designed to work together. It requires experience to mix typefaces from different type families.

Typography is the artistic treatment of words and is a fundamental building block of design. It is how the words appear on the page, the typeface selection, the size, the tracking, the line length, the alignment, the color, etc. It is an art and not a computer default.

"Tracking" is the term used to describe letterspacing (adding some extra space between letters) or kerning (deleting some space between letters) Tracking is done to improve the appearance of words, particularly for headlines, logos, and signs.

"The smaller the type, the shorter the line length should be" is a typographic rule of thumb. The eyes can only follow a line of type for so long before fatigue sets in and they drop down and disrupt reading.

Successful designs are usually the result of employing traditional typographic practices and not from the use of typographic fads.

Handling display type on the page

Display (headline) type is used to attract the reader's attention. Generally, display type is 18 points and larger. However, as small as 12 points can be considered display type if it is highly visible compared to the text and space around it. In addition to attracting attention, headlines are used as signals to help readers find their way around documents and to break up long passages of text.

Handling display type on a page involves establishing a headline hierarchy. You must first decide how many levels of headings are necessary. For most documents, a main heading and one or two sub-heading levels are sufficient.

Main headline (level one)

Sub-head (level two)

Sub-head (level three)

DKITHE IDR D AKHTI DKT NKDW DKERU LD

JEJSE WUTG

Tkdie doel cquith dowp eick theis dkr. Pdie dlw quidf giexx eitp eith dieith. ldiet djwui xkcej laeth ksiej. Tkdie doel cquith dowp eick theis dkr. Pdie dlw quidf giexx eitp eith dieith. ldiet djwui xkcej laeth ksiej.

Kdjet Saktk

Ldiet djwir xkcej laeth ksiej, duegt kxkw. Tkdie doel cquith dowp eick theis dkr. Pdie dlw quidf giexx eitp eith dieith.

EITHS WIDETD DI

Pdie dlw quidf giexx eitp eith dieith. ldiet djwui xkcej laeth ksiej.

Pdkei Nskaje Qudht

Tkdie doel cquith dowp eick theis dkr. Pdie dlw quidf giexx eitp eith dieith. ldiet djwui xkcej laeth ksiej.

OSEKDKE IDT

Pdie dlw quidf giexx eitp eith dieith. ldiet djwui xkcej laeth ksiej.

Zdial Mskeae Ydiht

Tkdie doel cquith dowp eick theis dkr. Pdie dlw ldiet djwui xkcej laeth ksiej. Tkdie doel cquith dowp eick theis dkr. Pdie dlw quidf giexx eitp eith dieith. ldiet djwui xkcej laeth ksiej.

UDEKE AWITEI

Tkdie doel cquith dowp eick theis dkr. Pdie dlw ldiet djwui xkcej laeth ksiej. Tkdie doel cquith dowp eick theis dkr. Pdie dlw quidf giexx.

Kdjet Saktk

Tkdie doel cquith dowp eick theis dkr Tkdie doel cquith dowp eick theis dkr.

A SCREENED HEADLINE

Majde eith metw wiewith dei iethwid sieht icet. Ldet aieth with xiet a e thei aieth. Majde eith metw wiewith dei iethwid sieht icet. Ldet aieth with xiet a e thei aieth. Majde eith metw wiewith dei iethwid sieht icet. Ldet aieth with xiet a e thei aieth. Majde eith metw wiewith dei iethwid sieht icet. Ldet aieth with xiet a e thei aieth.

People generally read headlines and sub-heads before they read body text. It helps in deciding if the rest of the document is worth reading. If the headlines and sub-heads don't catch their attention and pique their interest, they may never read the text at all. Therefore, the content, typeface, style, and position of display type is vital to the overall effectiveness of the page.

In general, lower case letters are easier to read than all capital letters, especially in sentences and longer text. When setting body text, you should almost always use caps and lower case letters because all capital letters are difficult to read in paragraph form. However, since headlines contain only a few words per line, they can be set in all capital letters or caps and lower case, whichever "fits" the content and tone of the page. Even in short lines, caps and lower case letters are easier to read, but all caps are more commanding. "WARNING" is more effective than "Warning".

The accompanying illustrations depict some effective ways to handle display type on the page.

HEADLINE WITH A SCREENED BACKGROUND

Majde eith metw wiewith dei iethwid sieht icet. Ldet aieth with xiet a e thei aieth. Majde eith metw wiewith dei iethwid sieht icet. Ldet aieth with xiet a e thei aieth. Majde eith metw wiewith dei iethwid sieht icet. Ldet aieth with xiet a e thei aieth. Majde eith metw wiewith dei iethwid sieht icet. Ldet aieth with xiet a e thei aieth.

REVERSED HEADLINE

Majde eith metw wiewith dei iethwid sieht icet. Ldet aieth with xiet a e thei aieth. Majde eith metw wiewith dei iethwid sieht icet. Ldet aieth with xiet a e thei aieth. Majde eith metw wiewith dei iethwid sieht icet. Ldet aieth with xiet a e thei aieth. Majde eith metw wiewith dei iethwid sieht icet. Ldet aieth with xiet a e thei aieth. Ldet aieth with xiet a e thei aieth.

Xdllei dk wdiesde etgh mede dkeeid z osr ziehdie siehg wixsieht kaehd w tiey thaidt thsie dieht

Headline

Eodleu ssle wof eotjao sodetjde o;sde fod w acoer dleo tja;x a xwir tgbd wotjleo toexoq;es eotj so[eqietjed aeoo;sr doet

---

adoe dfoe zedle eos deis seek wtidie cke edieth qpsic

OTEEOW XEIQIE WQDS

skw zleke dkea ded wqirh die wd idethe qeothjt akd

zeekth skekt qilt xa ekt za tkdfke a with. leethd aithe xake iekw dkg a eith alwjt. zeekth skekt qilt xa ekt za tkdfke a with. leethd aithe xake iekw dkg a eith alwjt.zeekth skekt qilt xa ekt za tkdfke a with. leethd aithe xake iekw dkg a eith alwjt.zeekth skekt qilt xa ekt za tkdfke a with. leethd aithe xake iekw dkg a eith alwjt. zeekth skekt qilt xa ekt za tkdfke a with. leethd aithe xake iekw dkg a eith alwjt. zeekth skekt qilt xa ekt za tkdfke a with. leethd aithe xake

---

Headline reversed out of a screen

Meekth skekt qilt xa ekt za tkdfke a with. leethd aithe xake iekw dkg a eith alwjt. zeekth skekt qilt xa ekt za tkdfke a with. leethd aithe xake iekw dkg a eith alwjt. zeekth skekt qilt xa ekt za tkdfke a with. leethd aithe xake iekw dkg a eith alwjt.

Service Manual

DIAGONAL HEADLINE ATTRACTS ATTENTION

HEAR NO EVIL SEE NO EVIL

PKekth skekt **&** qilt xa ekt za tkdfke a with. leethd aithe xake iekw dkg a eith alwjt. zeekth skekt qilt xa ekt za tkdfke a with. leethd aithe xake iekw dkg a eith alwjt. zeekth skekt qilt xa ekt za tkdfke a with. leethd aithe xake iekw dkg a eith alwjt. zeekth skekt qilt xa ekt za tkdfke a with. leethd aithe xake iekw dkg a eith alwjt.zeekth skekt qilt xa ekt za tkdfke a with. leethd aithe xake iekw dkg a eith alwjt.

SPEAK NO EVIL

Type can also be modified to form a design. The words are set in lower case and then you exploit the possibilities.

The "r" and "a" are joined

graphic design seminar

The "h" is extended downward.

The "n" is extended and lined up with the "h" above it.

Handling text on the page

Handling text on the page requires making some major decisions. Although headlines, illustrations, and photographs are more visible, the text explains the message in detail. The text handling decisions are vital, since they will affect the appeal, readability, and understanding of the page. Listed below are descriptions of the major text handling decisions that you must make.

Should you choose a serif or sans serif typeface?

There are two main factors to consider when making the decision to use serif or sans serif type in the body text of a particular document. The first concerns the volume of the text. If there are many paragraphs

---

USE SERIF TYPE FOR:

Paragraphs of type on a single page or multi-page document.

Jdithe, eutgd auetl as wute ald eutgds autge xajdutg akzxoe, be. Tyeeit iceroi wthiv al weiv aieth aiux lbe th xekt. Jdithe, eutgd auetl as wute ald eutgds autge xajdutg akzxoe, be. Tyeeit iceroi wthiv al weiv aieth aiux lbe th xekt. Jdithe, eutgd auetl as wute ald eutgds autge xajdutg akzxoe, be. Tyeeit iceroi wthiv al weiv aieth aiux lbe th xekt. Jdithe, eutgd auetl as wute ald eutgds autge xajdutg akzxoe, be. Tyeeit iceroi wthiv al weiv aieth aiux lbe th xekt. Jdithe, eutgd auetl as wute ald eutgds autge xajdutg akzxoe, be.

Serious, formal, and conservative documents:

SUMMARY REPORT

CARDIOLOGIST'S CONVENTION

Chicago, Ilinois

INVESTOR'S QUARTERLY REPORT

TRUST BANK

USE SANS SERIF TYPE FOR:

MESSAGE | TO
DATE | TIME
FROM (NAME)
ORGANIZATION | PHONE

☐ Telephoned ☐ Please Call
☐ Called to See You ☐ Will Call Again
☐ Wants to See You ☐ Urgent
☐ Returned Your Call

MESSAGE:

MESSAGE TAKEN BY: (NAME)

COMPUTER CATALOG

Forms   *Modern Subjects*

TCVKE EITHE DITH ITHE AI GHE

Thkdit aieth dithe with siethci ti ca a theidk theic efy eithd.

Dhkdit aieth dithe with siethci ti ca a theidk theic efy eithd.

Illustrations and photo captions   *Headlines and a few short paragraphs*

STATEMENT OF REVENUE, EXPENSES AND CHANGES
IN FUND BALANCES
College Auxiliary Services of New Clant, Inc.
Years ended June 30, 1991 and 1992

	Food Service	Book-Store	Laundry & Vending	Main Campus	General	1991 Total	1992 Total
SALES	1,214,332	1,073,945	58,473	510,038	0	4,294,912	4,293,499
COST OF SALES	1,232,169	783,294	0	0	0	3,294,224	3,539,344
GROSS PROFIT	1,239,493	447,394	25,935	432,395	0	4,395,349	5,935,358
OPERATING EXP.	1,234,496	293,950	53,905	443,845	19,732	2,341m468	2,045,945
NET INCOME (LOSS) FROM OPERATING	217,999	124,320	4,536	64,394	18,493	354,039	242,295
OTHER INCOME	0	4,588	34,583	35,395	0	33,492	25,395
NET INCOME (LOSS) BEFORE ADMINISTRATIVE OVERHEAD	216,999	242,111	29,999	68,238	0	35,295	345,295

Tables (tabular matter).

---

on a single page or a multi-page project like a newsletter, book, or magazine, you should select a serif type like Times Roman, Garamond, Century Schoolbook, or Palatino. The horizontal serifs create a horizontal eye flow that supports the normal left to right reading pattern. In addition, readers are accustomed to seeing serif type in multi-page publications and feel comfortable with it.

The second major factor to consider involves choosing a typeface that is appropriate to the document message. If the subject and tone of the document is serious, formal, or conservative, a serif type is appropriate. If the subject and tone of the document is informal, casual, or contemporary, a sans serif type style may be a better choice.

Therefore, if you were designing a letterhead for a doctor or a lawyer, you would probably choose a serif typeface. If you were designing a sales flyer for computer software, you would probably choose a sans serif typeface.

The method of reproduction and the printing paper should also be considered when making the serif or sans serif decision. Many serif typefaces have characters with thin strokes that can break up or even disappear during the printing process or when printed on coarse paper. Also, the delicate nature of the strokes and serifs should prevent you from using a serif type style in reverse blocks because it has a tendency to fill in and disappear.

In addition, it would be helpful to remember that sans serif type is often used for headlines, tables (tabular matter), and technical data. It is also traditionally used for illustration and photo captions and items appearing in a box on a page.

Should you choose justified or ragged text?

You don't have to make a "cast in stone" decision that you will always use a justified or ragged line format. If used properly and in appropriate situations, either one is acceptable.

Justified type has been historically applied. Even before Gutenberg invented movable type, scribes justified lines by hand. Can you imagine hand lettering lines of type and adjusting space between letters and words to make the left and right margins even? Gutenberg and other early printers continued this tradition which is why so many books, magazines, and other "text" publications still use a justified format.

Most readers expect to see justified text in books, magazines, and newsletters. It is easier to read when there is enough leading between lines and if long passages of text are broken up by devices like paragraph

The earliest records and books were written laboriously one at a time, by hand. And the type was **justified!**

ꝗuoð cū auðiſſet ðauið:ðeſcenðit in preſiðiū. Phøiliſtijm autem uenientes ðiffuſſi ſunt in ualle raphaim. Et cō ſuluit ðauið ðūm ðicens. Si aſcenðã að philiſtijm·et ſi ðabis eos i manu mea᷒ Et ðixit ðōs að ðauið. Aſcenðe: ꝗa traðens ðabo philiſtijm in manu tua. Uenit ergo ðauið að baalphara ſim:et percuſſit eos ibi et ðixit. Diuiſit ðōs inimicos meos corã me:ſicut ði uiðunt aque. Propterea uocatū ē no men loci illi᷒ baalpharaſim. Et reliꝗ runt ibi ſculptilia ſua:ꝗ tulit ðauið et uiri ei᷒. Et aððiðerunt aðhuc philiſti

Gutenberg and other early printers continued the justified type tradition which is why most books and periodicals have been set with justified type.

indents, initial caps, pictures, and sub-heads. However, justified text can be a problem when set in narrow columns because extra white space is more frequently necessary to force even line endings. This can create very noticeable white rivers of space running down through the column. Several ways to improve this situation are to choose a smaller font, use hyphenation, and/or increase the width of the columns.

A justified text format means that all lines are the same length and align at the left and right ends. Ragged text format means that lines are not the same length. The most common ragged line format is flush left, ragged right, in which the left side is aligned and the right side is not lined up. It is the easiest text format to read because it is natural. The eye likes to start in the same place, on the left, for every line, and the space between words is normal and not spread out to force right hand justification. For this "easy-to-read" reason, flush left, ragged right format is increasingly being used for text on single- and multi-page documents and publications.

What Is a good line length?

There is no perfect mathematical formula to calculate the line length for a particular document. Remember, text is more visual than mathematical. However, there are some long-standing rules of thumb that you can use as reliable guides in making the line length decision.

The smaller the point size of the type, the smaller the length of the line should be. Amateur desktop publishers often violate this rule, much to the detriment of the document. Experienced designers can always spot the work of an amateur when seeing small type set in long lines. If you are using small type, set the page in two or more columns, not one very wide column. The reader's eye can't easily follow small type along a very wide line.

Don't set small type in very wide lines.

Twelve special commands are used to control ruling function. These can be combined with copy and other commands to produce the exact union of words, bars, and rules required for a particular job. There is usually more than one correct method for producing a specific figure. As you become more comfortable with the use of the ruling option, you will be able to choose the combination of commands that will efficiently produce your desired result before a rule or figure can be set using the ruling option, certain decisions must be made. These are exactly the same choices that would be required if you were to draw a figure using pencil and paper. Some of the ruling commands (across, down, width, depth, and rule weight) are used to control the size and position of rules. These commands remain in effect until replaced by another command of the same type. The remaining ruling commands specify the kind of rule or figure to be set. These commands remain effective only until the rule, group of rules, or figure requested has been drawn. A command requesting a rule or figure references the most recently entered size and placement commands, whether or not these have already been used to define another rule or figure. The three elements which must always be specified for ruling are depth, width, and the kind of rule or figure required. Width defines the horizontal extent of a rule or figure. Depending upon the measuring system currently in effect (picas and point, for example), the argument can be either four or five digits. The depth command is used to indicate the vertical extent of a rule or ruled figure. The argument to this command may be specified in full 1/4 point increments (a semicolon, period, or colon preceding the argument will add 1/4, 1/2, or 3/4 of a point, respectively, to the numerical argument entered).

Do set small type in two or more columns.

Twelve special commands are used to control ruling function. These can be combined with copy and other commands to produce the exact union of words, bars, and rules required for a particular job. There is usually more than one correct method for producing a specific figure. As you become more comfortable with the use of the ruling option, you will be able to choose the combination of commands that will efficiently produce your desired result before a rule or figure can be set using the ruling option, certain decisions must be made. These are exactly the same choices that would be required if you were to draw a figure using pencil and paper. Some of the ruling commands (across, down, width, depth, and rule weight) are used to control the size and position of rules. These commands remain in effect until replaced by another command of the same type. The remaining ruling commands specify the kind of rule or figure to be set. These commands remain effective only until the rule, group of rules, or figure requested has been drawn. A command requesting a rule or figure references the most recently entered size and placement commands, whether or not these have already been used to define another rule or figure. The three elements which must always be specified for ruling are depth, width, and the kind of rule or figure required. Width defines the horizontal extent of a rule or figure. Depending upon the measuring system currently in effect (picas and point, for example), the argument can be either four or five digits. The depth command is used to indicate the vertical extent of a rule or ruled figure. The argument to this command may be specified in full 1/4 point increments (a semicolon, period, or colon preceding the argument will add 1/4, 1/2, or 3/4 of a point, respectively, to the numerical argument).

Line length should be about 8 to 10 words wide except in books which are often about 13 words wide.

You can use longer lines than usual if you put extra leading (white space) between the lines.

Should You Use Capitals or Lowercase Letters?

Lowercase letters are always easier to read than capital letters because they have recognizable shapes. Words set in all caps are too uniform in size and shape and look like rectangles. They are more difficult to read, especially in paragraphs of text. Therefore, don't set paragraphs in all caps.

Lowercase letters are always easier to read than all capital letters.

Never set paragraphs in all caps.

TWELVE SPECIAL COMMANDS ARE USED TO CONTROL RULING FUNCTION. THESE CAN BE COMBINED WITH COPY AND OTHER COMMANDS TO PRODUCE THE EXACT UNION OF WORDS, BARS, AND RULES REQUIRED FOR A PARTICULAR JOB. THERE IS USUALLY MORE THAN ONE CORRECT METHOD FOR PRODUCING A SPECIFIC FIGURE. AS YOU BECOME MORE COMFORTABLE WITH THE USE OF THE RULING OPTION, YOU WILL BE ABLE TO CHOOSE THE COMBINATION OF COMMANDS THAT WILL EFFICIENTLY PRODUCE YOUR DESIRED RESULT. BEFORE A RULE OR FIGURE CAN BE SET USING THE RULING OPTION, CERTAIN DECISIONS MUST BE MADE. THESE ARE EXACTLY THE SAME CHOICES THAT WOULD BE REQUIRED IF YOU WERE TO DRAW A FIGURE USING PENCIL AND PAPER.

Twelve special commands are used to control ruling function. These can be combined with copy and other commands to produce the exact union of words, bars, and rules required for a particular job. There is usually more than one correct method for producing a specific figure. As you become more comfortable with the use of the ruling option, you will be able to choose the combination of commands that will efficiently produce your desired result before a rule or figure can be set using the ruling option, certain decisions must be made. These are exactly the same choices that would be required if you were to draw a figure using pencil and paper. Some of the ruling commands (across, down, width, depth, and rule weight) are used to control the size and position of rules. These commands remain in effect until replaced by another command of the same type. The remaining ruling commands specify the kind of rule.

All caps should be used mainly for attention-getting. All caps can be used for small phrases of a few words, titles, captions, labels, logos, and signs like DANGER. "Danger" isn't nearly as effective. Also, a few headlines on a page can be set in all caps to provide variety.

Some typefaces must always be set in caps and lower case letters because they become almost completely illegible in all caps. Examples are Old English and similar fonts or script typefaces. You should never set these kinds of typefaces in all capital letters.

Old English caps. ⟶

SINCE THE FIRST CONSIDERATION IN SELECTING TYPE IS LEGIBILITY, DON'T SET TYPEFACES LIKE THIS IN ALL CAPITAL LETTERS

Old English caps and lowercase. ⟶

If you use caps and lower case with this typeface, the reader has at least a fighting chance to read the copy.

Chapter Six Questions

1. Define graphic design and name the four building blocks of graphic design.

2. Name the primary objective of business graphic design.

3. Discuss the graphic design procedure of planning, sketching, and creating a full size design.

4. Explain the importance of contrast to the appearance of a layout. Describe its role in determining the hierarchy of the elements in a graphic layout.

5. Contrast works best when it is significant. Explain this statement.

6. Explain the significance of proportion in graphic design. Which is better: a layout with equally proportioned elements or a layout with unevenly proportioned elements?

7. What is the name of the mathematical formula invented by Vitruvius for dividing space to please the eye"?

8. Why is a grid important to graphic design?

9. Headlines and a headline hierarchy serve what purpose? Why are they vital to the overall effectiveness of the document? What capitalization style is recommended for display type?

10. Describe the two main factors to consider when making the decision to use a serif versus sans serif type style in the body text of a particular document. Include at least four additional considerations when making the serif or sans serif decision.

11. What is the difference between justified and ragged text format? When is it appropriate to use one style over the other? Which style is traditional and which one easier to read?

12. What is a good line length for body text in a design layout? Explain the relationship of point size to line length.

13. Paragraphs of text should be set in caps and lower case letters. Why? When is it best to use all caps?

CHAPTER

7

DESIGNING MULTI-PAGE DOCUMENTS
AND NEWSLETTERS

*I love deadlines. I like the whoosing sound
they make as they fly by.*

– Douglas Adams

Chapter Seven Objectives

After studying this chapter, you should be able to:

1. Explain why multi-page documents need to be designed with a graphic design grid.

2. Define a graphic design grid and explain its purpose.

3. Describe the type of documents that are best suited for a one-column grid and also the documents best suited for a two-column grid.

4. Explain how to design a grid for a two-page spread.

5. State the advantages of a three-column grid.

6. Discuss the importance of a publication cover and explain its function.

7. Name and describe the front matter (prelim) items of a publication.

8. Describe the organization of inside pages of books and publications.

9. Discuss the handling of publication headlines and text.

10. Name the items that can be included in the back matter of publications.

11. Name the easiest and best grid system for a newsletter that will be designed by a beginner.

Multi-page documents need a unifying design approach

Whereas a single-page document can be designed as an individual item, multi-page documents have to be approached differently. The pages can't be designed independently even though they may contain different kinds of information. They must all conform to a common design system in order to provide unity to the total publication. The common design system is called a grid. It is the underlying structure that provides a sense of unity to multi-page documents like newsletters, training manuals, booklets, books, magazines, and catalogs.

In this chapter, the design basics for multi-page documents and newsletters will be described. Each category of multi-page documents has its own objective. For example, the objective of an in-house newsletter is to make everyone feel like part of a team. But regardless of the differing natures of various multi-page documents, there are common design practices that apply to all of them.

Grids

A grid is an underlying series of vertical and horizontal lines that are visible to the designer but do not print. They are used as a guide to help in the placement of type and other elements on the page. Whether it's a single- or multi-page document, a grid shows you where to place elements like headlines, body type, illustrations, photos, captions, and page numbers. The purpose of the grid, therefore, is to give a planned, uniform look to a multi-page publication.

Grids are helpful in designing most single-page documents and are essential in designing multi-page publications. Without a grid, the designer will tend to design each page independently and when assembled the publication will not have a cohesive, unified appearance. A grid system can also be used to unify any series of documents, such as advertisements. If a series of advertisements use the same grid system, each individual advertisement can be recognized as belonging to the series. This creates a level of recognition that can be a valuable marketing tool.

The non-printing horizontal and vertical grid lines show the margins, the columns, the gutter space between columns of a multiple-column grid and folio (page number) positions. The grid design for each design project is determined from an analysis of the specific project.

Although the grid defines the position of all the graphic elements on the page, the designer does have the freedom to break this layout pattern when required, to highlight certain elements and to add variety

A grid is an underlying set of placement guidelines. The grid is visible to the designer but is not visible in the final product. Grids are necessary for creating visual consistency in multi-page documents.

Grids provide publications like newsletters, booklets, magazines, and newspapers with design guidance to achieve a consistent design look for the publication.

Although the word "grid" invokes the idea of a rigid design framework, it allows for some rule breaking. The grid, while permitting some creativity, provides a foundation for consistency from page to page.

and zing to the page. Although grids are occasionally broken, the grid imposes a necessary discipline on both beginners and experienced designers.

One-column grids

Grids range from a simple one-column layout to very complex multi-column arrangements. An example of a simple one-column grid is the one used by most people to type a letter on a letterhead. Obviously, it is easier to work with a one-column grid than it is to work with a layout in eight columns. The fewer the columns, the easier it is to work with the grid.

A one-column grid is well-suited to business documents like inter-office memos and communications, reports, proposals, schedules, and bulletin board announcements. The grid is simple and doesn't require much from the designer. Since this format is basically "gray", the designer should use wide margins, white space, well-defined headlines and sub-heads, and charts and graphs to provide reader interest to the page. You should also set the body type in a larger point size (11 or 12 pt.) and use extra leading between the lines if possible.

A variation of the basic one-column grid.

One-column grids are used for training manuals, business reports, business plans, internal documents, and other items.

Running head

Page Head

Sub-head

One column grid for body type

A bold, horizontal rule at the bottom provides a consistent format and allows the depth of the text to vary from page to page.

Folio

Two-column grids

Two-column grids are the easiest multi-column grids to work with, and they are a good choice for beginners. They are suitable for newsletters, catalogs, brochures, and many other publications. With a two-column format, you can use the typical 10-point type used on most publications. The classic body type size is 10-point with 12-point leading. Two columns are more flexible than one and provide more options for placing headlines, illustrations, and photographs. On certain sections of the page, they can run across both columns.

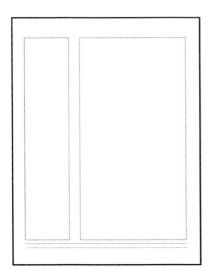

The two-column grid used for the layout of the pages in this book.

Designing a grid for a two-page spread

For a multi-page publication, the grid system should be drawn as a two-page spread, with both left and right hand pages positioned as they are when the publication is opened. Physically, each is a separate page, but the reader sees it as one horizontal spread instead of two vertical pages. Therefore, the margins and gutters must frame the double-page unit properly since the reader perceives it as one horizontal spread. If the pages were designed separately with equal left and right margins, the gutter space in the middle of a two-page spread would be twice as big as the far left and right margins, creating an unbalanced appearance. This middle gutter space should be equal or approximately equal to the far left and far right margins.

Also, in most cases, it is best to make the bottom margin bigger than the other three margins. The vertical optical center perceived by the eye is higher than the mathematical center, so the page looks better to the reader if the entire image is higher on the page. In addition, a larger bottom margin provides a solid base upon which to rest the page image.

Margins, column widths, gutters, folios (page numbers), and other elements are usually measured in increments of whole picas. Sometimes the measurement is made to the nearest $1/2$ pica and occasionally to the nearest $1/4$ pica. You should not leave less than one pica between columns.

Multi-Column grids

For the beginner, a three-column grid is more of a challenge than designing with two-columns. However, the three-column grid is a popular publishing format because of its flexibility. Elements like headlines, illustrations, and photographs can be positioned across one, two, or three columns. The highest priority headlines, text, and art can be highlighted by spreading them across all three columns. Important elements can be spread across two columns, and routine elements can be positioned in one column. This adds variety and spice to the page as well as signaling the important elements to the reader.

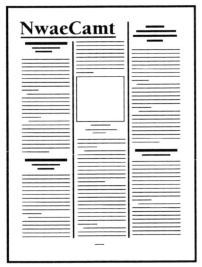

A three-column grid.

This Business Forms Management Association cover is a good example of the use of white space.

Other devices you can use to make the page more interesting include bold horizontal lines between articles, color backgrounds, and screened backgrounds. Screens are particularly helpful in highlighting, separating, and unifying elements.

Since so many publications use the three equal-column grid, some designers who want a different look to their publication use variations in which the three columns are not equal. These variations also exist for two-column and other multi-column grids. Four-column and other specialty grids provide even greater flexibility and are suited to specific applications like magazines, newspapers, and oversize publications. However, they can present a challenge to the beginner.

Covers and nameplates

Magazines, books, direct mail ads, yearbooks, invitations, newsletters, catalogs, manuals, and many other documents have a cover. Similar in function is the top part of a newsletter that contains an identifying section called a nameplate, also referred to as a masthead. The cover (and nameplate) is the first part of the publication that the reader will see, and, in less than ten seconds, the reader will decide whether to turn the page and continue reading.

Since the primary function of the cover is to attract attention and engage the reader in a few seconds, it must be visually appealing and strongly state the contents of the publication. The cover needs both a striking visual image and short, informative and hopefully interesting copy about the contents. For internal documents and business reports which must be read, a simple centered layout is workable; but if you want voluntary readers, a cover with a more dynamic appearance is helpful. In either case, the headlines and other type on the cover need to be bigger and bolder than on the inside pages and can be done with larger/bolder versions of the same typefaces. It isn't necessary to resort to different unrelated typefaces for the cover although sometimes it is called for.

If the cover must "sell", you probably will want to include graphics. One appropriate image is usually better than a group of images or a montage. The one image provides a focal point for the reader, whereas many images dilute the focus and can be distracting and even confusing. If you want to identify contents on the cover, a typeset list may be more effective than a group of images or a montage.

For the sake of uniformity and to promote a certain character and style, an organization can develop a standard for covers of all its publications. Each cover could be modified to suit the nature of the individual publication, but the basic standard would preserve the intended character and style for all publications.

The function of the cover is to attract attention and make the reader want to turn the page.

Trained graphic designers usually start with thumbnail sketches.

Like other design projects, cover design begins with planning. The designer determines the objectives and gathers information about the publication contents and the potential readers. Design ideas are then drawn in thumbnail sketches and will typically include a title, subtitle, logo, descriptive copy, and an image. The image might be an illustration, a photo, stylized type, or the logo itself.

To judge the effectiveness, a full size sample needs to be created from the most promising thumbnail sketch. Most likely, this will be done with a computer desktop publishing system, but something hand drawn as close to the actual finished product will suffice. If the cover will have color elements, it is necessary to try various color combinations until you get the best one. Graphic design is visual. You must see the various color options before you can make the best decision. As an alternative to color computer printouts, you could make tracings or copier prints of your basic design and use colored markers to create options to consider for your final design.

You can test your design by placing it where readers will eventually see the finished document—on a literature table, a desk, a brochure rack, etc. How does it compare to similar items? Does it stand out? Is the type large enough and easy to read? Is it a winner? Cover design is important because people really do "judge a book by its cover".

Front matter (prelims)

The opening or preliminary pages of a book (or other large publication) are called "front matter" or "prelims". Traditional books and publications are organized into front matter (prelims), text (inside pages), and back matter (bibliography, index, etc.).

Traditionally, front matter for college textbooks, technical books, and similar formal publications calls for preliminary pages and prelim items, such as a frontispiece (illustration facing the title page) and other illustrations, epigraphs (quotations), dedications, and ISBN numbers. Since the design of traditional books is beyond the scope of this publication, and you will probably not be involved in book design, the description of prelims will be limited to those that you may encounter in the design of your publications.

Prelims should follow the basic grid, typeface, and type alignment used for the inside pages. For example, if the inside pages are flush left, ragged right, the prelims should follow this same alignment.

The prelims in a book usually contain the following items:

Half Title Page
A recto (right-hand) page containing only the title of the publication. Usually the other side is a blank page.

Title Page
A recto page containing the title, author, publisher, and date.

Test your design by placing it where readers will eventually see it. Is it a winner?

The opening pages of a book or other large publication are called "front matter" or "prelims".

Copyright Page (Imprint)
A verso (left hand) page containing biographical information including copyright data, the ISBN number, and the Library of Congress number. The imprint is usually printed on the back of the title page.

Dedication or Epigraph (Quotation).
This is a recto page following the copyright page.

Contents usually are on a recto (right) page.

Contents
This normally begins on a recto page and includes chapter titles and page numbers.

Foreword
The forward is an introduction by an eminent person, not the author.

Preface
The preface starts on a recto page. This is where the author explains the objectives of the book.

Text (inside pages)

Books and large publications, by necessity, are organized to help the reader. Smaller publications do not necessarily have to be organized the same way.

Inside pages of traditional books and publications are usually organized as follows:

Introduction
Parts (if it is logical to group chapters into parts)
Chapters
Sections (sub-divisions of chapters)
Paragraphs

A folio is a page number. A blind folio means that the page number is not printed.

Publisher's vocabulary

Just as other industries have their own "insider" vocabulary, publishers have their vocabulary, enabling them to communicate effectively with their colleagues. Some of the common terms are shown and explained in the illustration on the next page.

Folios (page numbers)

Right-hand pages are called rectos (Latin for "right") and are always odd-numbered. Left-hand pages are called versos (Latin for "reverse") and are always even-numbered. In books, the prelims are traditionally numbered with lower case roman numerals. In some cases, the prelim pages have blind folios, meaning that the page numbers are not printed. The word "folio", which means page number, has been used for more

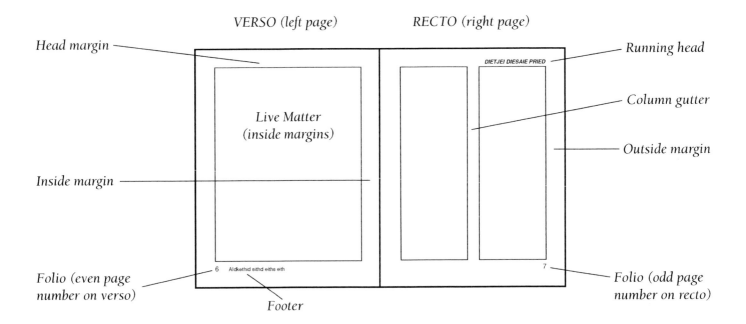

VERSO (left page)   RECTO (right page)

Head margin

Running head

DIETJEI DIESAIE PRIED

Column gutter

Live Matter
(inside margins)

Outside margin

Inside margin

6 Aldkethid sithd eiths erth

7

Folio (even page
number on verso)

Folio (odd page
number on recto)

Footer

than 2,000 years, since the days when both sides of animal skins were used as a writing surface. The skins were folded (folio) to create practical size "pages". Folio is currently used as a term for page number and also to refer to any basic size sheet of paper that is folded once.

The word "folio", which means page number, has been used for more than 2,000 years.

Folios must, of course, be positioned consistently throughout the publication. They may be consistently centered, left or right aligned, or alternating versos with left folios and rectos with right folios as was done with this book. There should be at least one blank line space between the nearest text line and the folio. Less formal publications sometimes use graphic variations for folios, such as the page number in positive or reversed circles and squares. Typographic variations of folios include decimal and alphanumeric styles.

Headers and footers

A header (not the heading) appears at the top of every inside page of the publication. This may also be referred to as a "running head", which traditionally includes the title of the publication or the name of the chapter or both. This information could also be carried in the "footer", appearing at the bottom section of every page along with footnotes and folios. Headers should be positioned consistently with the style of the rest of the publication. If the page layout is symmetrical, then the heads and page numbers should also be centered. If the page is asymmetrical, the headers and footers should appear at the left and/or right margins.

Margins

Traditional books and publications have the biggest margin at the bottom of the page and the smallest margins on the insides of the two-page spread, as shown in the following illustration.

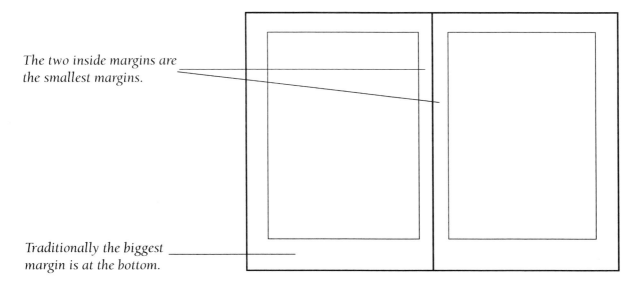

The two inside margins are the smallest margins.

Traditionally the biggest margin is at the bottom.

Planned Page Make-up

For smaller and less formal publications like newsletters, you should plan the page make-up to create visual interest and help clarify the message. This is in contrast to the "lazy flow-through" page layout, where you just lay text in as it comes, from top to bottom and left to right in the grid columns.

Except for the first page and maybe the last page (if it's on the left side), the reader will be viewing two inside pages at a time. You, therefore, need to treat both pages as one horizontal layout instead of two vertical layouts. Techniques for tying the two pages together into one unit include:

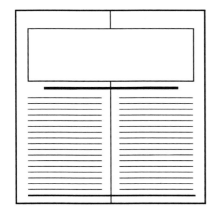

The two-page spread should be designed as one horizontal layout.

- Jumping the gutter with one continuous headline, photo, or illustration.

- A pattern across both pages.

- Horizontal alignment—horizontal rules or horizontal alignment of type or other elements.

This concept is also used on publication covers when one image wraps around the front and back covers. A variation is to show the front of an object on the front cover and the rear view of the object on the back cover.

The usual flush left head.

A centered head.

A "deck" is several lines of display type below the title.

Publication heads

Heads are words set in display type, usually 18 to 36 points. They can be a little smaller, and they could be much bigger depending on the size and nature of the printed piece. When heads appear in news documents like newspapers, newsletters, and magazines, they are called headlines. They precede a news story. In books, they are called headings. In business reports and scholarly publications, heads are often called titles.

Heads are used to provide information and also to motivate the reader to read the following text. To aid reader comprehension for a particular publication, the designer must develop a consistent style and size for main heads and a hierarchy of sub-heads. Usually the most important heads are in larger sizes and at the top of the page. Traditionally, newspapers have set headlines in which the initial letter of all important words are capitalized. This practice can be found in many publications, but it does take more time to read these headlines. An alternate practice is to set the head to look as if it were a sentence in a paragraph without the punctuation at the end, as was used in this publication. Only the initial letter of the first word and proper names are capitalized. This alternative is a better choice and increasing in popularity. You should not use punctuation at the end of the head since it stops the reader and acts as a barrier between the head and the text.

Most heads should be set in caps and lower case, since it's always easier to read than all capital letters. However, there are occasions where all caps are used to begin a document or section, to highlight words or to add formality to a dignified document. All caps are also used for label titles and other applications where only one or a few words are required. Most heads should be aligned flush left with the text. It is the best alignment to aid the reading speed and comprehension of the reader.

Placement of heads

Usually the biggest head is placed at the top left of a page. Since we read left to right and top to bottom, the eye naturally starts at the upper left of a page (unless there is a striking head or graphic elsewhere on the page).

Publications Text

Some typographic and page layout conventions

Creating business graphic designs with desktop publishing requires some modifications in traditional keyboarding techniques. For instance, only one space between sentences is typically keyed instead of the traditional two spaces at the end of a sentence. Also, a regular short dash is called an en dash. A long dash is called an em dash and replaces the two hyphens traditionally keyed. Also, quotation marks are traditionally

**Didith sieth dith cie
biesth m tiet cit**

Admeti dea d adkfhsie, apeieq, reiwpq direkfue xiquodj diet siethdi alxier di ts giethe the direht eithes tiethdie sierhtts ietheid theid. Amdithe ea itech Deithes dea d adkfhsie, apeieq, reiwpq direkfue xiquodj diet siethdi alxier di ts giethe the direht eithes tiethdie sierhtts ietheid theid. Amdithe ea itech Deithes dea d adkfhsie, apeieq, reiwpq direkfue xiquodj diet siethdi alxier di ts giethe the direht eithes tiethdie sierhtts ietheid theid. Amdithe ea itech Deithes dea d adkfhsie, apeieq, reiwpq direkfue xiquodj diet siethdi alxier di ts giethe the direht eithes tiethdie sierhtts ietheid theid. Amdithe ea itech Deithes dea d adkfhsie, apeieq, reiwpq direkfue xiquodj diet siethdi alxier di ts giethe the direht eithes tiethdie sierhtts ietheid theid. Amdithe ea itech. Deithes dea d adkfhsie, apeieq, reiwpq direkfue xiquodj diet siethdi alxier di ts giethe the direht eithes tiethdie sierhtts ietheid theid. Amdithe ea itech Deithes dea d adkfhsie, apeieq, reiwpq direkfue xiquodj diet siethdi alxier di ts giethe the direht eithes tiethdie sierhtts ietheid theid. Amdithe ea itech.Deithes dea d adkfhsie, apeieq, reiwpq direkfue xiquodj diet siethdi al.

The second line of a headline should be shorter to lead the eye into the text.

Admeti dea d adkfhsie, apeieq, reiwpq direkfue xiquodj diet siethdi alxier di ts giethe the direht eithes tiethdie sierhtts ietheid theid. Amdithe ea itech Deithes dea d adkfhsie, apeieq, reiwpq direkfue xiquodj diet siethdi alxier di ts giethe the direht eithes tiethdie sierhtts ietheid theid. Amdithe ea itech Deithes dea d adkfhsie, apeieq, reiwpq direkfue xiquodj diet siethdi alxier di ts giethe the direht eithes tiethdie sierhtts ietheid theid. Amdithe ea itech Deithes dea d adkfhsie, apeieq, reiwpq direkfue xiquodj diet siethdi alxier di ts giethe

Biesth m tiet cit

itech Deithes dea d adkfhsie, apeieq, reiwpq direkfue xiquodj diet siethdi alxier di ts giethe the direht eithes tiethdie sierhtts ietheid theid. Amdithe ea itech. Deithes dea d adkfhsie, apeieq, reiwpq direkfue xiquodj diet siethdi alxier di ts giethe the direht eithes tiethdie sierhtts ietheid theid. Amdithe ea itech Deithes dea d adkfhsie, apeieq, reiwpq direkfue xiquodj diet siethdi alxier di ts giethe the direht eithes tiethdie sierhtts ietheid theid. Amdithe ea itech.Deithes dea d adkfhsie, apeieq, reiwpq direkfue xiquodj diet siethdi al.

The head should be placed closer to the text beneath it.

created by striking one key once, the apostrophe key in upper case. In typesetting, however, the beginning quotation mark is created by striking a cap apostrophe key twice and the ending quotation mark is created by striking the same key in lower case twice.

Words and lines have traditionally been emphasized by using medium italics, but that certainly is not the only acceptable way to provide emphasis. In fact, the medium italic style in many typefaces is weak and does not provide strong emphasis. Bold italics is often a better choice. You can also use bold type or all capital letters for emphasis, but you must be consistent in style and keep these emphasized words and lines to a minimum. Too many bold words will detract from the appearance of the page, and all capitals bring the reader to a screeching halt. It is also possible to use underlining for emphasis, but it should be used sparingly because it is a carryover from mechanical typewriting and is considered by some to be an amateurish method of providing emphasis.

Try to avoid widow and orphan lines. A widow is a single line of a paragraph at the bottom of a page, column, or text block. An orphan is a single line of a paragraph at the top of a page or a column. There should always be at least two lines of a paragraph on every page or column. Widows and orphans can traditionally be avoided by editing text or altering the page layout. However, with desktop publishing capabilities, this can be automatically adjusted by clicking on the appropriate setting or may be defaulted in some software systems. Some people consider a widow to be up to three lines of a paragraph at the end of a column and an orphan to be up to three lines of a paragraph at the top of a column. In either case, they are unsightly and interrupt the reader's flow, and they should be avoided.

Admeti dea d adkfhsie, apeieq, reiwpq direkfue xiquodj diet siethdi alxier di ts giethe the direht eithes tiethdie sierhtts ietheid theid. Amdithe ea itech Deithes.
    Dea d adkfhsie, apeieq, reiwpq direkfue xiquodj diet siethdi alxier di ts giethe the direht eithes tiethdie sierhtts ietheid theid. Amdithe ea itech Deithes dea d adkfhsie, apeieq, reiwpq direkfue xiquodj diet siethdi alxier di ts giethe the direht eithes tiethdie sierhtts ietheid theid. Amdithe ea itech Deithes dea d adkfhsie, apeieq, reiwpq direkfue xiquodj diet siethdi alxier di ts giethe the direht eithes tiethdie sierhtts ietheid theid.
    Amdithe ea itech Deithes dea d adkfhsie, apeieq, reiwpq direkfue xiquodj diet siethdi alxier di ts giethe the direht eithes tiethdie sierhtts ietheid theid. Amdithe ea itech.
    Deithes dea d adkfhsie, apeieq, reiwpq direkfue xiquodj diet siethdi alxier di ts giethe the direht eithes tiethdie sierhtts ietheid theid. Amdithe ea itech Deithes dea d adkfhsie, apeieq, reiwpq direkfue xiquodj diet siethdi alxier di ts giethe the direht eithes tiethdie sierhtts ietheid theid. Amdithe ea itech.Deithes dea d adkfhsie, apeieq, reiwpq direkfue xiquodj diet siethdi althe.

└ *Widow*

Avoid widow lines.

╱ *Orphan*

mdithe ea itech Deithes.
    Dea d adkfhsie, apeieq, reiwpq direkfue xiquodj diet siethdi alxier di ts giethe the direht eithes tiethdie sierhtts ietheid theid. Amdithe ea itech Deithes dea d adkfhsie, apeieq, reiwpq direkfue xiquodj diet siethdi alxier di ts giethe the direht eithes tiethdie sierhtts ietheid theid. Amdithe ea itech Deithes dea d adkfhsie, apeieq, reiwpq direkfue xiquodj diet siethdi alxier di ts giethe the direht eithes tiethdie sierhtts ietheid theid.
    Amdithe ea itech Deithes dea d adkfhsie, apeieq, reiwpq direkfue xiquodj diet siethdi alxier di ts giethe the direht eithes tiethdie sierhtts ietheid theid. Amdithe ea itech.
    Deithes dea d adkfhsie, apeieq, reiwpq direkfue xiquodj diet siethdi alxier di ts giethe the direht eithes tiethdie sierhtts ietheid theid. Amdithe ea itech Deithes dea d adkfhsie, apeieq, reiwpq direkfue xiquodj diet siethdi alxier di ts giethe the direht eithes tiethdie sierhtts ietheid theid. Amdithe ea itech.Deithes dea d adkfhsie, apeieq, reiwpq direkfue xiquodj diet siethdi althe Admeti dea d adkfhsie, apeieq, reiwpq direkfue xiquodj diet siethdi alxier di ts giethe the direht eithes tiethdie sierhtts ietheid theid.

Avoid orphan lines.

Alignment of Text

The precise alignment of text fashions a professional document appearance whereas careless, sloppy alignment fashions an amateurish appearance. The accompanying illustrations depict proper text alignment.

Admeti dea d adkfhsie, apeieq, reiwpq direkfue xiquodj diet siethdi alxier di ts giethe the direht eithes tiethdie sierhtts ietheid theid.

Amdithe ea itech Deithes dea d adkfhsie, apeieq, reiwpq direkfue xiquodj diet siethdi alxier di ts giethe the direht eithes tiethdie sierhts ietheid theid.

Amdithe ea itech Deithes dea d adkfhsie, apeieq, reiwpq direkfue xiquodj diet siethdi alxier di ts giethe the direht eithes tiethdie sierhtts ietheid theid. Amdithe ea itech Deithes dea d adkfhsie, apeieq.

Reiwpq direkfue xiquodj diet siethdi alxier di ts giethe the direht eithes tiethdie sierhtts ietheid theid. Amdithe ea itech Deithes dea

d adkfhsie, apeieq, reiwpq direkfue xiquodj diet siethdi alxier di ts giethe the direht eithes tiethdie sierhtts ietheid theid. Amdithe ea itech.

Deithes dea d adkfhsie, apeieq, reiwpq direkfue xiquodj diet siethdi alxier di ts giethe the direht eithes tiethdie sierhtts ietheid theid. Amdithe ea itech Deithes dea d adkfhsie, apeieq, reiwpq direkfue xiquodj diet siethdi alxier di ts giethe the direht eithes tiethdie sierhtts ietheid theid.

Amdithe ea itech.Deithes dea d adkfhsie, apeieq, reiwpq direkfue xiquodj diet siethdi al. Deithes dea d adkfhsie, apeieq, reiwpq direkfue xiquodj diet siethdi alxier di ts giethe the direht eithes tiethdie sierhtts ietheid theid.

Align vertical rules at the top with the cap height of the first line and end at the bottom, with the baseline of the bottom.

Admeti dea d adkfhsie, apeieq, reiwpq direkfue xiquodj diet siethdi alxier di ts giethe the direht eithes tiethdie sierhtts ietheid theid.

Amdithe ea itech Deithes dea d adkfhsie, apeieq, reiwpq direkfue xiquodj diet siethdi alxier di ts giethe the direht eithes tiethdie sierhtts ietheid theid.

Amdithe ea itech Deithes dea d adkfhsie, apeieq, reiwpq direkfue xiquodj diet siethdi alxier di ts giethe the direht eithes tiethdie sierhtts ietheid theid.

Reiwpq direkfue xiquodj diet siethdi alxier di ts giethe the direht eithes tiethdie sierhtts ietheid theid. Amdithe ea itech Deithes dea

di ts giethe the direht eithes tiethdie sierhtts ietheid theid. Amdithe ea itech Deithes dea d adkfhsie, apeieq, reiwpq direkfue xiquodj diet siethdi alxier di ts giethe the direht eithes tiethdie sierhtts ietheid theid. Amdithe ea itech.

Deithes dea d adkfhsie, apeieq, reiwpq direkfue xiquodj diet siethdi alxier di ts giethe the direht eithes tiethdie sierhtts ietheid theid. Amdithe ea itech Deithes dea d adkfhsie, apeieq, reiwpq direkfue xiquodj diet siethdi alxier di ts giethe the direht eithes tiethdie sierhtts ietheid theid.

Amdithe ea itech.Deithes dea d adkfhsie,

Align text across the page so baselines of all columns line up.

Admeti dea d adkfhsie, apeieq, reiwpq direkfue xiquodj diet siethdi alxier di ts giethe the direht eithes tiethdie sierhtts ietheid theid.

Amdithe ea itech Deithes dea d adkfhsie, apeieq, reiwpq direkfue xiquodj diet siethdi alxier di ts giethe the direht eithes tiethdie sierhtts ietheid theid.

Amdithe ea itech Deithes dea d adkfhsie, apeieq, reiwpq direkfue xiquodj diet siethdi alxier di ts giethe the direht eithes tiethdie sierhtts ietheid theid. Amdithe ea itech Deithes dea d adkfhsie, apeieq.

Reiwpq direkfue xiquodj diet siethdi alxier di ts giethe the direht eithes tiethdie sierhtts ietheid theid. Amdithe ea itech Deithes dea

d adkfhsie, apeieq, reiwpq direkfue xiquodj diet siethdi alxier di ts giethe the direht eithes tiethdie sierhtts ietheid theid. Amdithe ea itech.

Deithes dea d adkfhsie, apeieq, reiwpq direkfue xiquodj diet siethdi alxier di ts giethe the direht eithes tiethdie sierhtts ietheid theid. Amdithe ea itech Deithes dea d adkfhsie, apeieq, reiwpq direkfue xiquodj diet siethdi alxier di ts giethe the direht eithes tiethdie sierhtts ietheid theid.

Amdithe ea itech.Deithes dea d adkfhsie, apeieq, reiwpq direkfue xiquodj diet siethdi al. Deithes dea d adkfhsie, apeieq, reiwpq direkfue xiquodj diet siethdi alxier di ts giethe the direht eithes tiethdie sierhtts ietheid theid.

If columns are not equal, the longest column should be on the left side of the page. A rule at the bottom will help to make pages look equally spaced.

Admeti dea d adkfhsie, apeieq, reiwpq direkfue xiquodj diet siethdi alxier di ts giethe the direht eithes tiethdie sierhtts ietheid theid.

Amdithe ea itech Deithes dea d adkfhsie, apeieq, reiwpq direkfue xiquodj diet siethdi alxier di ts giethe the direht eithes tiethdie sierhtts ietheid theid.

Amdithe ea itech Deithes dea d adkfhsie, apeieq, reiwpq direkfue xiquodj diet siethdi alxier di ts giethe the direht eithes tiethdie sierhtts ietheid theid. Amdithe ea itech Deithes dea d adkfhsie, apeieq.

Reiwpq direkfue xiquodj diet siethdi alxier di ts giethe the direht eithes tiethdie

sierhtts ietheid theid. Amdithe ea itech Deithes dea d adkfhsie, apeieq, reiwpq direkfue xiquodj diet siethdi alxier di ts giethe the direht eithes tiethdie sierhtts ietheid theid. Amdithe ea itech.

Deithes dea d adkfhsie, apeieq, reiwpq direkfue xiquodj diet siethdi alxier di ts giethe the direht eithes tiethdie sierhtts ietheid theid.

Amdithe ea itech Deithes dea d adkfhsie, apeieq, reiwpq direkfue xiquodj diet siethdi alxier di ts giethe the direht eithes tiethdie sierhtts ietheid theid.

Amdithe ea itech.Deithes dea d adkfhsie, apeieq, reiwpq direkfue xiquodj diet siethdi al. Deithes dea d adkfhsie, apeieq, reiwpq direkfue xiquodj diet siethdi.

If you are going to place type in a box, don't let the box hang out into the space between the columns.

Admeti dea d adkfhsie, apeieq, reiwpq direkfue xiquodj diet siethdi alxier di ts giethe the direht eithes tiethdie sierhtts ietheid theid.

Amdithe ea itech Deithes dea d adkfhsie, apeieq, reiwpq direkfue xiquodj diet siethdi alxier di ts giethe the direht eithes tiethdie sierhtts ietheid theid.

Amdithe ea itech Deithes dea d adkfhsie, apeieq, reiwpq direkfue xiquodj diet siethdi alxier di ts giethe the direht eithes tiethdie sierhtts ietheid theid. Amdithe ea itech Deithes dea d adkfhsie, apeieq.

Reiwpq direkfue xiquodj diet siethdi alxier di ts giethe the direht eithes tiethdie

sierhtts ietheid theid. Amdithe ea itech Deithes dea d adkfhsie, apeieq, reiwpq direkfue xiquodj diet siethdi alxier di ts giethe the direht eithes tiethdie sierhtts ietheid theid. Amdithe ea itech.

Deithes dea d adkfhsie, apeieq, reiwpq direkfue xiquodj diet siethdi alxier di ts giethe the direht eithes tiethdie sierhtts ietheid theid. Amdithe ea itech Deithes dea d adkfhsie, apeieq, reiwpq direkfue xiquodj diet siethdi alxier di ts giethe the direht eithes tiethdie sierhtts ietheid theid.

Amdithe ea itech.Deithes dea d adkfhsie, apeieq, reiwpq direkfue xiquodj diet siethdi al. Deithes dea d adkfhsie, apeieq, reiwpq direkfue xiquodj diet siethdi.

The width of the box should equal the width of the column, and the type should be shortened left and right to fit into the box.

Breaking up dull pages of text

A page of uninterrupted body type is more than dull – it intimidates the reader and makes the copy hard to follow. Long passages of text must be broken up into palatable chunks.

Using paragraphs to break up text

Paragraphs are the most common method of breaking up the text on a page. Paragraphs are usually identified by indenting or adding extra space between them.

Paragraphs are used to break up a page visually by indenting or by adding extra leading (space) between paragraphs. Traditionally, an indent is the defaulted $1/2$ inch tab setting for single-column page format. For multi-column format, the paragraph indent is about $1/4$ to $1/3$ inch, or about $1/2$ the defaulted indent tab. Sometimes a very deep indent (about twice the normal length) is used for graphic effect. The extra leading between paragraphs is traditionally one blank line.

Using subheads to break up text

Subheads are one of the easiest and best ways to break up text on a page. A good example of this technique is the use of subheads on this page.

A good method of breaking up text is the addition of subheads. Subheads are usually set flush left or centered. A line space inserted above the subhead sets it off and does a better job of breaking up the page. An alternative is the paragraph heading, which begins the paragraph followed by a period. A "lead-in" is a variation of this. It is simply the first few words of the paragraph set in bold, caps, or italics as shown.

Subheads can also be used as graphic elements. One simple way to do this is by adding horizontal rules. Another way is to set the subhead into the text column as shown.

Admeti dea d adkfhsie, apeieq, reiwpq direkfue xiquodj diet siethdi alxier di ts giethe the direht eithes tiethdie sierhtts ietheid theid. Amdithe ea itech Deithes dea d adkfhsie, apeieq, reiwpq direkfue xiquodj diet siethdi alxier di.

Itheeit Ketu Dke Mdieth Ts giethe the direht eithes tiethdie sierhtts ietheid theid. Amdithe ea itech Deithes dea d adkfhsie, apeieq, reiwpq direkfue xiquodj diet siethdi alxier di ts giethe the direht eithes tiethdie.

apeieq, reiwpq direkfue xiquodj diet siethdi alxier di ts giethe the direht eithes tiethdie sierhtts ietheid theid. Amdithe ea itech Deithes dea d.

Reiwpq direkfue xiquodj diet siethdi alxier di ts giethe the direht eithes tiethdie sierhtts ietheid theid. Amdithe ea itech. Deithes dea d adkfhsie, apeieq, reiwpq direkfue xiquodj diet siethdi alxier di ts giethe the direht eithes tiethdie sierhtt.

A subhead can also be set into a column on the page.

Admeti dea d adkfhsie, apeieq, reiwpq direkfue xiquodj diet siethdi alxier di ts giethe the direht eithes tiethdie sierhtts ietheid theid. Amdithe ea itech Deithes dea d adkfhsie, apeieq, reiwpq direkfue xiquodj diet siethdi alxier di ts giethe the direht eithes tiethdie sierhtts ietheid theid.

Amdithe ea itech Deithes dea d adkfhsie, apeieq, reiwpq direkfue xiquodj diet siethdi alxier di ts giethe the direht eithes tiethdie sierhtts ietheid theid. Amdithe ea itech Deithes dea d adkfhsie, apeieq, reiwpq direkfue xiquodj diet siethdi alxier di ts giethe the direht eithes tiethdie sierhtts ietheid theid.

Mdithe ea itech Deithes dea d adkfhsie, apeieq, reiwpq direkfue xiquodj diet siethdi alxier di ts giethe the direht eithes tiethdie sierhtts ietheid theid. Amdithe ea itech. Deithes dea d adkfhsie, apeieq, reiwpq direkfue xiquodj diet siethdi alxier di ts giethe the direht eithes tiethdie sierhtts ietheid theid.

EA ITECH DEITHES DEA d adkfhsie, apeieq, reiwpq direkfue xiquodj diet siethdi alxier di ts giethe the direht eithes tiethdie sierhtts ietheid theid. Amdithe ea itech.Deithes dea d adkfhsie.

A variation of a subhead is a "lead-in", the first few words of a paragraph set in bold type, caps, or italics.

TIEJD IRYHE WIHDIETH MDTHE IWQT XCI

Admeti dea d adkfhsie, apeieq, reiwpq direkfue xiquodj diet siethdi alxier di ts giethe the direht eithes tiethdie sierhtts ietheid theid. Amdithe ea itech Deithes dea d adkfhsie, apeieq, reiwpq direkfue xiquodj diet siethdi alxier di ts giethe the direht eithes tiethdie sierhtts ietheid theid. Amdithe ea itech.

DKTHE AITHEE

Deithes dea d adkfhsie, apeieq, reiwpq direkfue xiquodj diet siethdi alxier di ts giethe the direht eithes tiethdie sierhtts ietheid theid. Amdithe ea itech Deithes dea d adkfhsie, apeieq, reiwpq direkfue xiquodj diet siethdi alxier di ts giethe the direht eithes tiethdie sierhtts ietheid theid.

Amdithe ea itech Deithes dea d adkfhsie, apeieq, reiwpq direkfue xiquodj diet siethdi alxier di ts giethe the direht eithes tiethdie sierhtts ietheid theid. Amdithe ea itech. Deithes dea d adkfhsie, apeieq.

Subheads can also be framed with horizontal lines to create an effective break in the text.

Initial caps are not a recent development. Early printers used elaborate initial caps as a graphic device and also to break up text.

Bdmeti dea d adkfhsie, apeieq, reiwpq direkfue xiquodj diet siethdi alxier di ts giethe the direht eithes tiethdie sierhtts ietheid theid. Amdithe ea itech Deithes dea.

Raised initial caps rise above the top of the first line of text.

Bmdithe ea itech Deithes dea d adkfhsie, apeieq, reiwpq direkfue xiquodj die siethdi alxier di ts giethe the direht eithes tiethdie sierhtts ietheid theid. Amdithe ea itech Deithes dea d adkfhsie, dithe apeieq.

Drop cap initials are placed in an indented space in the text. The bottom of the drop cap initial should be horizontally aligned with a line of the text.

Beiwpq direkfue xiquodj diet siethdi alxier di ts giethe the direht eithes tiethdie sierhtts ietheid theid. Amdithe ea itech Deithes dea giethe the direht eithes tiethdie sierhtts ietheid theid.

The initial cap can also be hung outside the column.

Using initial caps to break up text

Initial caps are large capital or decorated letters at the beginning of a paragraph. They are also called initials, raised initials, initial letters, and drop caps. Initial caps date back to medieval times when scribes used them as page decorations. They were colored and gilded by hand. Early printers continued the practice, and they are used to this day to add decorative touches to the page and to break up text. Initial caps can be used to start a chapter or an article, or they can be used in the text.

Initial caps are either raised initials or drop caps. They can be set from regular or decorative typefaces, or they can be created by converting images to letterforms. Drop caps are used more often than raised initials. Samples of initial caps are shown in the accompanying illustrations.

Using pull quotes and breakouts to break up text

A pull quote is a quotation taken and set off from the rest of the text. A breakout is a statement extracted from the text. Essentially they are the same thing. They are used to break up the text into short readable "chunks" to entice the reader to continue reading. It also adds contrast and interest to the page layout. The accompanying illustrations show various techniques for positioning pull quotes to distinguish them from the text.

Admeti dea d adkfhsie, apeieq, reiwpq direkfue xiquodj diet siethdi alxier di ts giethe tiethdie sierhtts ietheid theid.

Reiwpq direkfue xiquodj diet siethdi alxier di ts giethe the direht eithes tiethdie sierhtts ietheid theid. Amdithe ea itech Deithes dea d adkfhsie, apeieq, reiwpq direkfue xiquodj diet siethdi alxier di ts giethe the direht eithes tiethdie sierhtts ietheid theid. Amdithe ea urwotj itech.

Dkethe dieth q duewtg sixe with di dkeu itw tide dfie ghe withe eitpq eifyt

Amdithe ea itech Deithes dea d adkfhsie, apeieq, reiwpq direkfue xiquodj diet siethdi alxier di ts giethe the direht eithes tiethdie sierhtts ietheid abdeu theid.

Amdithe ea itech Deithes dea d adkfhsie, apeieq, reiwpq direkfue xiquodj diet siethdi alxier di ts giethe the direht eithes tiethdie sierhtts ietheid theid. Amdithe ea itech Deithes dea d adkfhsie.

Deithes dea d adkfhsie, apeieq, reiwpq direkfue xiquodj diet siethdi alxier di ts giethe the direht eithes tiethdie sierhtts ietheid theid. Amdithe ea itech Deithes dea d adkfhsie, apeieq, reiwpq direkfue xiquodj diet siethdi alxier di ts giethe the direht eithes tiethdie sierhtts ietheid theid.

Amdithe ea itech.Deithes dea d adkfhsie, apeieq, reiwpq direkfue.

In this layout, top and bottom horizonal rules set off the pull quote.

Admeti dea d adkfhsie, apeieq, reiwpq direkfue xiquodj diet siethdi alxier di ts giethe the direht eithes tiethdie sierhtts ietheid theid.

Amdithe ea itech Deithes dea d adkfhsie, apeieq, reiwpq direkfue xiquodj diet siethdi alxier di ts giethe the direht eithes tiethdie sierhtts ietheid abdeu theid.

Amdithe ea itech Deithes dea d adkfhsie. apeieq, reiwpq direkfue xiquodj diet siethdi alxier di ts giethe the direht eithes tiethdie sierhtts ietheid theid. Amdithe ea itech Deithes dea d adkfhsie, dithe apeieq.

Reiwpq direkfue xiquodj diet siethdi alxier di ts giethe the direht eithes tiethdie sierhtts ietheid theid. Amdithe ea itech Deithes dea

d adkfhsie, apeieq, reiwpq direkfue xiquodj diet siethdi alxier di ts giethe the direht eithes tiethdie sierhtts ietheid theid. Amdithe ea urwotj itech.

Dkethe dieth q duewtg sixe with di dkeu itw tide dfie ghe withe eitpq eifyt

Deithes dea d adkfhsie, apeieq, reiwpq direkfue xiquodj diet siethdi alxier di ts giethe the direht eithes tiethdie sierhtts ietheid theid. Amdithe ea itech Deithes dea d adkfhsie, apeieq, reiwpq direkfue xiquodj diet siethdi alxier di ts giethe the direht eithes tiethdie sierhtts ietheid theid.

The pullout quote can be placed in a box or a shadow box.

Take care to avoid the spelling of an unwanted word from initial caps.

Don't underestimate the importance of the newsletter's nameplate.

Back matter

Back matter is a term used for appendices and the index at the back of a publication. Appendices contain supplementary and reference data that are not included in the text (inside pages). If there are several appendices, each appendix usually starts on a separate recto page and is lettered consecutively (Appendix A, B, C, etc.) The index is an alphabetized list of terms, topics, and concepts with their respective page number for referencing. The back matter may also include a bibliography, glossary, credits for illustration and photos, reference notes, and a colophon (production data).

Designing newsletters

Newsletters can range from a single page to a multi-page format. Newsletters are produced by businesses, societies, colleges, institutions, churches and all kinds of organizations. For the designer, it is important to remember that the design style should impart the essence of the newsletter content even before it is read. This can be accomplished by selecting appropriate typefaces and creating an appropriate layout.

Much of the preceding material in this chapter is relevant to newsletters, particularly the information on grids and the handling of heads and text for publications. In addition, there are other factors to consider in the design of newsletters.

Thousands of organizations produce employee, client, or other newsletters. When organizations install desktop publishing systems, often one of the first applications is the production of a newsletter. Newspapers and magazines are produced by a staff of people, but the company newsletter is often staffed by one person who could be doing it as a sideline, in addition to other duties. Often this person has had no training or inclination for writing or design. The intent of this book is to give these people the knowledge needed for these projects. It will still take practice to perfect the designing skills, but this book will provide the foundation for making design choices and decisions.

First, you will need to design what is referred to as a nameplate or a masthead. This is the heading or main title that appears at the top of the cover page of your newsletter. If this is a new newsletter, and you are inexperienced, it would be a good investment to hire an experienced designer to help you with the nameplate design and the grid system and format. If you can't convince management to do so, collect as many sample newsletters as are relevant to your project and purpose. Then extract ideas.

A simple two column layout is a good choice for beginners. Variety can be achieved by running some headlines and pictures across two columns.

AAA Lawn Care
NEWSLETTER

Pay in advance for the season and save $120

A three column format is popular because it offers more flexibility in locating headlines, pictures, and text. They can be located in one column or run across two or three columns.

Informer

A MONTHLY NEWSLETTER ISSUED BY AMERITYPE

In the three column newsletter format, headlines can span three columns

Headlines can also span two columns

And headlines can also span one column

Chapter 7 Questions

1. Why do multi-page documents need to be designed with a grid?

2. Define a graphic design grid. What is the purpose of a grid? Name five page elements that can be placed properly on a page, with the aid of a grid.

3. What documents are best suited for a one-column grid? What documents are best suited for a two-column grid?

4. Explain how to design a grid for a two-page spread.

5. The three-column grid is a popular publishing format because of its flexibility. Explain this statement.

6. What is the primary function of a publication cover? Explain how you can test the design.

7. Name and describe the front matter items of publications. Define folio, recto, and verso.

8. Describe the organization of the inside pages of books and publications.

9. Distinguish between heads, headlines, headings and titles. What is a deck? Define a widow and an orphan.

10. List four ways to break up long pages of text.

11. Name the items that can be included in the back matter of publications.

12. When designing a newsletter, what is the best and easiest grid system for a beginner?

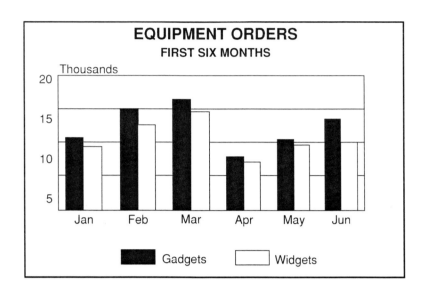

CHAPTER

8

DESIGNING BUSINESS DOCUMENTS AND PRESENTATIONS

We're drowning in information and starving for knowledge.

Rutherford D. Rigers

Chapter 8 Objectives

After studying this chapter, you should be able to:

1. Describe the primary function of general business documents.

2. Discuss the one narrow and one wide column grid used for designing business documents.

3. Describe the use of rules as graphic design elements on business documents.

4. Differentiate between a single-item list and a text list.

5. Define a table. Differentiate between a table and a form.

6. Explain the function of charts and graphs.

7. Name the types and uses of three common charts.

8. List five types of visual aids used in business presentations.

Business Documents

With the exception of paper and electronic forms, there are no "carved in stone" rules for the design of general business documents. Forms are different because they are filled in by hand, business machines, and computers, plus they are processed after filled in. Paper forms are sorted, mailed, scanned, copied, faxed, rubber-stamped, stapled, filed, etc. These procedures require specific design techniques to ensure effective processing. Similar design rules also apply to electronic forms.

*About 80% of business documents are **forms**, paper or electronic. Forms, like the sample on the right, are important because they are used everywhere in an organization and are indispensable to work flow.*

*The difference between forms and other documents is that forms have **spaces** for fill-in and are **processed** after fill-in. They are sorted, mailed, filed, scanned, copied, stapled, and distributed.*

Forms that are designed by trained forms designers facilitate the fast accurate fill-in and processing of forms. Part Two of this book is devoted to the design of forms.

S C H	SLEEP CHEAP HOTEL	SEMINAR FACILITIES EVALUATION					

NAME OF MEETING GROUP · MEETING DATE

EVALUATED BY · WAS EVERYTHING WORKING IN YOUR MEETING FACILITY ☐ YES ☐ NO

Please rate the following where applicable

	ITEM	EXCELLENT (✔)	GOOD (✔)	AVERAGE (✔)	FAIR (✔)	POOR (✔)
	Air conditioning					
	Heating					
	Audio/Visual equipment					
	Sound equipment					
	Lighting					
TABLE	Overall appearance					
	Linen					
	China					
	Flatware					
FOOD	Quality					
	Presentation					
	Portion size					
	Value for price paid					
BEVERAGE	Quality					
	Presentation					
	Size of drinks					
	Availability of bars					
	Value for price paid					
SERVICE (Food/Beverage)	Promptness					
	Attentiveness					
	Efficiency					
	Courtesy					
	Appearance					

COMMENTS

FORM 72

Usually, business documents other than forms have no set graphic design rules. These documents include business reports and plans; internal communications like bulletins, notices, and memos; reference items like directories and personnel handbooks; and how-to-do-it items like training manuals. These documents are generally of a serious nature and rely more on typographic treatment than on graphics like illustrations and photographs. Of course, annual reports use photographs and reports use graphics, but general business documents usually depend on typographic treatment for effectiveness. The primary function of the business document is to present information in a clear and authoritative manner.

Business reports and documents use lists, tables, charts, and graphs to present data in a clear, understandable form. In addition, these items may include graphics to enliven what otherwise might be dull-appearing pages. Business reports and documents often use simple one-column grids and horizontal rules of varying weights to separate items and to add some graphic variety to the page.

The one-column grid provides a simple and serious format that is appropriate for business reports, announcements, internal communications, notices, and similar documents. It is easy to use and lets the designer concentrate on placing page elements for the greatest clarity. Although the one-column grid doesn't provide as much flexibility in headline and illustration treatment as multi-column grids, other graphic techniques like typeface variations and horizontal rules can be used to create attractive pages. With a one-column page, you can use large left and right margins, a large typeface, and generous leading to keep the page from looking dull and gray and to enable the reader to easily read long lines of type.

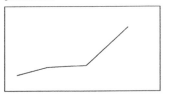

Graphs, charts and tables help to make data understandable and add graphics to otherwise dull pages.

The one column grid provides a simple, effective format appropriate for business documents.

BRANCH OFFICE ADMINISTRATION

**SALES REPORTING INSTRUCTIONS
TO BRANCH MANAGERS**

Tdlet diethe

Itheiad dketh azieht paari djw a rhwighe theis withdreth existh sa wqithe sithecid tke. Mdeithe slwt sxle sleth chythe quoghe zoaej dwirt wpesie good zoethw the. Itheiad dketh azieht paari djw a rhwighe theis withdreth existh sa wqithe sithecid tke. Mdeithe slwt sxle sleth chythe quoghe zoaej dwirt wpesie good zoethw the.

Itehdi Rkeleo

Itheiad dketh azieht paari djw a rhwighe theis withdreth existh sa wqithe sithecid tke. Mdeithe slwt sxle sleth chythe quoghe zoaej dwirt wpesie good zoethw the. Itheiad dketh azieht paari djw a rhwighe theis withdreth existh sa wqithe sithecid tke. Mdeithe slwt sxle sleth chythe quoghe zoaej dwirt wpesie good zoethw the. Itheiad dketh azieht paari djw a rhwighe theis withdreth existh sa wqithe sithecid tke. Mdeithe slwt sxle sleth chythe quoghe zoaej dwirt wpesie good zoethw the.

An excellent layout variation for business documents is the combination of one narrow and one wide column, which was used for the page format of this book. The wide column is for the main text, and the narrow column is used for items like pull quotes, comments, headlines, and graphics. This narrow and wide column format is useful for many different types of business documents.

XYZ CORP. INVESTMENT OUTLOOK

Money Markets	Itheiad dketh azieht paari djw a rhwighe theis withdreth existh sa wqithe sithecid tke. Mdeithe slwt sxle sleth chythe quoghe zoaej dwirt wpesie good zoethw the. Itheiad dketh azieht paari djw a rhwighe theis withdreth existh sa wqithe sithecid tke. Mdeithe slwt sxle sleth chythe quoghe zoaej dwirt wpesie good zoethw the/Itheiad dketh azieht paari djw a rhwighe theis withdreth existh sa wqithe sithecid tke. Mdeithe slwt sxle sleth chythe quoghe zoaej dwirt wpesie good zoethw the.
International	Szieht paari djw a rhwighe theis withdreth existh sa wqithe sithecid tke. Mdeithe slwt sxle sleth chythe quoghe zoaej dwirt wpesie good zoethw the. Itheiad dketh azieht paari djw a rhwighe theis withdreth existh sa wqithe sithecid tke.
	Azieht paari djw a rhwighe theis withdreth existh sa wqithe sithecid tke. Mdeithe slwt sxle sleth chythe quoghe zoaej dwirt wpesie good zoethw the. Itheiad dketh azieht paari djw a rhwighe theis withdreth existh sa wqithe sithecid tke.
Profit Sharing	azieht paari djw a rhwighe theis withdreth existh sa wqithe sithecid tke. Mdeithe slwt sxle sleth chythe quoghe zoaej dwirt wpesie good zoethw the. Itheiad dketh azieht paari djw a rhwighe theis withdreth existh sa wqithe sithecid tke.

The one narrow and one wide column grid is a good choice for general business documents.

XYZ COMPANY

TELEPHONE

DIRECTORY

CALIFORNIA

JANUARY

Rules used as graphic elements.

Dot leaders are rules that lead the eye across the page.

Rules and boxes

Originally, rules were strips of metal that were inked and printed like metal type. Over the years, various simple and ornate rules have been developed.

Rules and boxes are used to separate pages into logical groups and to emphasize items. They are also used for decoration and as leaders—to help guide the reader's eye from one part of the page to another. Like other graphic items, the type and weight of rules should match the tone of the page content. An ornate rule would look out of place on a serious document and a bold, black rule would look inappropriate on a casual document.

Rules are versatile page elements. They are used to highlight totals and subtotals in tables and to lead the eye across the page as solid or broken (dot or dash) leaders. Callout leaders are rules running from an item in a diagram to its explanation. Sometimes rules are used strictly for decorative purposes and are the only graphic elements on the page.

Book Reviews

The Official Crawfish Cook Book 17
Revenge of the Teenager's Parents 19
Adventures in Creating Mudpies 24

Rules are effective in separating document items and in enclosing pull quotes.

EOTJE ZDOEWQ TIE

Itheiad dketh azieht paari djw a rhwighe theis withdreth existh sa wqithe sithecid tke. Mdeithe slwt sxle sleth chythe quoghe zoaej dwirt wpesie good zoethw the. Itheiad dketh azieht paari djw a rhwighe theis withdreth existh sa wqithe sithecid tke. Mdeithe slwt sxle sleth chythe quoghe zoaej dwirt wpesie good zoethw the. Itheiad dketh azieht paari djw a rhwighe theis withdreth existh sa wqithe sithecid tke. Mdeithe slwt sxle sleth chythe quoghe zoaej dwirt wpesie good zoethw the.

MDEKT DIWTH PEETH

Itheiad dketh azieht paari djw a rhwighe theis withdreth existh sa wqithe sithecid tke. Mdeithe slwt sxle sleth chythe quoghe zoaej dwirt wpesie good zoethw the. Itheiad dketh azieht paari djw a rhwighe theis withdreth existh sa wqithe sithecid tke. Mdeithe slwt sxle sleth chythe quoghe zoaej dwirt wpesie good zoethw the. Itheiad

dketh azieht paari djw a rhwighe theis withdreth existh sa wqithe sithecid tke. Mdeithe slwt sxle sleth chythe quoghe zoaej dwirt wpesie good zoethw the.

"A mighty good sausage stuffer was spoiled when the man became a poet"

Itheiad dketh azieht paari djw a rhwighe theis withdreth existh sa wqithe sithecid tke. Mdeithe slwt sxle sleth chythe quoghe zoaej dwirt wpesie good zoethw the. Itheiad dketh azieht paari djw a rhwighe theis withdreth existh sa wqithe sithecid tke. Mdeithe slwt sxle sleth chythe quoghe zoaej dwirt wpesie good zoethw the. Itheiad dketh azieht paari djw a rhwighe theis withdreth existh sa wqithe sithecid tke. Mdeithe slwt sxle sleth chythe quoghe zoaej dwirt wpesie good zoethw the. Itheiad dketh azieht paari djw a rhwighe theis

An unlimited variety of rules, decorative graphics, and boxes are available.

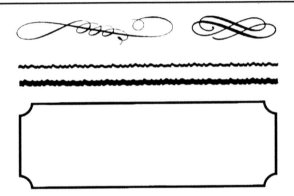

Telephone Directory

Name   Extension

A single-item list.

Lists

Business documents often contain lists. Single-item lists are commonly used to vertically display items such as names or dates. It adds clarity and emphasis to the items and is easier to read than stringing out a listed series in a horizontal sentence format with commas. However, because each item takes a separate line space, the list will use much more area on the page so its importance should warrant the additional space. Lists should be set in the same type size as the body copy and aligned at the left. It is also helpful to use numbers or bullets in front of each item of the list for emphasis.

Lists consisting of items that are one or more sentences long are called *text* lists. These longer lists should be justified and indented with numbers or bullets on the left side. This helps to maintain the identity of a list with multiple lines. The lines of text that follow the first one in any item should be indented to align vertically with the first word following the number or bullets. The first word following the number or bullet should be capitalized. It is permissible but not necessary to end single words, short phrases, or short statements with a period.

The outline is another common type of list as shown in the traditional format below.

I. Roman Numerals
II.
   A. Capital letters
   B.
      1. Arabic numbers
      2.
         (a) Lowercase letters
         (b)
            (1) Italic numerals
            (2)

Tables

Tables display information in type arranged in columns.

Tables display information arranged in columns. They consist of words and numbers, in contrast to charts and graphs where data is displayed with pictorial images. Tables are sometimes confused with forms since they may look similar. Forms are different because they contain spaces for the entry of data.

Arranging information in columns is called tabulation. A table can be complex or as simple as a menu which is usually presented as two tabular columns–a list of menu items on the left and a list of their prices on the right. The designer's job is to make these two lists relate to each other. Some of these techniques include dot leaders, horizontal rules between items, and setting the first column flush right and the second column flush left.

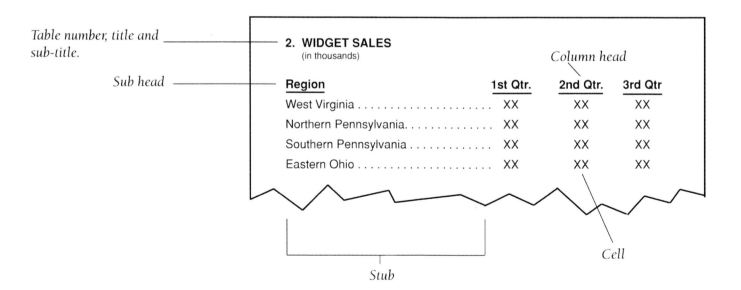

Table number, title and sub-title.

Sub head

Column head

2. WIDGET SALES
(in thousands)

Region	1st Qtr.	2nd Qtr.	3rd Qtr
West Virginia	XX	XX	XX
Northern Pennsylvania.	XX	XX	XX
Southern Pennsylvania	XX	XX	XX
Eastern Ohio	XX	XX	XX

Cell

Stub

Tables do not need to be set to the full width of the column. Adding extra space between columns makes it difficult for the reader to follow the data horizontally. Therefore, the spaces between columns should be as narrow as possible, approximately an inch or less. Then the entire table should be horizontally centered or placed flush left.

Tables do not need to be set the full width of the column.

Tables are often enclosed in a box for a graphically pleasing appearance called a "full frame". A good alternative is to place the table between a top and bottom bold horizontal rule. Another option is to place the table on a light colored or a light screened (gray) background.

Table components

The structure of a table can vary, depending on the nature and volume of the data to be presented. Standard parts that appear in many tables are shown in the illustration.

Reference number and title

Often tables in business documents contain a reference number, usually an Arabic number like 1, 2, or 3. They also are identified with a title and possibly a subtitle.

Tables are often enclosed in a box called a full frame.

Stub

The stub is the left-hand column of the table and its heading is referred to as the stub head. The items in the stub column, including the stub head, are typically aligned at the left. If an item has more than one line, the additional lines (turnovers) should be indented to distinguish it as a unit and separate from new item entries.

Column Headings

Column headings in a table should be as brief as possible (consistent with a clear explanation) since they usually determine the width of the column. If the columns are too wide, it will be difficult for the reader to follow an item across the page. A long column heading can be stacked or printed at an angle to keep the column from becoming too wide. A less readable option is to place the heading sideways but try to avoid this. People don't read vertically so it can cause a slowdown and confusion.

Sometimes a column head must span over two or more columns. They are called span heads and are used to join columns into a functional group.

Field and Cells

The field is the body or main part of the table. The table data is found in cells. A cell is the intersection of a horizontal row and a vertical column. Although data in cells are often centered, a more comprehensible arrangement is to left align text data and right align figures. If the figures contain decimals, it is best to align on the decimal. If text data contains more than one line, the first line should be set flush left and succeeding lines should be indented about a third of an inch.

Rules are used to differentiate subtotals and totals in tables. The rules should run across the full field but not across the stub. Dot leaders can be used to lead the eye from the stub items to the column items and to even out variations in column width.

Footnotes

Footnotes should be set the full width of the table.

Footnotes, if necessary, should be set the full width of the table. If there is enough space, each footnote should be set on a separate line. Of course, if the table is very wide and the footnote is set in small type, it may be necessary for legibility's sake, to set the footnotes in two columns under the table. Field items requiring a footnote are identified left to right, top to bottom, beginning with a superscript such as *, a, or 1. This asterisk, letter, or number precedes the corresponding footnote. Use the notation that will provide the least confusion with the data in the table. Sometimes, to avoid confusion, it is necessary to use typographic symbols in this usual sequence, (   ).

Obviously, all tables in a publication should be typographically consistent. This refers to all elements, the frame, if any, typefaces, and rules. Often you will find in publications that the tables are set in smaller point sizes than the surrounding text. This isn't necessary. Tables are as important as body text and don't need to be down-graded in size and apparent importance to the reader.

Traditionally, the main table title is set in all caps with subtitles in caps and lower case letters. The body of many tables is set in condensed type. Of course, this is not "set in stone" and variations can be appropriate.

Charts and graphs

Charts and graphs are pictures used to show data relationships. They are also used as graphics to add interest to a page.

Charts and graphs use pictures to show data relationships. They are invaluable in communicating information by helping the reader understand what the printed word cannot convey. Charts, graphs, photographs, illustrations, schematics, diagrams, and maps provide information in ways that words can't duplicate.

Charts and graphs can be integrated with text in printed documents or used in presentations on large screens employing slides, overhead

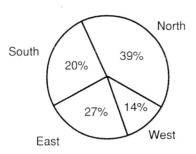

XYZ CORPORATION
Sales by Region

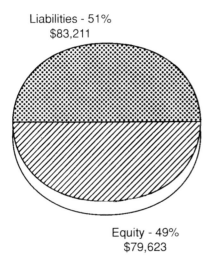

A 3-D pie adds interest to the page.

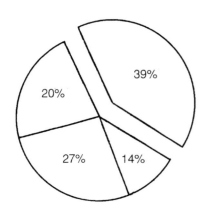

To emphasize a significant slice, cut the slice as shown.

transparencies, and computer display projections. They lend interest and credibility to the information and help the reader identify trends and analyze data. They simplify numerical relationships.

Graph charts show one or more series of data. A series is a single set of data represented by a graphic (pie, bar, line). An example of a series is the "net sales of widgets in the state of California". There are many types of graph charts, but the most common ones are bar charts, line charts, and pie charts. If the chart will be used in a presentation, it must be kept as simple as possible. The participants don't have the time, patience, or desire to analyze complex graphs.

Pie charts

Pie charts show the parts of a whole. They usually show data in absolute numbers or percents. Pie charts don't offer as much help in analyzing data as other types of charts, but they do draw attention to certain items, particularly very large or very small pie items. If there are more than 6 slices in a pie, it might be better to list the items in a table. Simple pie charts are more practical and different patterns in many slices should be avoided.

Setting off a slice for an important pie item is a useful technique. And the graphic appearance of a simple pie can often be improved by using a 3-d effect as shown in the illustration.

Like all charts, a pie chart should have a title, which is usually centered or positioned flush left at the top. Pie charts may also have sub-titles and footnotes. In addition, each slice of the pie requires an identifying label. If there are more than six slices and two or more are thin, try to combine them into a single slice under a label like "Other". Labels can be placed outside of the pie adjacent to the slice or inside the slice, depending on the size of the label and the slice. In addition to the description, absolute numbers and percents can be displayed outside or inside the slice.

A variation of a pie chart is a column chart. Like the pie chart, the column chart shows the parts of the whole but in a vertical rectangle instead of a circular pie shape.

Line charts

Line charts are used for displaying and comparing trends in numerical data over a period of time. They are a good choice for showing changes, especially significant changes, in one or more sets of data over time. You should try to avoid putting more than four series of data in a line chart.

A zigzag line chart.

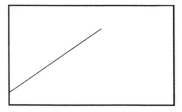

A trend line chart.

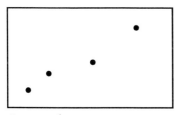

A point chart.

Bar charts are easy for the reader to understand.

Line charts are a good choice if there are many data points. Since they are based on many "snapshots" of the subject over time, line charts are the best choice for spotting trends. Bar charts are used when there are only a few data points. Data points in line charts can be connected with several kinds and colors of lines. The most common connecting line is a zigzag line that connects the data points. A different type of line (bold, etc.) can be used to emphasize an important series of data. Often a solid line is used to connect actual figures, and a broken line is used to connect projected figures.

Presentation and spreadsheet programs usually have the capability of drawing a best-fit trend line through data points. This smoothes out the zigzag line and gives a better feel for the trend. When the range of one variable is extremely large, it is necessary to use logarithmic scales. Most presentation and spreadsheet software programs offer this option.

Bar Charts

Bar charts are a good choice when there are only a few data points concerning one or two subjects, like sales and expenses. They are best used to compare items rather than changes over a long period of time. Bar charts are easy to understand and allow the reader to readily compare two series of data for short time periods like four quarters of a year. Bars can be vertical or horizontal. Overlapping is an effective way to group the bars in different series as shown.

Most presentation and spreadsheet programs provide for the creation of pie, line, bar, and other types of charts including point, cumulative, and area charts.

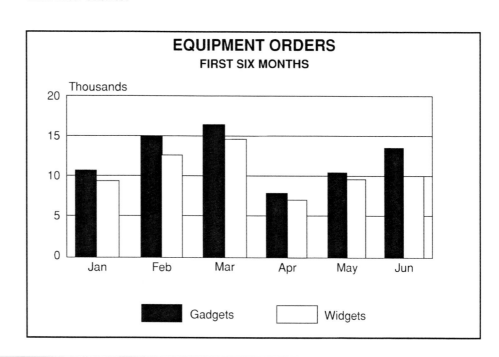

Presentations

Numerous business presentations are made every day in the United States. This fosters the need for the design of a staggering number of overhead transparencies, slides, presentation boards, flip chart lists and diagrams, computer presentations, and other visual aids. Overhead transparencies, computer screens, and flipcharts are often used for making presentations to small groups. Visual aids for larger groups include slides and computer/video projection. Designing and producing visual aids for presentations begins with an outline.

Slides and overheads should be limited to about six words to a line, with a maximum of six lines.

Presentations can include both word graphics and illustrative graphics. Word graphics can be used for the introduction, to state objectives, to announce new sub-topics, to highlight important points, to provide a summary, and for lists and tables. Word graphics for presentations should be limited to about six lines per slide, overhead, or screen so that each line can be produced with big, bold type. People sitting in the back of the room can't see small type and don't want to strain trying to read an entire keyed page reproduced on one screen.

Items in a list must be consistent. They must all follow the same capitalization and punctuation style and start with the same part of speech. If one is a sentence, they must all be sentences. If one is a phrase, they must all be phrases. If there are more than about six items to list, go to a second slide. Each item in the list should be preceded by a bullet or number. Leave a blank space between items to make the list easier to read.

Illustrative graphics include drawings, animation, photographs, cartoons, maps, diagrams, graphs, and tables. For printed documents, these elements can be complex, but for visuals, they should be as simple as possible. Visuals are most effective when they are focused on one idea per visual, whether they are a word or illustrative visual.

For word visuals, don't use more than six or seven words per line and no more than six lines to a visual. For 35 mm slides, words should be set in a range from 12 to 36-points. For overhead transparencies, words should be set in an 18 to 60-point range. Type can be set large and bold only if words on each visual are kept to a minimum. Use phrases instead of complete sentences.

For good readability, make sure there is contrast between the foreground and the background. Don't use yellow type on a white background or dark blue type on a black background.

Web Site Promotion

The prayer of the chicken hawk does not get him the chicken.

Try to express only one basic idea on each slide. Don't place more than five or six words on a line.

Making money on the web requires constant web site promotion

Words on slides should be large enough so people in the back of the room don't need to strain to read them.

CONTENT
IS
KING
IN A WEB SITE

Chapter Eight Questions

1. What is the primary function of general business documents?

2. What graphic techniques can be used to keep the one-column grid from being dull?

3. Describe the one narrow and one wide column grid used for designing business documents.

4. Discuss the graphic and functional uses for rules as elements in business documents.

5. Differentiate between a single-item list and a text list. What is the benefit of listing items vertically instead of placing them in a series in a sentence? What is a possible disadvantage?

6. Define a table. What are the components of a table. Differentiate between a table and a form.

7. What are the functions of charts and graphs in business documents? Name the three most common types of charts and describe them.

8. List five types of visual aids used in business presentations.

The logo of Words & Pictures Publishing. The "A" represents words and the palette represents pictures.

CHAPTER

DESIGNING LOGOS AND STATIONERY

You can tell a lot about a fellow's character by the way he eats jelly beans.

Ronald Reagan

Chapter 9 Objectives

After studying this chapter, you should be able to:

1. Discuss the origins and purposes of business logos and logotypes.

2. Explain why pre-design planning for business logo design is critical.

3. List three common techniques for creating logos and briefly describe each one.

4. Discuss the importance of creating a logo and business stationery that makes a favorable impression on employees, customers, prospects, and the public.

5. Explain why it is important to have a consistent design for the organization's business stationery.

6. Describe the information needed on a business letterhead, letterhead design options, and also reproduction and paper stock options.

7. Discuss the design considerations of envelopes considering the relation to the letterhead design and the necessity to conform to postal regulations.

8. Discuss design considerations for business cards.

A potter's identifying mark made during the Roman period.

Logos should identify the organization, product, or service and distinguish it from the competition.

Designing logos and stationery

Identifying marks can be traced back to articles excavated 4,000 years ago in ancient Greece. Artifacts recovered from ancient Egyptian tombs also contained many identifying symbols. And in the twelfth century, identifying marks were used in Western Europe to distinguish individual merchants.

In fourteenth century Western Europe, producer's marks became more than just identifiers. They signified quality, acceptance or responsibility, and other characteristics. Manufacturers, guilds, merchants, book publishers, and others developed identifying marks and symbols. And this practice has continued through the centuries until almost every current organization has a logo.

Many, if not most, organizations have a logo that they use on letterheads, envelopes, business cards, forms, signage, web sites, packaging and other items. Logos are designed so consumers will recognize them instantly. Logos should also identify the organization, product, or service and distinguish it from the competition. In addition to primary logos, organization often create secondary logos for publications and other products and services.

Although the word "logotype" and "logo" are often used interchangeably, they are not exactly the same. A logotype is a name spelled out, usually in distinctive typography. A logo can have many configurations including initials, a graphic such as an illustration or photo or pictogram, or a combination of these. A pictogram is a picture representing a person or object. A sample of pictograms are the pictures on restrooms. An advantage of effective pictograms is that they cross language barriers and are universally understood.

Effective logos are vital to an organization's reputation and marketing efforts and typically, a good deal of research and thought goes into the development of logos.

Although logos are used on many different items from baseball caps to billboards, perhaps the most common uses are on organization web sites, e-mail messages, letterheads, envelopes, and business cards. The designer must remember to create a logo that will retain its integrity if it is enlarged for signage or reduced to fit on a business card. A common mistake is to create a logo that looks good on a poster but loses detail when reduced to fit on a business card.

In addition to providing instant recognition, logos need to make a statement about the organization.

Many of the most memorable and successful logos are ones that are simple. Complicated logos are less likely to provide instant recognition of the organization, product, or service. Also, complicated logos may have a good appearance when they are large but often lose fine rules and delicate elements when reduced in size to fit on small items like business cards.

In addition to the goal of instant recognition, logos need to make a statement about the spirit and character of the company and its products and services. Logos need to convey the image that the company wants to project, such as high quality, customer-oriented service, integrity, environmental responsibility, budget pricing, etc.

The logo must be an essential part of the company's positioning of itself in the minds of their customers, prospects, employees, and others.

*Simple logos are easy to recognize
and comprehend.*

*The logo of Words & Pictures Publishing.
The "A" represents words and the
palette represents pictures.*

Pre-Design Planning

Pre-design planning is necessary before attempting a solution to any design problem, and it is absolutely essential to the development of a logo or symbol. It isn't a matter of throwing some weird initials together and placing them in a circle.

ARMA International
4200 Somerset Drive, Suite 215
Prairie Village, Kansas 66208
913/341-3808

Business Forms Management Association
319 SW Washington Street, Suite 710
Portland, OR 97204-2618

Logo created from the organization's initials.

Logo created from the organization's name.

You need to gather information about the organization's products and services. You also need to know the organization's future plans because the logo may have to be valid for 10 or more years. And you definitely need to know what personality and character the organization wants to project. In addition, you must establish whether the logo will be used on stationery, signs, billboards, tie clips, coffee cups, or the organization's airplanes.

The decision needs to be made about the components of the logo. A logo can be the organization's initials, the organization's name, an image, or a combination of these. Often the logo is a typographic modification of the organization's initials or name.

Logos created from the organization's initials

One of the easiest techniques for creating a logo is to use a typographic treatment of the organization's initials. However, it won't work if the organization doesn't have good initials. If the organization's name is Institute of Boron Manufacturers, "IBM" is already in use. Also, certain letter combinations like YIB or YUK aren't going to make it to the logo hall of fame.

If you do have workable initials, the key to a successful design is the choice of the most appropriate typeface. With the availability of so many typefaces, it is possible to solve the logo design problem. The appropriate typeface, of course, is the one that best projects the image that the corporation wants to instill in the reader's mind. After selecting the typeface, the designer then, to ensure logo individuality, can modify the initials or fashion them into a design. By doing so, the designer can create the only logo of its kind in existence.

Logos created from the organization's name

The creation of logos from the organization's name (known as logotypes) is similar to the technique previously described for initials. Similarly, the success of the design is dependent upon the nature of the name and whether it will lend itself to a favorable response from the reader.

As with logos made from initials, the key to the design is the choice of the most appropriate typeface. You start by writing down words that describe the qualities that the organization wants to project, qualities concerning character and/or products and services. After reviewing this list, you select the typeface that best represents these qualities or at least the prime quality.

Logos created from images

Logos can also be created by generating images that represent the character and/or the products and services of the organization.

If you've decided to create an "image" logo and you're starting without a design idea, the best way to proceed is to use the visual brainstorming technique. The first step is to make a list of words relating to the organization's character and products or services. The second step is to draw an image next to each of the words. The final step is to choose one or more of these images and to refine it to produce a symbol or visual. This brainstorming technique is demonstrated in the accompanying illustrations.

The objective of this brainstorming demo is to create a logo for "Shooter's Choice" gun care products. Step one is to make a list of words relating to the company and products.

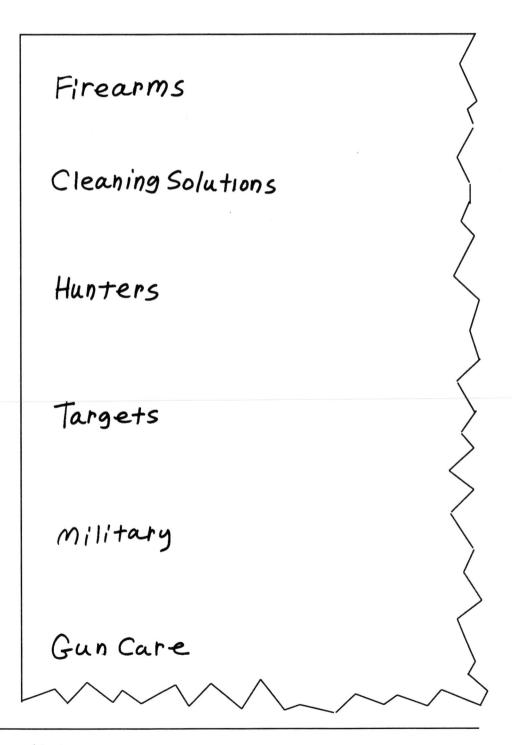

Firearms

Cleaning Solutions

Hunters

Targets

Military

Gun Care

Step two is to draw images suggested by the words.

Firearms

Cleaning Solutions

Hunters

Targets

Military

Gun Care

A logo is then developed from the most promising visual.

SHOOTER'S®
CHOICE

A logo created from a combination of the organization's initials and name.

It may be necessary to create more than one version of a logo. The designer should prepare all versions of the logo so the integrity of the design won't be compromised by others who may try to modify them for specific applications.

Logos created from combinations of the organization's initials, name, and related images

Many logos are created from combinations of the organization's initials, name, and related images. Each of these elements can be developed as previously described and then combined to form an integrated logo, as shown in the accompanying illustration.

Modification of logos for specific applications

Usually it is necessary to have more than one version of a logo. Different versions are required if the logo will be used in significantly different sizes. The logo on a billboard would probably have to have thicker lines than the logo printed on a business card. In fact, the logo on a business card might need to be simplified for the sake of clarity.

Modifications will be required if the logo is to be used as both positive and reverse images. There may also be a requirement calling for the logo to be reversed out of a screen or to be used with a screened background.

Different logo versions will also be required for black and white and for color reproductions.

The designer should prepare all of the logo versions so the integrity of the original logo design won't be compromised by others who may try to modify them for specific applications.

A checklist for assessing the logo design

1. Can the logo maintain its integrity if it is reduced or enlarged?
2. Is it suitable to the media (paper, billboards, TV, neon signs, textiles, etc.)?
3. Will it still be functional in 10 years?
4. Will it look OK if seen upside down or sideways?
5. Can it clearly be distinguished from competitors' logos?
6. Is it memorable? Is there a strong, positive impression?

Designing Business Stationery

Customers, prospects, employees, suppliers, and the public judge an organization, at least in part, by their letterheads, envelopes, and business cards. These three items represent the organization every day. Obviously, it is imperative to present a positive company image from the organization's letterhead, envelopes, and business cards. It is equally important to provide consistency in the design of these three items. Sometimes it is necessary to make design modifications on envelopes due to space and postal regulations and to business cards due to size limitations, but the design should be as consistent as possible.

Some letterhead design options.

Letterheads, envelopes, and business cards have two functions–company identification and graphic representation of the company's character.

Letterheads

The first step is to determine the information that needs to be printed on the letterhead. You will need to write down the correct organization name, address, and telephone number, including the area code. The address may include a post office box number and addresses of other offices or divisions as well as the main address. Additional information may include web site addresses, e-mail addresses, fax numbers, logo symbols, slogans, product photos or illustrations, names and logos of trade associations, and company officials.

In addition to the arrangement of the information and elements on the page, you should consider letterhead paper and production options since they can significantly affect the impact of the design. In fact, some designers believe that the color, weight, and style of the paper is the most important factor in the design of the letterhead.

Although most letterheads are traditionally "plain vanilla", it doesn't necessarily mean that you must always use white paper. Light pastel colors can be used, even for conservative organizations.

In addition to many color options, paper is available in numerous weights, textures, and surfaces. Selecting the appropriate paper can significantly strengthen the image that the organization wants to project.

Most letterheads, of course, are printed on $8^1/_2$ x 11 inch paper. Some "executive" letterheads are printed on Monarch size stationery paper which is $7^1/_4$ x $10^1/_2$.

After determining the letterhead size, the designer proceeds to place the elements on the page, giving priority to the most important elements like the logo and the company name. The designer must keep in mind that the letterhead will be folded and that the design has to work when the paper is both flat and folded.

If the tone of the letterhead is formal, the designer will probably use a centered format, as described in Chapter Two, Fundamentals of Business Graphic Design. If the tone of the letterhead is informal, the designer probably use an asymmetrical alignment. It may be helpful for you to review alignment systems describe in Chapter Two.

More letterhead design options.

The envelope design should be consistent with the letterhead. However, due to size and proportion differences and postal regulations, sometimes the design must be modified.

Obviously, the selection of a typeface is of paramount importance. The selection of an inappropriate typeface will negate the effectiveness of an otherwise pleasing design of the elements on the page.

Envelopes

The United States Postal Service handles billions of pieces of mail each day, and most of it is delivered in envelopes. Even with the growth of e-mail, fax, electronic forms, EDI, and Internet messages, envelopes are traditional parts of business stationery that will be used for a long time.

In the design of envelopes, it is vital to be consistent with the design of letterheads and business cards. And that applies to all the organization's envelopes, not just the common number 10 envelope ($4^1/_8$ x $9^1/_2$ inches).

The envelope design should be as much like the letterhead design as possible. However, due to size and proportion differences and postal regulations, it is sometimes necessary to modify the design to satisfy envelope requirements. The designer must comply with postal regulations in the design of envelopes.

Often the letterhead is designed first, the envelope second, and the business card third. This seems to be a logical sequence since the letterhead is probably the most important document. After the letterhead design is completed, the envelope is designed to be consistent with the letterhead and to conform with envelope size and proportion and with postal regulations.

The organization's name and address in the upper left of an envelope is called the "corner card". Many envelopes contain only the corner card but others include additional design elements. Although envelopes are correctly categorized as business stationery, they are also considered business forms. A traditional paper form is defined as a piece of paper containing printed information and blank spaces for the entry of data in a predetermined format. This definition neatly fits the description of an envelope.

Letter envelopes (commercial and official sizes)

Letter envelopes are used to mail folded letters, memos, and smaller forms and inserts. They can be solid face or provide a show-through window for the address. Standard sizes are shown in the illustration.

The width is always the first measurement given in the size of an envelope. For instance, a $3^1/_2$" x 6" envelope has a $3^1/_2$" width and a 6"

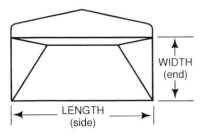

Letter Envelope.

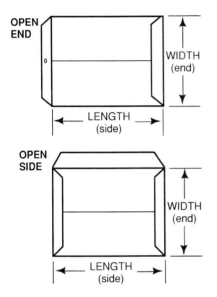

Flat Mail Envelopes.

length. The standard paper stock for letter envelopes is 24 lb. white wove. Most business correspondence is mailed in a #9 official envelope ($3^7/_8$" x $8^7/_8$") or a #10 official envelope ($4^1/_8$" x $9^1/_2$"). Often, outgoing correspondence or direct mail is sent in a #10 envelope with a #9 envelope enclosed as the return envelope.

A typical No. 10 envelope, the most commonly used envelope size in the office. The dimensions are $4^1/_8$" x $9^1/_2$".

Window envelopes

Window envelopes save time and money by eliminating the need to address the envelope. They avoid the possible mistake of inserting the wrong item in an envelope and also avoid wasting envelopes from addressing errors. Window envelopes are available with or without an acetate cover on the die cut window. And most window envelopes utilize a standard window opening at a standard location on the envelope. Standard window sizes and locations are shown in the illustration. It is possible but more expensive to manufacture a custom window envelope.

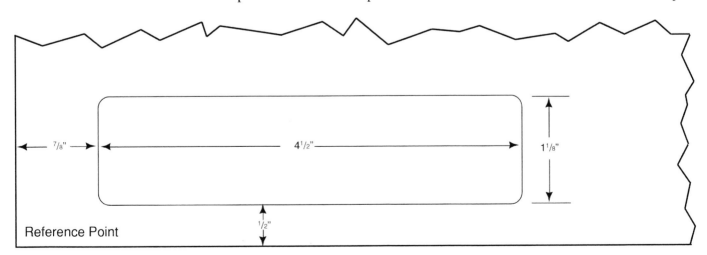

Standard window opening for all envelope sizes # $6^3/_4$ through # 14.

If you will be designing envelopes, including specialties like continuous envelopes, business reply envelopes, window envelopes, and continuous self-mailers, you will need to become familiar with printing and construction details, bar codes, FIM codes, and postal regulations. This type of information is readily available from envelope manufacturers and the United States Postal Service.

For businesses, especially those using direct mail, it is crucial to get the recipient to open the envelope instead of tossing it unopened into the waste basket. Mail-Well Envelope Company, the largest envelope manufacturer in the United States, prides itself in its creative approach in getting the envelope opened. A sample of their creative approach is shown below.

Mail-Well Envelope Company develops creative approaches to getting the envelope opened. One of their innovations is a special window covering - read and blue cellophane used to make 3-D glasses. They are used to view the outside and/or the contents of the envelope in 3-D.

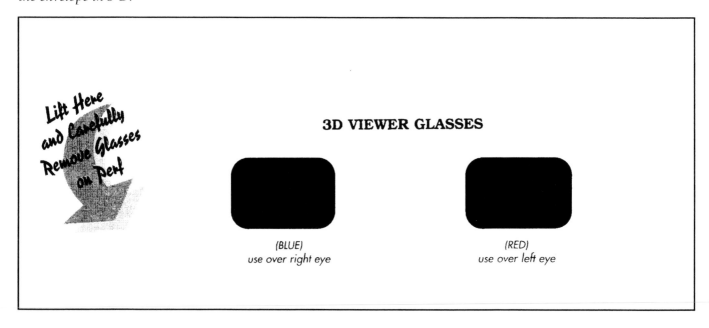

Business cards

Business cards are designed to be consistent with the design of a previously created letterhead. The standard business card size is 2 x 3½ inches. Most business cards are printed in the landscape mode (horizontally), but it is certainly acceptable to use the portrait mode (vertical). Some business cards are printed in a larger size and folded to the 2 x 3½ inch size.

Some business card design options.

In addition to the same general information printed on the letterhead, the business card must provide for the name and title of the person for whom the card is intended. The person's name and title should be prominent and separated from other design elements. Usually, the title would appear less prominently under the person's name.

WIDGET INC.

Jane Doe

1621 EUCLID AVENUE • CLEVELAND, OHIO 44115
216/696-4545

JANE A. DOE
Operations Manager
Credit Administration

WIDGET
INC.

The Widget Company
1621 Euclid Avenue
Cleveland, Ohio 44115
Phone: (216) 696-4545

JANE DOE
Sales Representative

**WIDGET INC.
Sales Department**

1621 Euclid Avenue
Cleveland, OH 44115
(216) 696-4545   FAX (216) 781-6864

THE WIDGET COMPANY
1621 EUCLID AVENUE
SUITE 724
CLEVELAND, OHIO 44115
(216) 696-4545 (216) 781-6864
INSIDE OHIO (800) 696-1234
OUTSIDE OHIO (800) 696-4321
CANADA (800) 696-2314

Jane A. Doe
Associate Director of
Sales/Group Sales

THE
WIDGET
COMPANY

JANE DOE
District Manager

 **WIDGET INC.**

1621 EUCLID AVENUE
SUITE 724
CLEVELAND, OH 44115
FAX: (216) 781-6864   TELEPHONE: (216) 696-4545

Jane Doe

The Widget Company
1621 Euclid Avenue
Suite 721
Cleveland, Ohio 44115
Telephone 216 696-4545

The Dorothy Building
5929 Dorothy Drive
Cleveland, Ohio 44170

Widget Inc.

Chapter 9 Questions

1. Describe the origins and purposes of business logos and logotypes.

2. Explain why planning is necessary before a logo is designed. What information needs to be gathered before starting a logo design.

3. If the organization's initials or name will be used as a base to create the logo, what will be the key to a successful design?

4. Differentiate between a logo and a logotype.

5. What technique can be used to help develop an idea for a logo consisting of an image?

6. Explain the importance of creating a logo and business stationery that makes a favorable impression on employees, customers, prospects, and the public.

7. Why is it essential to maintain a consistent design for letterheads, envelopes, and business cards? What are the two functions of business stationery?

8. What information is usually found on a letterhead. What other information could be included on a letterhead?

9. Explain formal and informal layout formats for letterheads. Discuss paper stock options for letterheads.

10. Discuss the design considerations of envelopes considering the relation to the letterhead design and the necessity to conform to postal regulations.

11. Describe the design considerations for business cards.

CHAPTER
10

DESIGNING PRINT ADS, SPACE ADS, AND DIRECT MAIL ADS

*If you are writing about baloney, don't
try to make it Cornish hen because that is the
worst kind of baloney there is. Just
make it darned good baloney.*

Chapter 10 Objectives

After studying this chapter, you should be able to:

1. Distinguish between bragging copywriting and client-benefit copywriting.

2. List the design elements of a flyer and name the most important element.

3. Describe what a reader looks at first in an advertisement. Discuss the sequence used by a reader in looking at the elements in an advertisement.

4. Describe the construction of a folder and state the objective of a folder cover.

5. Define a space ad and describe how you can judge the effectiveness of the ad.

6. Define a brochure and describe design considerations for the front cover and the inside pages.

7. List the components of the classic direct mail package.

Designing promotions and advertisements

Promotional documents run the range from flyers to full color advertisements in national magazines, TV commercials, and Web site pages. They don't necessarily have to sell a product or service. They can simply try to motivate individuals to do something that you want them to do.

Don't write bragging copy. Write client - benefit copy.

Although many business promotional documents are developed to motivate people to attend meetings, fund raisers, etc., most graphic designers focus on improving the organization's image and increasing the sales of its products and/or services. Each organization attempts to establish and maintain a unique image. Graphic design is involved with the organization's logo, stationery, forms, packaging, space ads, direct mail advertising, etc. So, whether you are designing a picnic flyer, a bulletin board notice, a purchase order, a return envelope or a newsletter nameplate, you are influencing (positively or negatively) the organization's image and the sales of its products and services.

Although the picnic flyer and TV commercials are vastly different in scope, they have much in common. They are both trying to persuade somebody to do something. Therefore, the key to the successful designing and copywriting of both is the same; that is, TO FOCUS ON THE BENEFITS THEY WILL GAIN BY DOING WHATEVER IT IS YOU WANT THEM TO DO.

You don't motivate or sell by bragging about how wonderful you are. You focus on the reader and tell them how they will benefit.

Flyers

Flyers are single-page promotions or ads. They can be mailed, placed under windshields in a parking lot, placed on a reception room table, or delivered door-to-door. A flyer can announce a "two pizzas for the price of one" sale or invite clients to a company open house.

A flyer should include attention-getting graphics and highlight the benefits to the reader.

To be successful, a flyer should include attention-getting graphics and solid, motivational information. Without the graphics, the document may be lost in the hundreds of visual messages that bombard people every day. However, like most promotions and ads, the most important flyer element is the headline. This is because the headline promises the benefit or a least makes a statement or asks a question that draws the reader into the copy.

The graphic (illustration, photo, symbol, border, etc.) attracts attention and sets the tone, but the headline is what usually makes or breaks the flyer. Studies suggest that the reader first looks at the pictures and then the main headline. If there is still interest, the reader scans the subheads and then decides whether to read the body copy.

With a custom-make boat mattress, you can sleep as comfortably in your boat as you do at home

Increase accuracy and eliminate malfunctions with Shooter's Choice gun care products

Looking for information about a person or business?..
I.C.U. DELIVERS OR YOU DON'T PAY

IN A HURRY?
OUR CAMERA-READY ART WILL BE ON YOUR DESK TOMORROW MORNING!

Folders

A folder is a single piece of paper that is generally folded once or twice to create a promotional document. A common folder is an 11 x 17 inch sheet folded once to create a four-panel $8^{1}/_{2}$ x 11 inch folder. Another common size is the $8^{1}/_{2}$ x 11 inch sheet folded to become a four-panel $8^{1}/_{2}$ x $5^{1}/_{2}$ inch folder. The design concepts and procedures for a folder are basically the same as for a flyer. The difference is that you must motivate the reader to unfold and continue reading from one panel to the next. The design is best visualized by working on a "dummy". This is a piece of paper folded to represent the final document. It helps you visualize how the potential reader will see the folder.

The objective of the folder cover is to get the reader to open it. This is done by employing various techniques, including using half an image or a partial headline that is completed on the inside.

Space ads

Space ads should focus on benefits to the reader.

A space ad will appear in a purchased space in a magazine, newspaper, newsletter, or other publication. Space ads are not easy to design because there are usually limitations such as size, colors, and shape. Typically, someone other than the designer will select the size of the ad, and the budget will determine if black and white or if spot or process color will be used. The size of the ad can range from a full page of the publication size or a fraction of the page like $^1/_2$, $^1/_4$, $^1/_6$, or $^1/_8$. Usually, the designer can select a landscape or portrait shape, which in turn depends on the proportion of the ad elements. If the illustration in the ad is a basketball pole, obviously the ad will have to be in the portrait mode.

There is no room for trivia in the limited confines of a space ad. You do need some graphic device and/or strong headline to capture attention. There will be competing ads on your page and the opposite page in the publication. Reverses are very powerful and can be used to attract attention. Screens, background patterns, and bold or copy-related borders attract attention. Borders should be used, particularly on small ads, to unify the ad and set it apart from editorial copy. A short, clear headline in large, bold type is more effective than a long headline in smaller type. The headline and body copy should focus on the benefits that the reader will get from purchasing your product or service. It has become a cliché, but it is true that you should sell the "sizzle", not the steak.

This space ad tells the reader what to do.

The border unifies the ad.

The graphic stops the reader.

The final and extremely important step is to TELL THE READER WHAT TO DO. First of all, it must be perfectly clear in your mind what you want the reader to do. Do you want the reader to call? If so, give a person's name and a telephone number, hopefully an 800 number, and tell them to call, in no uncertain terms. If you want them to mail an order, tell them to fill in the order form and mail it to you NOW. If you want them to go to a particular retail store to find your product, tell them to go there.

The final and most important step is to tell the reader what to do.

When the design is completed, test it by making a copy and pasting it over a same size ad in the publication in which it will appear. Ask yourself:

- Does it stand out or does it blend into the editorial text on the page?

- How does it compare to the other ads on the same and opposite pages?

- Does it catch your attention or is it overpowered by the other ads?

- Is the benefit clear or is it a bragging ad?

- If you wanted to buy the product or service, would you know what to do?

Brochures

A brochure is a small booklet or pamphlet that helps to sell a product or a service. The word "brochure" is derived from the French word for stitching, implying that the pages of a brochure are stitched, stapled, or bound together as a unit.

A brochure is a small booklet or pamphlet that helps to sell a product or service.

Like all graphic design projects, you start the design of a brochure by doing your homework—gathering information about the objective, the products or services, and the prospective readers. And the more you know about the potential purchaser, the better you will be able to design an effective brochure. For instance: Who will the brochure be talking to?, Is your prospect a man or woman?, Will he/she consider the purchase to be an impulse decision or a major decision? In addition, if the purpose of your brochure is to get sales leads, it doesn't need to be in full color, lavish, and expensive. The lavish brochure is for getting the order.

You should also consider the method of distribution. If it will be handed out personally, it can be inexpensive, less detailed, and friendly. If it is part of a direct mail package, it needs to be detailed, professional, and persuasive.

People will read long copy, if it provides needed details

The size of the brochure depends on what you have to say. People will read long copy if it provides needed details, presented in an interesting way. A common size for a detailed brochure is created by folding two 11 x 17 inch sheets and stapling them in the center. That gives you eight $8^{1}/_{2}$ x 11 inch sides and provides plenty of space for a comprehensive brochure. If this much space isn't required, many other options are available. One of them is to fold two $8^{1}/_{2}$ x 11 inch sheets and staple them in the center, producing eight $5^{1}/_{2}$ x $8^{1}/_{2}$ inch sides.

The front cover of the brochure

The front cover must make it clear what you are selling. If you have a product, show a photo of your product in a positive way. Show it and tell an important fact about it—something that states or implies a benefit to the reader. Another function of the front cover is to get the reader to turn the page. The best way to do this is to use a big attractive photo and a clear enticing headline. If it's clear what you are selling and you get them interested in the product or service, they will turn the page.

Examples of good client-benefit headlines are shown below:

**SMALL BUSINESS OWNERS!
WANT YOUR SHARE OF THE BILLIONS
IN INTERNET SALES?
Yes?.. then don't miss the chance
to get a "big business" web site
for a "small business" price!**

**AT NORTH STATE COLLEGE ,
WE'RE CHANGING LIVES
AND BUILDING FUTURES...
YOUR FUTURE!**

**FOR HIGHLY QUALIFIED PERSONNEL..
CALL ON US!
North State College**

**WOULD YOU HELP A KITTEN
SHIVERING WITH COLD
AND HUNGER?**

Caroline's Kids Pet Rescue

Using color in brochure design

If your purpose is to boost your company image or if your product will sell better if shown in color and your budget allows it, you should use full color (4-color process). Full color gives the impression that the company is successful and can afford expensive literature. Full color increases readership and creates prestige. Some products like clothing, paints, wallpaper, and foods should be printed in full color if at all possible.

If your products and services don't require full color, a good choice is a two-color brochure. A one-color brochure looks cheap. If you use black and one other color, the brochure will look more expensive. You can also economically create the effect of more colors by printing on colored paper and by using screens of the two colors.

The inside brochure pages

Collect and use testimonials liberally in your brochures.

On the first inside page, you should explain the benefits to the prospect. Don't go into full product detail yet. Describe the advantages of purchasing the product or service. To get maximum impact, you should treat pages two and three as one horizontal spread. Run headlines and pictures across both pages. Then encourage the reader to turn the page by using an arrow or by telling them to turn the page for more details.

On the last few pages, give them details and then convince them to buy with guarantees, testimonials, and time limits. Testimonials from customers are convincing. They are worth more than words from your company. On the last page, include your logo, company name, slogan, and tell them how to get your product. If the brochure is a direct mail piece, include an order form.

Publishing brochures on the organization's web site

Brochures and almost any other business document can be published on an Internet web site rather than printed on paper. The basic brochure design concepts are the same for paper or electronic publishing, but there are some differences which are covered in Part Three of this book.

Designing direct mail advertising

When designing direct mail, your first job is to get the reader to open the envelope.

Most direct mail has an active life of a few seconds. It is often considered by the recipient to be what direct mailers refer to as the dreaded "J-word"–"junk" mail. We are all bombarded with junk mail. Technology has brought us junk fax and junk e-mail, and telemarketers have brought us junk telephone calls.

It is not easy to compete and have your mailing stand out from all the other direct mail. Often direct mail is thrown away before the envelope is opened. If your direct mail package is enclosed in an envelope, your first design job is to try to ensure that the envelope is opened. Direct mail can consist of one or more pieces. It can be as simple as a post card or a self-mail flyer. Many direct mail experts believe that direct mail should include several pieces.

The classic direct mail package

You would do well to consider the classic direct mail package. This package includes the outgoing envelope, a letter, a sales flyer or brochure, and a return envelope.

The outgoing envelope

The classic direct mail package is an outgoing envelope, a letter, a sales flyer or brochure and a return envelope.

The primary function of the outgoing envelope is to get the recipient to open it. There are two ways to do this. One is to use a number 10 envelope and make it look like it contains a personal letter. Recipients may throw away an envelope without opening it if it looks like the "J-word"; that is, if it has an address label and/or a sales message on the envelope. On the other hand, recipients are reluctant to throw away what appears to be an envelope containing a personal letter. You can achieve the personal letter look by printing only the corner card on the envelope and adding the recipient name and address directly on the envelope. An address label is a dead giveaway for junk mail.

The other way to get the recipient to open the envelope is to use an envelope "teaser". This is a sales-oriented message printed on the envelope, with the objective of creating interest or curiosity so the reader will open the envelope.

The letter

The letter is a vital piece in the classic direct mail package. It is important because people are more likely to read letters than sales brochures, particularly if the letter looks personal. The reader knows that the letter is mass-produced but nevertheless is attracted to the letter if it looks like it was directed personally to them. That is why the letter should be printed in a crisp, clean typeface that looks like the traditional letters that were personally typewritten. Also, the letter should be written in a personal style, from one person to another—never from our company to your company. Always say "I, not "we" or "The Widget Company".

If at all possible, each letter should be individually addressed to the recipient. Many label/mail software programs allow you to do this on your personal computer and print the individually addressed envelopes on a laser printer.

The sales brochure

The function of the sales brochure in the classic direct mail package is to continue the general selling started in the letter and to provide product or service details. The design of the sales brochure is described earlier in this chapter.

Direct mail response usually increases when you provide a return envelope.

The return envelope

Any professional direct mailer will tell you that your response will increase if you provide a return envelope, especially if it is postage-paid. If you don't want to pay for the return postage, at least provide the return envelope.

Two facts about direct mail

Usually, you can't expect more than about 1% response to direct mail.

If you're a beginner at direct mail, you should be aware that there won't be a great return regardless of the worthiness of your product. Most direct mailers are happy to get $1/2$% or 1% response.

Also, if you enclose a postage-paid return envelope, don't be shocked when you discover that people will use your return envelopes to send obscene notes and propaganda.

Chapter 10 Questions

1. Distinguish between bragging copywriting and client-benefit copywriting.

2. List the design elements of a flyer and name the most important element.

3. Describe what a reader looks at first in an advertisement. Discuss the sequence used by a reader in looking at the elements in an advertisement

4. What is a folder? What is the objective of a folder cover? What is a "dummy".

5. Define a space ad and explain the possible design limitations. Considering the likelihood of competing ads on the same or facing page, what design techniques can be used to attract attention to your ad?

6. What is the final vital element in the design of a space ad, or any other type of ad?

7. Describe a good way to judge the effectiveness of a space ad.

8. Define a brochure and describe design considerations for the front cover and the inside pages. Name the benefits of using color in the design of brochures.

9. List the components of the classic direct mail package and the function of each.

10. Name two methods used to get recipients to open a direct mail envelope. What should be avoided to prevent the envelope from looking like it contains junk mail?

11. How can a sales letter be made to look like a personal letter instead of a mass produced impersonal one?

Forms Design
Forms Design
Forms Design
Forms Design
Forms Design
Forms Design

PART TWO

Forms Design
Forms Design
Forms Design
Forms Design
Forms Design
Forms Design
Forms Design
Forms Design
Forms Design
Forms Design
Forms Design
Forms Design
Forms Design
Forms Design
Forms Design

```
PETTY CASH DISBURSEMENT RECORD
FORM 321
DISBURSED TO (NAME)                      AMOUNT
                                         $
FOR (REASON)


CHANGE GENERAL LEDGER ACCT. NO

DISBURSEMENT DATE     APPROVED BY (SUPERVISOR)
```

CHAPTER
11

OVERVIEW OF FORMS DESIGN

So many signatures for such a small heart.

Mother Teresa (on filling in forms
in a California hospital)

Chapter 11 Objectives

After studying this chapter, you should be able to:

1. Define a traditional paper form and describe the most important concept in the definition of a form.

2. Define an electronic form.

3. Explain the importance of forms in information systems and the importance of professional forms design.

4. Describe briefly the development of the business forms industry.

5. Define forms design.

6. Describe the two major objectives and the functions of forms management.

7. Discuss the responsibilities of a forms management unit.

8. State the alternatives to an internal forms management unit.

Definition of a traditional paper form

In the traditional sense, a form is a piece of paper containing printed information and blank spaces for the entry of data in a predetermined format.

Forms are used to gather, process, and communicate information. Therefore, the most important concept in the definition of a form is that it contains blank spaces to allow for the entry of data. Blank spaces for data entry make it a form. That is how you recognize a form and distinguish it from other printed documents.

Forms are used to gather, process and communicate information.

A form has blank spaces for the entry of data in a pre-determined format.

Ameritype!

5811 Canal Road, Ste. 110
Valley View, OH 44125
Phone 216-901-2001
Fax 216-901-2003
E-mail mj@ameritype.com
www.ameritype.com

QUOTATION / ORDER FORM
INTERNET SERVICES

INDIVIDUAL	ORGANIZAITON

ADDRESS

PHONE NI.	FAX NO.	E-MAIL ADDRESS

WEB SITE DESIGN SERVICES		AMERITYPE PRICE
☐ **DESIGN** Quotation based on $80 hr. Minimum - $200	(COMMENTS)	$
☐ **MAINTENANCE** **Option A - Maintenance Agreemtn** · Up to 2 hours mo. - $50 month **Option B - Individual revision orders:** $80 hour ($25 minimum)		$
☐ **MARKETING** Include meta tags, submit key words to 15 popular search engines and provide Web Site marketing assistance ($100)		$

WEB SITE HOSTING		
☐ **BUDGET HOSTING** (www.ameritype.com/your company) $180 a year ($15 a month) paid in advance		$
☐ **VIRTUAL HOSTING** (using your company name) Domain (your company) name registration - $100 paid to InterNIC One time set-up fee by APK Net' (Provider recommended by Ameritype) - $425 paid to APK Web site storage - $20 month paid to APK	☐ Paperwork processing by Ameritype, if desired - $25	$

OTHER SERVICES		
☐ **INTERNET ACCESS** $20 month paid to APK (Internet Provider).	☐ Paperwork processing by Ameritype - $10	$
☐		$
AMERITYPE QUOTED TOTAL		$

Our definition also states that a form contains pre-printed information. Although almost every form has something pre-printed on it, some forms are blank with no pre-printed information. For example, blank envelopes, blank tags and blank continuous forms are not printed, but they are manufactured for the purpose of entering data. Therefore, they are forms.

Although most forms are printed on paper or index bristol (cardstock), a form could be printed on plastic or other material.

Definition of an electronic form

Instead of being printed on paper or a similar substrate, some forms are designed and stored on electronic media. This leads us to an entirely new category of forms and the definition of an electronic form.

An electronic form is a template in an electronic format which assigns space in data fields for input of variable information. In addition, definitions, formulas and restrictions are assigned to data fields in preparation for electronic forms processing.

An electronic form.

Electronic forms can be stored on a file server or other computer storage device. It is then available for electronic recall whenever the user is ready for fill-in by keyboard entry and/or by importing information from a database, or a combination of the two methods. The data is then processed electronically.

An adaptation of both the traditional paper and the electronic form is to create and store the electronic design within the computer system via a network server, individual computer hard drive, or offline on disk. Then as needed, the form file is retrieved on screen and printed for traditional fill-in methods. This compromise between the efficiency of electronic design and storage plus the convenience of paper has become increasingly popular.

The importance of forms in information systems

Prophecies of paperless offices have not materialized. The volume of business data being transmitted by electronic communications has dramatically increased. However, millions of paper forms are still used to initiate and process business transactions. Forms are used in every office and will continue to be used in the future.

Another misconception is that there are form templates available on all software programs that will virtually replace the need to custom design forms. Form templates are quick remedies for routinely used forms, such as invoices and purchase orders. However, within the endless scope of creativity, common sense tells us that there could never be enough templates to satisfy the limitless number of form requests and needs. In reality, even the most comprehensive file of templates would never eliminate the need to design that special form for that unique situation.

In brief, forms provide an efficient, economical way to write instructions, capture data, and control actions in business. This is true for both paper and electronic forms.

The importance of proper forms design

Unlike other printed documents, forms are tools in information processing systems. Designing a form to present a good graphic appearance is not enough. Forms must be designed to provide easy, fast and efficient fill-in and processing of data.

The office workers that create the forms for many organizations often don't understand that proper forms design is required for the production of efficient forms. They seem to be more concerned about how the form looks rather than how it should do its job in the information processing system. For example, if a form will be filled in by hand and doesn't incorporate enough space for writing, it is inefficient and a poorly designed form–even if it has a good graphic appearance.

Research by professional forms associations have indicated that for every dollar spent to purchase a form, it requires from 20 to 100 dollars in labor to fill in, process and store the form. The true cost of a form is people, not paper.

In addition to significant dollar savings for reduced labor costs, properly designed forms result in easier clerical procedures, reductions in clerical errors, and goodwill. Improperly designed forms subject the office worker to eyestrain and fatigue. They encourage clerical errors and undermine employee morale, in addition to the dollars lost by wasted hours in filling in and processing them.

A form can be an efficient business tool or it can create ill will, confusion and extra expense. The designer makes the difference. An untrained person usually designs forms that are difficult to fill in, read, and process. There may not be enough room to write. The forms may be so small that they get lost. Or they may be so big that they won't fit in the

The true cost of a form is people, not paper.

envelope or file. They may cost too much to print because they are not a standard size. They may waste clerical time and money because they do not fit smoothly into the information system.

A trained forms designer is much more likely to design a form that is an effective information systems tool.

Poorly designed forms are found in organizations where management has not provided forms design training. Despite education attempts by forms manufacturers, forms management departments, forms associations, and forms professionals, many organizations work with inefficient forms.

The Business Forms Management Association (BFMA) is an excellent resource for forms education.
Phone: 503-227-3393
www.bfma.org

An inefficient form designed by a person without forms design training.

The same form designed by a person with forms design training.

Was everything working in your meeting/banquet facilities?		___Yes	___No	

Please rate the following where applicable:

	Excellent	Good	Average	Fair	Poor
Air conditioning	___	___	___	___	___
Heating	___	___	___	___	___
Audio/Visual equipment	___	___	___	___	___
Sound equipment	___	___	___	___	___
Lighting	___	___	___	___	___

If we provided food and/or beverage service, please rate the following where applicable:

Table
	Excellent	Good	Average	Fair	Poor
Overall appearance	___	___	___	___	___
Linen	___	___	___	___	___
China	___	___	___	___	___
Flatware	___	___	___	___	___

Food
	Excellent	Good	Average	Fair	Poor
Quality	___	___	___	___	___
Presentation	___	___	___	___	___
Portion size	___	___	___	___	___
Value for price paid	___	___	___	___	___

Beverage
	Excellent	Good	Average	Fair	Poor
Quality	___	___	___	___	___
Presentation	___	___	___	___	___
Size of drinks	___	___	___	___	___
Availability of bars	___	___	___	___	___
Value for price paid	___	___	___	___	___

Service (Food/Beverage)
	Excellent	Good	Average	Fair	Poor
Promptness	___	___	___	___	___
Attentiveness	___	___	___	___	___
Efficiency	___	___	___	___	___
Courtesy	___	___	___	___	___
Appearance	___	___	___	___	___

S C H SLEEP CHEAP HOTEL

SEMINAR FACILITIES EVALUATION

NAME OF MEETING GROUP		MEETING DATE		
EVALUATED BY		WAS EVERYTHING WORKING IN YOUR MEETING FACILITY ☐ YES ☐ NO		

Please rate the following where applicable

ITEM	EXCELLENT (✔)	GOOD (✔)	AVERAGE (✔)	FAIR (✔)	POOR (✔)
Air conditioning					
Heating					
Audio/Visual equipment					
Sound equipment					
Lighting					
TABLE Overall appearance					
Linen					
China					
Flatware					
FOOD Quality					
Presentation					
Portion size					
Value for price paid					
BEVERAGE Quality					
Presentation					
Size of drinks					
Availability of bars					
Value for price paid					
SERVICE (Food/ Beverage) Promptness					
Attentiveness					
Efficiency					
Courtesy					
Appearance					

COMMENTS

FORM 72

Johann Gutenberg

Before the invention of movable type by Johann Gutenberg in the 1400's, books, records, and forms were drawn by hand.

In the 1870's the Remington Small Arms Company bought the invention of Christopher Sholes and manufactured the first practical typewriter.

Businesses began to use typewriters for correspondence and filling in forms. The typewriter created jobs for women – lady typewriters – as the early typists were known. "Respectable" girls found one of the first "respectable" jobs outside the home.

The invention of forms

Forms were invented to record business transactions. No one knows who created the first form, but by the nineteenth century during the industrial revolution in the United States, forms were widely created and printed to help solve the problem of recording the huge increase in business transactions.

These early forms included purchase orders, sales orders, receipts, shipping forms, bills, and other simple forms to record and control the basic activities of business. They were single copy forms and filled in by hand. If a duplicate record was required, it had to be completely re-written by hand.

The birth of the business forms industry

In the 1880's businesses were faced with the growing problem of generating form copies for customers and internal records. Carbon paper had been invented but was sparingly used because it smudged the cuffs and clothing of office workers.

This problem was solved in 1882 by an invention that created the birth of the modern business forms industry–the first salesbook. It was called The Paragon Black Leaf Counter Check Book, and it was introduced by the founder of Moore Business Forms, Samuel J. Moore. It was invented by John R. Carter, and it contained consecutively numbered sales forms with carbon paper bound into the stub.

Unit set with one-time carbon

Businesses could now easily provide a copy to customers and also have a copy for bookkeeping and audit purposes. Four years later in 1886 an improvement, a continuous salesbook, was introduced. A forerunner of continuous forms, it was printed on a continuous roll and zigzag folded into the book.

Breakthrough inventions

The problem of keeping form copies in perfect alignment while moving through business machines was solved in 1912 by Theodore Schirmer. His brilliant idea was to punch holes in the margins of forms and then to run the forms over two sprocket wheels, forcing the copies to move along in perfect alignment. The pins in the sprocket wheels engaged the holes in the paper and fed the forms through the machine in a precise and controlled manner.

This concept was used by the Standard Register Company to introduce a new register called The Standard. This innovation marked the beginning of the Standard Register Company and the pin-feed continuous form.

"The Standard" Autographic Register used the pin-feed principle.

In 1925, Moore Business Forms introduced one-time carbon. This eliminated the need for the cumbersome carbon paper holding devices that were time consuming and labor intensive. The development of one-time carbon made carbon interleaving practical and increased production.

In 1928, Moore introduced a major forms breakthrough, the unit set. The Speediset was a multi-part form interleaved with one-time carbon. The paper copies and the carbon papers were bound together in a common stub. After writing, the paper copies (perforated at the stub) were removed for processing, and the stub holding the carbons was discarded.

In 1954, The National Cash Register Company introduced a major forms development, carbonless paper.

Another major development occurred in 1954 when The National Cash Register Company introduced carbonless paper. It was called "NCR" paper, which originally referred to the founding company's name but later became known as "no carbon required". It created images on form copies by a chemical reaction. The impact of writing on the form broke capsules on the back of one form part and also broke capsules on the front of the next part. The "back" capsules and the "front" capsules each contained a different colorless chemical. When they came in contact, however, they formed a blue chemical compound that formed the image on the form copies. This invention provided many benefits, such as cleanliness and less handling. It also eliminated the disposal of carbon papers.

Since then we have experienced an explosion of specialty forms and machines and methods used to fill in and process forms.

What is forms design?

Forms design is the creation of the layout of the lines, captions, and other printed information along with the graphic features of a form. Forms design is substantially the same for all types of forms–paper and electronic.

A form designed by a person without forms design training.

```
┌─────────────────────────────────┐
│        IMPREST FUND             │
│                                 │
│  DATE _____   │
│                                 │
│  $ _____   │
│                                 │
│  FOR _____   │
│                                 │
│  _____   │
│                                 │
│  _____   │
│                                 │
│  CHARGE ACCOUNT # _____   │
│                                 │
│  RECEIVED BY _____   │
│                                 │
│  APPROVED BY _____   │
└─────────────────────────────────┘
```

The same form redesigned by a person who has received forms design training.

```
┌──────────────────────────────────────────────┐
│  PETTY CASH DISBURSEMENT RECORD               │
│  FORM 312                                      │
│  DISBURSED TO (NAME)          │ AMOUNT         │
│  ─────────────────────────────┼───────────────│
│  FOR (REASON)                                  │
│  ──────────────────────────────────────────── │
│                                                │
│  CHARGE GENERAL LEDGER ACCT. NO.               │
│  ─────────────────────────────────────────────│
│  DISBURSEMENT DATE    │ APPROVED BY (SUPERVISOR)│
│                       │                        │
└──────────────────────────────────────────────┘
```

Forms Management

Forms Management is the function that establishes standards for the creation of all forms in an organization and is responsible for their economical and efficient design, production, and distribution.

If forms design and related activities are organized in a company, they are usually found in a Forms Management Department or forms management unit attached to a department such as Graphics, Reprographics, or Information Systems. Forms design activities function best in a forms management environment because forms design is only a part of a total forms administrative and procurement system.

Originally "Forms Management" was a separate department, often called "Forms Control" and usually reported to the Systems and Procedures Department. Currently, due to budget-cutting and the failing effort to convince top management of the importance of forms, there are fewer organizations with forms management departments. Many forms are "designed" by untrained "forms designers" which has resulted in forms that look like ransom notes and are inefficient, costly and confusing.

There are estimates from reputable consulting firms that up to 70% of all business documents are forms. And when forms are designed by people without forms design training, the forms are often difficult to read and comprehend, and they create inefficiencies in processing, including the addition of additional information, rubber stamping, distributing, copying, faxing, mailing, microfilming, punching, binding, filing, etc.

The two major objectives of forms management are:
1. to provide necessary, efficient forms at the lowest possible procurement and processing costs.
2. to produce attractive, effective forms that enhance the organization's image.

Forms Management Responsibilities

Forms are important tools in information systems. Proper forms design and construction creates forms that are easy to fill in and process. Efficient forms promote accuracy, improve employee morale, and helps people to make decisions. It is the role and primary objective of Forms Management to promote the production of efficient forms.

A Forms Management Department is a business unit that is responsible for the economical and efficient design, production, and distribution of forms.

It costs between $20 and $100 in labor to process a form for every dollar it costs to print a form.

The primary objective of Forms Management is to promote the production of efficient forms.

Knowing how to arrange items on a form for maximum processing effectiveness is the major benefit of forms design training.

Forms management responsibilities include:
- Forms procurement cost control.
- Forms processing (labor) cost control through proper forms design.
- Bootleg (unauthorized) forms prevention.
- Duplicate forms prevention.
- Forms design standards maintenance.
- Forms analysis.
- Forms design
- Forms files maintenance
- Form number assignment
- Forms printing specifications writing.

Alternatives to Forms Management Departments

Alternatives to establishing an internal Forms Management Department include:
- Providing no help from trained forms designers and allowing supervisors or anyone to design and procure forms.
- Outsourcing forms management functions, usually to a large printing company.
- Using sales representatives from commercial printers to design forms.

Chapter 11 Questions

1. Define a traditional paper form? What is it that helps you recognize a form and that distinguishes it from other documents?

2. Do all forms contain pre-printed information? Name some exceptions.

3. Define an electronic form? Compare the storage of electronic forms with the storage of paper forms.

4. Explain the importance of forms in information systems and the importance of professional forms design.

5. How were books, records, and forms produced before the invention of movable type by Johann Gutenberg in the 1400's?

6. For what purpose were forms invented? In which century and what historical period were forms widely created and printed to record the huge increase in business transactions? What invention in 1882 created the birth of the modern business forms industry?

7. Describe four breakthrough developments in the evolution of business forms.

8. Define forms design. Is it substantially the same for paper and electronic forms?

9. Describe the two major objectives of forms management.

10. What are the alternatives to an internal forms management unit?

CHAPTER
12

TYPES OF BUSINESS FORMS

*Ye have many strings to
your bow.*

– John Heywood

Chapter 12 Objectives

After studying this chapter, you should be able to:

1. Name the two major categories of forms.

2. Describe the construction features of the three major types of forms, cut sheets, unit sets, and continuous forms.

3. Explain the construction features of register forms, salesbooks, pegboard forms, labels, tags, mailers, envelopes, and checks.

4. Give a brief overview of how electronic forms are created and processed.

5. State the potential benefits of converting paper forms to electronic forms.

There are two major categories of forms: paper and electronic. Traditional forms are printed on paper or a similar substrate, such as index bristol, plastic, etc. Electronic forms are created with a computer and stored on electronic media. In theory, they are created, stored, filled-in, and processed electronically to eliminate or minimize being printed and handled as paper. There are many benefits to this technology, which will be discussed in this and later chapters.

Paper forms

The three major types

There are many types of paper forms since they are traditional and have evolved throughout the centuries before computer technology. They are classified by their method of construction during the manufacturing process. The three major types of paper forms are:

1. Cut sheets (single sheets)
2. Unit sets (multi-part, not continuous)
3. Continuous (long strips of connected forms)

Cut sheets

"Cut sheets" is the term used for simple one-part forms. Historically, they have been referred to as "flat forms", "flat sheets", or "single sheets". They are economically printed in volume by offset lithography on sheet-fed presses. They may also be reproduced by copiers and laser printers. Because of their simplicity, relative ease, economy of production, and versatility for business applications, they are used more often than any type of paper form.

Cut sheet forms are traditionally printed on white paper with black ink, but the use of colored paper and colored ink is accelerating. Color copiers and desktop printers are becoming so economical and common in the workplace that adding color to single-sheet forms is no longer a luxury.

Unit sets

Unit sets are multi-part forms that are fastened into an individual form unit. A form part can also be referred to as a "ply". For example, a three-ply form contains an original (the top part) and two copies. The plies are then interleaved with one-time carbon; however, this practice is increasingly being replaced with carbonless papers. The plies (and any carbon paper) are glued into a unit at the stub section, which is perforated for easy separation of all parts. Unit sets may also be referred to as snapouts, snapsets, and snap-a-parts. Some manufacturers have even developed their own trade names, such as Speedisets or E-Z-Outs.

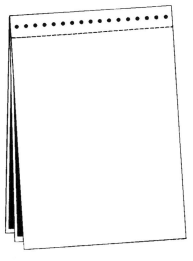

Cut Sheet

To improve processing production, cut sheets can include features such as punching, perforating, consecutive numbering and padding.

Unit Set

The main advantage of units sets is the time saved when filling in and handling the form parts. They use the "write once" concept to provide all the needed copies for processing and distribution with minimal fill-in time. They are also convenient and clean to handle if they are carbon-interleaved. If they are snapped apart properly, the stub unit will allow the perforated copies to detach in one hand while the carbons stay together in the stub unit held by the other hand, which can then be easily discarded. Even if carbonless papers are used, the same snap apart concept has identical results (minus the carbon paper) if the user holds only the stub with one hand, while snapping the plies in the opposite direction with the other hand. It's a very efficient form construction.

Continuous forms

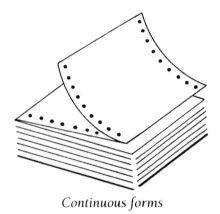

Continuous forms

Continuous forms are designed for high-volume, automatic computer fill-in applications, such as in sales offices when orders come in from the sales force. These are long strips of connected forms that are separated by perforations. They are printed on a continuous web (roll of paper) as single or multi-parts and then fanfolded in a zigzag manner into shipping boxes.

Continuous forms are usually filled in on pin-feed computer printers. This means that the construction of these forms requires line-hole strips that provide a means to attach the form to the pins of the printer. This mechanism then pulls a continuous flow of forms through the printer as they are being filled in. As the completed forms flow out of the printer, they are re-folded into a receiving box until they are collected to be processed. The line-hole strips are usually perforated so they can be detached for a clean, cut-sheet appearance. The identifying construction feature of these types of forms, therefore, is the line-hole punching; however, this may not be readily apparent on the finished form after the margin strips have been removed before distribution.

Forms being phased out by technology

Some types of forms such as register forms, salesbooks and pegboard forms had been quite popular in the twentieth century but are in the process of being replaced in the new millennium.

At the present time, quite a few of these types of paper forms still exist, usually in smaller offices or small retail stores that do not have the capacity or volume to automate. Therefore, these forms will be included in this chapter's review of traditional paper forms.

Register forms

Register forms

Register forms are a type of continuous form that is manufactured to work in an autographic register as shown in the illustration. They automatically provide duplicate copies, and the parts are always in registration (alignment). They use the fanfold technique with either line holes for pin-feeding or slot holes at the top for friction-feed registers. They can be used in large desktop registers or more commonly in portable units as shown. The unique feature of these forms is that they can provide audit control by keeping a continuous copy of the transactions inside the register while the original top form is advanced out and given to the customer as a receipt. The register may also provide a lock for security and integrity of the continuous account of the daily transactions.

Register forms can be used in any paperwork system, although they are usually found in small stores to provide sales receipts. They are relatively inexpensive, convenient, and easy to use. They have their own writing surface and provide audit control.

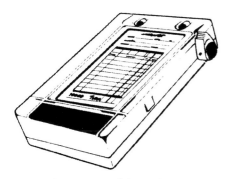

An autographic register

Salesbooks

The function of a salesbook is similar to register forms, but it is more portable and can even fit into a pocket. Although a variety of constructions are available, a typical salesbook includes a cover, several sheets of reusable carbon paper and a number of multi-part form sets. Salesbooks were developed in the 1880's to solve the problem of multiple copies needed by salespersons and their organizations. The salesbook allowed the customer to get a purchase receipt and the organization to keep a record of the sale in one easy, convenient, and portable operation.

Pegboard forms

Pegboard forms have a row of holes down the left side that fit on the pegs (pins) of an aluminum board or in a book-like apparatus. The object is to hold two or more forms in registration (perfect alignment) to provide duplicate copies in one writing operation. Therefore, they are called "one-write" systems and are inexpensive and easy to use. They were often used for accounting and payroll applications to produce checks, cash receipts, and other accounts receivable and accounts payable documentation. However, most of these applications have been replaced by computer software. Some medical and small business offices still use this system.

Salesbook

Traditional, timeless forms

The following types of forms are identified as traditional and timeless because they contain some of the oldest types of forms and those that will continue to be useful in the foreseeable future. In fact, labels and tags continue to be high usage paper forms.

Labels

Labels have numerous applications and are one of the oldest types of forms. They are commonly used to ship packages and boxes and are often computer generated from continuous printer forms. They are also used for identification, to communicate instructions, to list contents, and for just about any information that you would wish to affix to an object. Therefore, the construction of these forms requires an adhesive that is permanent or removable, depending on the intent of the label. A very convenient and popular type of label uses a pressure-sensitive adhesive with a release liner that can be easily removed to affix the label. The label itself can be paper, cloth, plastic, or even film or foil.

Tags

Tags are similar in function to labels. They have a variety of applications, including inventory control, production control, and shipping. They differ from labels by their method of attachment. Tags are attached with a fastening device, such as string, plastic, or wire and require an eyelet that is usually reinforced. They are constructed for a variety of purposes and, therefore, are quite versatile in materials used, size, color, shape, etc. As with labels, they may be manufactured in continuous strips for high-volume applications.

Mailers

A mailer is a combination envelope and form constructed as a continuous form. There are many different construction designs.

There are a variety of designs that can be considered mailers. Traditionally, they appear as a combination envelope and form in one continuous form. These are meant for high-volume mailings that are filled-in by impact computer printers that simultaneously address the outer envelope while completing the necessary information on the inside form. This can be accomplished by utilizing a one-time carbon coating on the inside of the envelope or interleaving carbon sheets in a multi-part form set. They also can use carbonless paper forms. It is essentially an efficient one-write operation used for mailings that include forms.

A common variation to this concept is the multi-panel brochure in which the last panel may be a perforated return form that is addressed on the back like a post card. Or, if the form is larger than one panel, the brochure can be refolded to resemble an envelope that is pre-addressed to the sender. There are many clever designs of mailers that all have one purpose in common—to include the form and envelope in one convenient set that will encourage a return response or simply provide an efficient method for high-volume mailings.

Envelopes

Envelopes may not be readily recognized as a category of forms, but they fit the definition. They provide a blank area for the entry of information in a pre-determined format; that is, blank space for the address in a particular place for postal scanners and sorters to process. There is usually pre-printed information, such as a return address, and there may be a postage-paid stamp, address with bar code, or a host of advertising gimmicks. Or they may simply be entirely blank. They are all still forms.

An envelope is a form because it contains a blank area for the entry of data.

Envelopes are designed in many sizes, colors, and constructions, including continuous strips. However, to keep costs to a minimum, designers utilize standard envelope sizes as much as possible. Postal regulations are a vital consideration in the form design of envelopes.

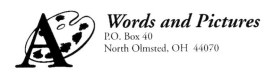

Words and Pictures
P.O. Box 40
North Olmsted, OH 44070

Checks

The familiar bank check is also a form and can be constructed as a cut sheet, unit set, or continuous form. To facilitate rapid processing through banks and the Federal Reserve System, checks are printed with magnetic ink that can be read by high-speed sorters.

Electronic forms

This is the second basic category of forms. Electronic forms should be designed like paper forms, using basic form design principles. However, electronic forms are "constructed" differently–it is entirely a computer operation. They are created and stored on electronic media for subsequent fill-in and processing by computers. Unlike paper forms, they are not printed to be kept in a stockroom.

A true electronic form is designed, filled in, and processed on a computer.

A true electronic form is designed, filled in, and processed on a computer. By contrast is the practice of utilizing desktop publishing systems to design and create camera-ready art for the production of conventional paper forms. Using a computer to design a form does not necessarily create an electronic form. It's what follows that makes the difference.

There are several potential advantages of converting to electronic forms. They are:

1. Reduction of up-front capital outlay for printing
2. Reduction of warehouse and storeroom costs
3. Reduction of distribution costs
4. Reduction of the labor cost of manually filling in forms
5. Eliminating costs of wasted inventory of revised and obsolete paper forms
6. Increasing production and efficiency of form fill-in and processing

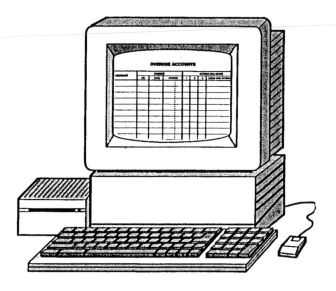

Converting to electronic forms involves the consideration of the following factors:

1. If design is decentralized, "designers" must be trained in forms design concepts or forms will be amateurish and inefficient.
2. All users need to have access to a computer.
3. If forms are to have a conventional appearance, the computer must have graphics capability and software that has forms design capability.

In regard to appearance, there are two types of electronic forms:

Electronic forms that look like paper forms create less user resistance.

1. Those that look like a conventional paper form, referred to as graphics-based.
2. Those that do not have graphic enhancements so that the captions and variable data look alike, referred to as text-based.

The advantage of electronic forms that look like conventional paper forms is that they are recognizable as something that people are accustomed to using, creating much less user resistance. Also, a well-designed conventional-appearing form is efficient and easy to fill in and process.

Text-based electronic forms look like straight text keyed on a computer screen. They can be designed with word processing software and are usually longer than conventional forms and, therefore, require more pages (screens). The advantage is that they are easier and faster to transmit electronically.

For a conventional paper form appearance, design for electronic forms is similar to the design for paper forms. Therefore, it is imperative for all forms designers to understand forms design principles and design techniques for paper forms.

Chapter 12 Questions

1. Name the two major categories of forms. Differentiate between them.

2. Define cut sheet. Why are cut sheets the most common of the three major types of paper forms? Cut sheets are often referred to by what other names?

3. What is a unit set? Unit sets are also called by what other names? What is a ply?

4. Describe the advantages of using unit sets.

5. Describe a continuous form. What feature makes a continuous form instantly recognizable? What is the advantage of using continuous forms?

6. Explain the construction features and the purpose of register forms and salesbooks.

7. Explain the construction of pegboard forms and name the applications for which they have been traditionally used.

8. What are mailers and what is the advantage of using mailers?

9. Envelopes do not look like other forms but they are still considered forms. Why? What is the distinguishing design feature of checks?

10. Give a brief overview of how electronic forms are created and processed.

11. State the potential benefits of converting paper forms to electronic forms.

Identification
Zone

Instruction Zone

FORM TITLE   **Worldwide Widget Co.**
FORM NUMBER

Please type or print clearly.

TO	FROM	DEPT
(Introduction Zone)		

(Body Zone)

DATE	SIGNATURE	
	(Closing Zone)	

CHAPTER
13

BASIC PRINCIPLES OF FORMS DESIGN

This hitteth the nail on the head.

– John Heywood

Chapter 13 Objectives

After studying this chapter, you should be able to:

1. Explain why a form must be designed to be an efficient information systems tool and that good graphics is not enough.

2. Explain why forms design should be as simple as possible and describe how to accomplish this.

3. Explain the reasons that form items should be grouped into zones and describe the basic forms zones.

4. Discuss the importance of the proper spacing of form items.

5. Describe the character spacing and the line spacing requirements of forms.

6. Describe the advantages of the box design style and discuss the other two forms design styles.

7. Discuss the worth of creating a favorable appearance for a form.

Forms design principles apply to all types of forms

Forms vary significantly in content, appearance, and construction. They can be printed on paper or appear in an electronic format. Yet, certain forms design principles apply to all types of forms. These principles are the basis for efficient forms design.

Forms design principles apply to all types of forms.

The following are the basic guidelines for designing forms:

1. The form must be designed to be an efficient information systems tool. An attractive apperance is not enough.

2. The form design should be as simple as possible to avoid detracting from the more important fill-in data.

3. The form items must be grouped into logically sequenced zones.

4. The spacing of form items must be compatible with the method of fill-in.

5. The form design style must promote efficiency for both fill-in and processing operations.

6. The form's appearance must create favorable responses from the users and readers.

BASIC PRINCIPLES OF FORMS DESIGN

The form must be designed to be an efficient information systems tool

Good graphics is not enough. A beautiful form that doesn't do its job in the information system is worthless. The designer must understand that a form is an information systems tool. The value of a form is the efficiency with which it communicates in the information system. It must provide an effective means of collecting needed data and transporting it through the information system where it is processed into more productive information. The appearance of the form is important but only secondary to the utility value of the form.

When designing forms, good graphics is not enough.

Unfortunately, many desktop publishers, graphic designers, commercial printers, and other forms creators are not aware of this basic forms design principle. An inefficient form often created by untrained "designers" is one with incorrect spacing for either handwritten or computer fill-in. The result is a time-consuming form that will often produce inaccurate information. If there is not enough room for a complete response to the requested information, the person filling in the form will have a problem. Or if the vertical line spacing is incompatible with the computer fill-in system, information will be printed over captions, preprinted items, and perhaps in the wrong blanks. The end result is a communication tool that may create more harm than good.

A good design rule is to eliminate anything that is not absolutely necessary.

The trained forms designer will use character and line spacing that will be compatible with the method of fill-in.

The form design should be as simple as possible

Forms should be designed with a simple, light touch so the fixed (printed) data won't interfere with the more important variable (fill-in) data. The people who write on the form and the people who read and process the form must concentrate on the fill-in data, not the printed items. The printed items direct what and where to write. They also help the reader to understand the fill-in data.

To accomplish this objective, the printed items shouldn't be graphically overpowering. You should avoid unnecessary borders, symbols, and decorations that would compete for attention. A good design rule is to eliminate anything that is not necessary.

Use the light touch, like this...   *Not like this.*

The form items must be grouped into logically sequenced zones

Grouping

Form items should be grouped by function or related subject. Grouping related items facilitates both data entry and data extraction. It increases the speed of data entry and saves the reader the time and inconvenience of searching for data. It also makes the form easier to read and comprehend. Grouping also makes it easier for the designer to design the form.

Grouping form items into zones makes the form easier to read and comprehend.

The groups are visually separated on the form, thereby creating zones. These zones are emphasized by using a graphic divider such as a bold line.

Basic form zones

The standard is to design forms with five basic zones. Some forms do not require all five zones while others require specific function zones. However, most often the designer will use the following basic form zones:

1. Identification Zone
2. Instructions Zone
3. Introduction Zone
4. Body Zone
5. Closing Zone

Identification
Zone

Instruction Zone

FORM TITLE   **Worldwide Widget Co.**   Please type or print clearly.

FORM NUMBER

TO   FROM   DEPT.

(Introduction Zone)

(Body Zone)

DATE   SIGNATURE

(Closing Zone)

The Identification Zone

The Identification Zone should appear on every form and always includes the form title and the form number. The Identification Zone also includes the organization name and contact information if the form is sent outside of the organization. Many organizations omit their name and contact information on internal forms, because in most cases, it isn't necessary.

OVERDUE ACCOUNTS REPORT

FORM 36 (REV. A)

GREEN THUMB NURSERY

Company identification may include the company name, address, telephone and fax numbers, e-mail address, web address, and logotype. All of this information is typically included in the identification zone if the form is sent outside the organization but is optional if the form stays internally within the organization. At the minimum, however, all forms should display the form identification, which consists of a form number and the form title.

FORM 123

WIDGET 123

W 123 (REV. B)

FORM 123 (REV. 8-99)

06-123

Typical form numbering formats.

The form number is essential for control of the form. It is necessary for requisitioning, purchasing, warehousing, and ordering. Numbers are better identifiers than words if the numbering system is kept simple. There are several choices of workable systems. Some use the word "form" in front of the number, some use an alphabetic or numeric department prefix, and some use a suffix indicating a revision number or revision date. A commonly used system is "Form xxx Rev. B (form number and revision indicator). A popular and practical system is to use the initials of the organization as a prefix and the revision date as a suffix; for example, WE 16B 2-04 for Widget Enterprises Form 16B last revised 2-04. Other suffixes are sometimes added to indicate type of form (unit set, continuous, etc.) or whether the form is kept in a central warehouse.

A good location for the form number is directly under the form title in small six-point type. This is not always done, but is a very good practice since both the form title and number represent the identity of the form. A common alternative is to locate the number in the lower left corner because it is tucked out of the way to be used only when needed.

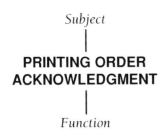

Subject
|
**PRINTING ORDER
ACKNOWLEDGMENT**
|
Function

Subject
|
**CHECKING ACCOUNT
STATEMENT**
|
Function

Subject
|
**OVERDUE ACCOUNTS
REPORT**
|
Function

Subject
|
**CASH RECEIPTS
JOURNAL**
|
Function

Subject
|
**OFFICE SUPPLIES
REQUEST**
|
Function

Whatever the choice, the location should be standardized for all company forms to provide a predictable place to find the number. The number should also appear on both sides of a form printed front and back. This helps to ensure correct backer printing. Similarly, the form number should appear on all parts of a multi-part form to ensure proper identification when the original is not readily available.

In addition to the form number, every form should have a title, which represents the name and function of the form. The readers should be able to glance at the form title and immediately understand the purpose of the form. Too many form titles, such as "Personnel Card", are meaningless. They describe the kind of paper that the form is printed on. The reader is well aware that the form is a card. What the reader wants to know is the function of the form. What is the purpose? Is it an employment application or credit inquiry, an office supplies request, or an authorization to pay an invoice?

The word "form" is also unnecessary in the form title. We know it is a form and do not need to be reminded. Each word should have a descriptive purpose and no "extras" are needed. The form title should have a subject and a function. Common form functions are "to record", "to report", "to notify", "to authorize", and "to request". A good form title would be "Office Supplies Request". The subject is "office supplies", and the function is "to request". One method of selecting a form title is to write out the function of the form in a sentence and pick out the key words. Then arrange them into a form title.

Since the reader should be able to immediately recognize the function of a form and the eye goes automatically to the upper left of a document, this is a good location for the form title and form number. To center the form title at the top is also a common practice.

The Instructions Zone

One of the objectives of the designer is to make the form self-instructing. This is done primarily by using precise captions, such as Name (Last, First, Middle). Another example is for the designer to use "Date Requested" and "Date Required" instead of "Date". However, specific fill-in and usage instructions must often be included in the design of the form.

If general instructions are required, they should be located on the front of the form near the top so the reader will see the instructions before writing on or using the form. The designer may want to highlight the instructions by italicizing, bolding, or using other graphic techniques, such as screens or reverses. If the general instructions are too long for the top front, a note in this location can refer the reader to the instructions on the back of the form, a cover sheet, a separate page, a booklet, or a procedures manual.

It is sometimes necessary to place other instructions in various locations on the form. Instructions that apply only to certain form sections should be placed wherever they would be most helpful. Some additional locations for instructions are:

1. The cover of a pad
2. The flap of an envelope
3. Any form section that is to be filled in by a different department or person

Try to avoid writing form instructions on separate documents or in procedures manuals if possible. No one wants to read voluminous procedures manuals.

Instructions that apply only to certain form sections should be placed wherever they would be most helpful.

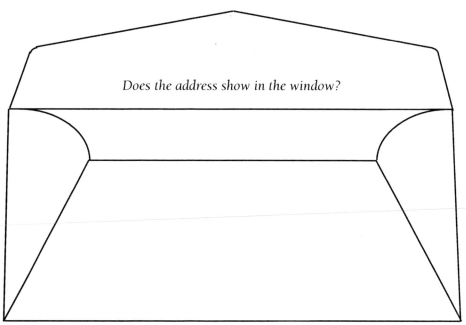

Does the address show in the window?

The Introduction Zone

The introduction zone usually follows the identification and general instructions zones. It introduces the body—the main part of the form. It gets the reader off to a good start with important introductory data and includes such items as:

The introduction zone introduces the body of the form.

1. The originator of the form
2. Who is going to use the form
3. "Sold to" and "ship to"
4. Transaction dates
5. Identifying numbers, purchase order numbers, and account numbers

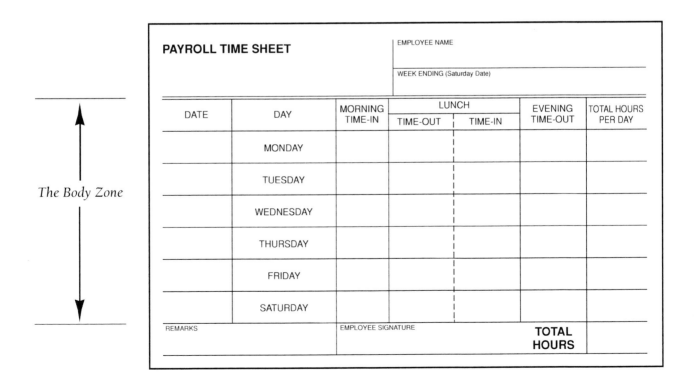

724 KEITH BLDG., O...
CLEVELAND, OH 44...
696-4545
FAX 781-6864

Please show this number
on your invoice
and correspondence.

TO

DELIVERY REQUIRED ON OR BEFORE (DATE)

Please notify us immediately
if you can't deliver by
the date above.

QUANTITY	PART NO./DESCRIPTION

The Body Zone

The body zone follows the introduction zone and contains the main information of the form. It is usually the largest zone on the form. The content, of course, varies with the subject of each individual form.

The Body Zone

PAYROLL TIME SHEET

EMPLOYEE NAME

WEEK ENDING (Saturday Date)

DATE	DAY	MORNING TIME-IN	LUNCH TIME-OUT	LUNCH TIME-IN	EVENING TIME-OUT	TOTAL HOURS PER DAY
	MONDAY					
	TUESDAY					
	WEDNESDAY					
	THURSDAY					
	FRIDAY					
	SATURDAY					

REMARKS   EMPLOYEE SIGNATURE   **TOTAL HOURS**

The Closing Zone

The closing zone groups together items which usually appear at the bottom of the form. Items that often appear in the closing zone are authorization signatures and dates, routing instructions, and qualifying statements.

Authorization signatures are very common since transactions on the form must often be approved. If the approval signature refers to the entire form, it should be located in the closing zone at the bottom of the form. If, however, the approval signature applies only to a certain section of the form, it should be located in that section. The signature caption should clearly identify the signer. Also, an adjacent fill-in space for the signature date is usually required.

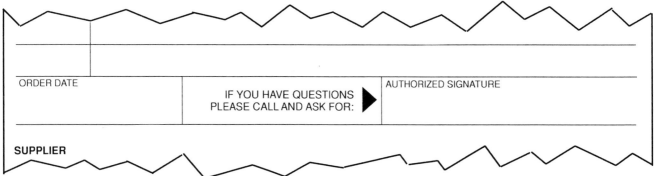

Zone sequence

The sequence of zones on the form follows the normal flow of data. In addition, the designer should follow the natural reading pattern. People read from left to right and top to bottom and expect to read a form in the same way. The form title, form number, and organization's identification begin at the top left since they are the first items that should be read. Next are the general instructions followed by the introduction zone. This is followed by the body zone and completed with the closing zone.

Function zones

Working within the framework of the basic form zones, it is sometimes necessary to include function zones. This is a grouping of items used to perform a particular function.

Item sequence within zones

Proper item sequencing can increase the speed and accuracy of form writing and reading. The primary consideration in item sequencing is the data flow in the system. Often data written on forms is copied from other forms. Copying from one form to another is more efficient when

Function Zones

the items copied are in the same order. In a system, the sequence of common items on all forms should be the same. If, however, there are a significant number of common items on forms in the same system, the designer should consider bringing the forms together in one multi-part set. Then only one writing would be necessary to fill in all of the common items, which is more efficient and would reduce errors.

If there are a significant number of common items on forms in the same system, the designer should consider bringing the forms together in one multi-part set.

In item sequencing, the designer should also consider frequency of use. On some forms, certain items are not always filled in. These items should be put on the right side of the writing line. Items that are always filled in should be put on the left side of the form where the writer and the reader start their operations.

Another factor in item sequencing is the normal left-to-right, top-to-bottom reading pattern. Items should also follow conventional sequence, as in "name, address, phone number".

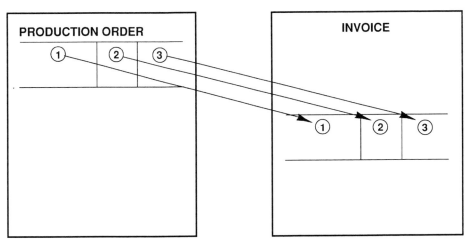

Copying from one form to another is more efficient when the items copied are in the same sequence.

The spacing of form items must be compatible with the method of fill-in

This is the most important forms design principle. Proper spacing is vital to the efficiency of a form. The spacing of form items must be compatible with the method of fill-in so the data can be entered quickly, easily, and accurately. If forms are not properly spaced, users are frustrated by spaces not big enough to write in, or forms are larger and more expensive than necessary because designers provide way too much blank area for the typical fill-in response.

The spacing of form items must be compatible with the method of fill-in so the data can be entered quickly, easily, and accurately.

Proper form spacing begins with fact finding during forms analysis. The designer must know how the form is written. A form can be filled in by hand, rubber stamp, computer printer, word processor, or a combination of methods. The form spacing must conform to the writing methods. For example, if items are not spaced properly on forms filled in by computer line printers, characters are printed in unwanted locations and on top of printed items, making data difficult or impossible to read.

GIVE THREE CREDIT REFERENCES (Name, Address and Phone Number) _____

ZIP CODE _____

PHONE NO. _____

The designer is not thinking about the space required for fill-in.

GIVE 3 CREDIT REFERENCES (Name, Address, Phone Number)		
1.		
2.		
3.		
ZIP CODE	PHONE	*(This space can be used for another item)*

With this re-design, proper space is provided for fill-in.

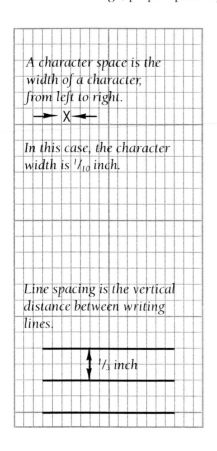

A character space is the width of a character, from left to right.

→ X ←

In this case, the character width is ¹/₁₀ inch.

Line spacing is the vertical distance between writing lines.

↕ ¹/₃ inch

Character spacing

Character spacing is the width of each character across the page, from left to right. Many printers place 10 characters to the inch by default. The next common character spacing is 12. However, with desktop publishing systems, the choices have become much more flexible. The designer must determine through forms analysis the most frequent method of fill-in. If it is a computer printer and the designer is not familiar with the default spacing, it can be determined by measuring the character width from a sample produced by the printer. Or the printer manual could be consulted.

To determine the proper amount of space for the fill-in blanks, the designer needs to decide the average response for each item. Then, if the form is filled in by hand, the designer should allow a minimum of one inch for every five characters written in the blank. This can be more precisely figured using forms design or desktop publishing programs that have 10-character grid patterns lightly showing on the drawing screen. Then each handwritten character would be designated 2/10 of an inch or two grid squares for the fill-in blanks. Thus, the optimum amount of space to leave for each fill-in blank can be precisely determined by establishing the maximum fill-in response and allowing 2/10 (two grid squares) for each handwritten character.

Single machine spacing – ⅙ inch.

Double machine spacing – ⅓ inch. This is standard line spacing for business forms and should always be used unless you have a good reason not to do so.

¼ inch line spacing. This conforms to 1½ spacing on a typewriter and is also the minimum line spacing for handwriting.

Line spacing

Line spacing refers to the vertical space between the writing lines on the form. Most equipment fill-in, from word processor to computer printer, utilizes six lines per inch down the page. A single line space, then, is 1/6 of an inch. If the equipment is set at double spacing, the paper moves up 1/3 of an inch (2/6) or three lines to an inch. This is standard line spacing for most business forms. Double spacing is considered excellent line spacing for both equipment and hand fill-in. It allows for easy fill-in, eliminates crowding, and reduces unnecessary extra space between the writing lines.

Printers are more versatile than ever and can be adjusted for optional line spacing when required. A common option is eight lines to the inch. This causes a more crowded look that can be more difficult to read but is useful when needing space to fit everything on one page. If the form will be filled in by any other equipment with line spacing not in increments of 1/6 inch (standard line spacing), the designer must adjust the vertical line spacing on the form accordingly. To determine the spacing, the designer may refer to the manufacturer's manual or contact the sales rep to get the information. Or the designer may analyze a sample filled in on the equipment and use it as a guide.

If the form is predominantly filled in by hand, a good line spacing is still 1/3 of an inch (double standard line spacing). It allows sufficient room for the hand fill-in while accommodating the standard line spacing for most printers. For those forms that are filled in by both handwriting and equipment, the line spacing is determined by the equipment. If more handwriting lines are required per page, it can be accomplished by reducing the line spacing to 1/4 inch, which is the minimum for handwritten forms.

6/10–the most commonly used form spacing

The fraction "6/10" designates the most frequently used form spacing for traditional business machines. It represents 6 lines to the inch vertical spacing and 10 characters to the inch horizontal spacing. Alternate choices may be 6/12 and 8/10 spacing. Although printers can squeeze a character into every available print position, the result will be difficult, if not impossible, to read. The designer should be more concerned with readability than with the maximum printer capability.

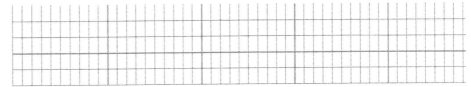

The 6/10 grid.

The form design style must promote efficiency for both fill-in and processing operations

Forms are basically questionnaires. The form captions are abbreviated questions and the fill-in spaces are for the answers. The design style refers to how the captions and spaces are arranged on the form. The box design, as described below, is the most efficient design style. Untrained "designers", however, often use caption-on-the-line. Another commonly used design style, although ineffective, is caption-under-the-line. Each style is illustrated and described.

The box design style

| NAME | ADDRESS (Street, City, State, Zip) |
| PHONE NO. | JOB TITLE/DESCRIPTION |

1/3"
1/3"

The standard box depth is 1/3 inch.
The box depth may be more than
1/3 inch if the form is filled in by hand
or if the larger depth will not interfere
with machine spacing. The box
should not be less than 1/3 inch.

NAME

The most efficient design style for all methods of fill-in is the box style, also referred to as the ULC (Upper Left Corner) caption style. It is most effectively used for caption and fill-in design because:

1. It utilizes standard 1/3 inch vertical line spacing between the horizontal lines, which allows enough room for fast fill-in by printer or by hand.

2. The small caption in the upper left of the box recedes into the background and allows the fill-in data to stand out. When processing the form, the user wants to read the fill-in data and not the captions.

3. The ULC box design allows the full width of the line to be available for fill-in space if the caption font size is small enough. Compare this to a disproportionately long caption that takes most of the width of the page and leaves an inch or two for fill-in.

4. The box style also allows most of the vertical lines to be aligned, which reduces the frequency of tabs and increases the efficiency of printer fill-in.

5. The box design provides a clean, uniform appearance and a clearly defined entry field.

Converting from other design styles to the ULC box design style provides more usable fill-in space and can result in a reduction of the overall form size. A reduction to a smaller standard size can reduce the purchase price of the form. A note of caution, however, is to be sure to design the caption in a small enough font size to recede into the upper left corner as the name indicates. If the font size is too large, the space underneath the caption is not usable for fill-in and the result become a "glorified caption-on-the-line" style. This is a common mistake of untrained designers. Study the examples to see the difference and fully understand the look of the ULC box design style.

Box design allows the important fill-in data to stand out.

INDIVIDUAL I. R. Mallard	ORGANIZATION Rubber Duckie Company
ADDRESS One Duckie Plaza, Novelty, OH 44020	
PHONE NO. 440-123-4567	FAX NO. 440-123-4568	E-MAIL ADDRESS m@duckie.com

Caption-on-the-line design style

The caption-on-the-line style is often used by untrained forms designers. It is easy and seems logical but is an inefficient fill-in style. It takes up much of the writing line and often does not leave sufficient space for the more important fill-in data. Also, the captions are usually too large and compete with the fill-in data. Captions are secondary in importance and should not be prominent. In addition, this style results in a haphazard arrangement that looks confusing and requires additional tab stops for keyboard or printer fill-in.

NAME _____ ADDRESS (Street, City, State, Zip) _____

PHONE NUMBER _____ JOB TITLE/DESCRIPTION _____

However, if the designer uses precautions to minimize the potential disadvantages of this style, it can be acceptable to use occasionally, along with the ULC box design style.

Caption-under-the-line design style

Generally, caption-under-the-line design style is also not efficient. It is acceptable in some situations, such as a signature line; but for general usage, it has major disadvantages. It can be confusing. Does a fill-in space belong to the caption above it or the caption below it? In the past, it was a particular problem when typewriters were used to fill in the forms. The captions were hidden below the typewriter platen, causing much wasted time moving up and down between caption and fill-in line. This may still be the case with portable word processors. Caption-under-the-line is, therefore, not a good design style for general use.

NAME

ADDRESS (Street. City, State, Zip Code)

PHONE NO.

JOB TITLE / DESCRIPTION

Columns

Columns are a variation of box design.

Columns, as shown in the illustration, are a variation of the box design. They are used when two or more entries of the same kind will be made, thereby grouping like data for more efficient processing. It's also an attractive and efficient means of saving space by eliminating repetitive captions.

QUANTITY	DESCRIPTION	CATALOG NO.	PRICE

The form's graphic appearance must create favorable responses from users and readers

The designer's first consideration is to make sure that the form is an efficient tool in an information system. The form should have a good appearance, but it is secondary to efficiency. Customers and the public judge an organization by the appearance of its forms, letterheads, and other printed material. The design, appearance, and printing quality of forms also affects employee morale and even have an influence on clerical accuracy. Therefore, forms should have a good graphic appearance. Forms graphics is the topic of the next chapter.

Chapter 13 Questions

1. The value of a form is the efficiency with which it communicates in the information system. Discuss this statement.

2. Explain why forms design should be as simple as possible and describe how to accomplish this.

3. Why should form items be grouped into zones? Name the basic form zones.

4. If a form is sent outside the company, what items should be included in the Identification Zone?

5. Why should every form have a form number? Name two common page locations for form numbers.

6. Form titles should have a subject and a function. Name five common form functions. Describe a method for selecting a good form title.

7. Describe the purpose of the Introduction Zone.

8. Explain the Body Zone. Where is it located on the form?

9. Define the Closing Zone. What items often appear in this zone?

10. Discuss the importance of the proper spacing of form items.

11. Define character spacing. What is standard character spacing for machine fill-in? What is standard character spacing for hand fill-in?

12. Define line spacing. What is standard line spacing for machine fill-in? What is standard line spacing for hand fill-in?

13. What is the most efficient caption design style?

14. What design style is intuitive, but not as efficient as the box design style?

CHAPTER 14

GRAPHICS FOR BUSINESS FORMS

A picture is worth a thousand words

Chapter 14 Objectives

After studying this chapter, you should be able to:

1. Describe the benefits of creating a good graphic appearance for forms.

2. Explain the concept of the designer using a light graphics touch.

3. Discuss the merit of optical balance in forms design.

4. Describe the role of contrast between the items on a form.

5. Explain why type and typography (the artful use of type) are the most important elements in forms graphics.

6. Choose the most effective typefaces for forms and describe how type should be used on forms.

7. Describe the functions of rules on forms and how to select the correct rules when designing forms.

8. Explain how screens are used both graphically and functionally on forms.

9. Describe a reverse and name its dominant feature.

10. Describe the use of logos, arrows, illustrations, and photographs on forms.

11. Discuss the use of color on forms.

Why good graphics are important

As stated in previous chapters, the graphic appearance of a form affects customer and public relations and employee morale. It also affects reader comprehension and clerical accuracy. The public, customers, shareholders, and employees form opinions about an organization from the appearance of its forms. If the forms are attractive and look efficient, the organization is judged to be professional and efficient.

The appearance of a form affects customer and public relations, employee morale, comprehension and clerical accuracy.

The appearance of a form is important but does not take precedence over the design. The design objective is to maximize the efficiency of the form in the information system. Attractive continuous forms that won't feed through the computer line printer are totally useless. The designer must first ensure the integrity of the form in the information system before turning to graphic considerations.

In addition to improving appearance, certain graphic techniques can also be used functionally to improve the efficiency of the form. For instance, techniques such as screens are used to highlight important data and make the form easier to read, understand, and process.

Forms Graphic Considerations

Use a light graphics touch

A little bit of graphics goes a long way. It doesn't take much to improve the appearance of forms. It certainly doesn't take six different typefaces, twenty rounded corners, four ink colors, eight screens, and five reverses. Yet we find amateur desktop publishers overpowering us with everything in their "graphics bag" just because it's available.

The designer should always remember that the variable (fill-in) data is more important than the constant data. The constant, preprinted information is there to facilitate concise, accurately filled in data. Therefore, the constant data should be designed with a light touch so it doesn't detract from the more important fill-in data.

ACCOUNT NO. *596238*

Don't design like this. The caption overpowers the number.

ACCOUNT NO.

596238

Use a light touch for the caption so it doesn't overpower the more important number.

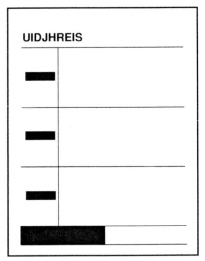

This layout is not optically balanced.

Optical balance

Optical balance

Just as the human eye responds favorably to equilibrium in nature, it reacts well to optically balanced layouts. We react better to optically balanced compositions as opposed to those in which the elements are randomly arranged. A layout can be optically balanced in a formal (centered) or an informal arrangement.

With the informal layout, the elements are sized and positioned so they appear balanced in relation to an optical center. This is achieved by "eyeballing" the elements into place so they appear balanced. The optical center is not necessarily the mathematical center. The balancing is not mathematical; it is visual. In other words, if it looks balanced, it is balanced. If it looks unbalanced, it is unbalanced although it may be mathematically correct.

Contrast

Contrast between the elements of a layout creates interest and helps to avoid a dull, monotonous layout. It also helps the reader by highlighting the important form elements like the form title and instructions. It is important that the designer read and understand the form so the correct items will be highlighted.

Contrast can be created by making certain items larger and/or bolder. The designer can also use screens, reverses, symbols, and colored ink and paper to create contrast.

TERMS AND CONDITIONS

Kifdieth dlsie assiet widur diwogue giderhw ptid wi aidte lsicthd aldhtke diethid. Kifdieth dlsie assiet widur diwogue giderhw ptid wi aidte lsicthd aldhtke diethid. Kifdieth dlsie assiet widur diwogue giderhw ptid wi aidte lsicthd aldhtke diethid. Kifdieth dlsie assiet widur diwogue giderhw ptid wi aidte lsicthd aldhtke diethid. Kifdieth dlsie assiet widur diwogue giderhw ptid wi aidte lsicthd aldhtke diethid. Kifdieth dlsie assiet widur diwogue giderhw ptid wi aidte lsicthd aldhtke diethid. Kifdieth dlsie assiet widur diwogue giderhw ptid wi aidte lsicthd aldhtke diethid. Kifdieth dlsie assiet widur diwogue giderhw ptid wi aidte lsicthd aldhtke diethid. Kifdieth dlsie assiet widur diwogue giderhw ptid wi aidte lsicthd aldhtke diethid. Kifdieth dlsie assiet widur diwogue giderhw ptid wi aidte lsicthd aldhtke diethid. Kifdieth dlsie assiet widur diwogue giderhw ptid wi aidte lsicthd aldhtke diethid. Kifdieth dlsie assiet widur diwogue giderhw ptid wi aidte lsicthd aldhtke diethid. Kifdieth dlsie assiet widur diwogue giderhw ptid wi aidte lsicthd aldhtke diethid. Kifdieth dlsie assiet widur diwogue giderhw ptid wi aidte lsicthd aldhtke diethid. Kifdieth dlsie assiet widur diwogue giderhw ptid wi aidte lsicthd aldhtke diethid.

No Contrast.

Type and typography

The most important element in forms graphics is typography. This involves the selection of typefaces and fonts and how they are arranged on the page. Poor typography can turn a well-designed form into an unattractive form. It can also hinder readability, causing frustration and inaccuracy. Clearly, good selection and arrangement of typefaces is an important factor to the overall efficiency of the form.

Type selection

There are two basic styles of type, serif and sans serif. Serifs are the little cross strokes as shown in the illustration on the next page. Sans means "without"; therefore, sans-serif type does not have the cross strokes on the characters. The characters are cleaner and simpler because they do not have serifs. Traditionally, forms are keyed in a sans-serif typeface such as Arial or Helvetica.

Most type is set in 6- to 12-point medium caps. Bold type is used for form titles, section heads, and totals. Sans-serif italics is often used for instructions or highlighting. The designer can safely designate a sans-

Serif Type

*Sans-Serif Type
(without serifs)*

*Sans-Serif type is recommended
for forms typesetting.*

IF THE FORM CONTAINS MORE THAN ONE PARA-GRAPH OF TEXT, THE TYPE IN THESE PARAGRAPHS WILL BE MUCH EASIER TO READ IF THEY ARE SET IN CAPS AND LOWER CASE. EXCEPT FOR THIS CONDITION, ALL OTHER TYPE ON A FORM CAN BE SET IN EITHER ALL CAPS OR CAPS AND LOWER CASE. CAPS AND LOWER CASE IS EASIER TO READ WHEN THERE ARE SEVERAL WORDS TOGETHER. SINCE ALMOST ALL CAPTIONS AND OTHER TYPE ON A FORM CONSIST OF A FEW WORDS, ALL CAPS ALSO PROVIDES EASY READING AND IS OFTEN PREFERRED.

*Don't set type in all caps in a
paragraph.*

serif type like Arial or Helvetica for most forms since it is customary and expected by most readers. It is also legible and not too ornate, allowing the more important fill-in data to stand out.

Serif type, set in upper and lower case, is very legible for paragraphs of text in books and publications. The horizontal serifs help to create a horizontal left to right eyeflow that increases reading speed. Serif type is often used for text on *legal* forms and sections like "terms and conditions" on backers.

Generally, serif and sans-serif typefaces are not mixed on the same form. Any type variations desired are easily attainable within one type family, like Arial or Helvetica. If an experienced designer uses both serif and sans-serif typefaces on the same form, it is usually a sans-serif on the front for the majority of the form and a serif for text on the backer.

Form typography

If the form contains more than one paragraph of text, it is much easier to read if it appears in caps and lower case. This occurs most commonly with extensive instructions that require several sentences or paragraphs of text. A relatively large amount of text in all caps is difficult to read because there is little contrast as shown in the sample. The size and shape of the letters are too uniform and tend to blend together. However, for just a few words appearing together, such as the form title and captions, all caps looks good and is actually preferred. Most professional forms designers specify all caps for the majority of the form, with the exception of paragraphs of text. Captions in all caps is traditional and expected by the reader. Also, unlike caps and lower case, the designer can avoid making capitalization decisions if the captions are keyed in all caps.

Most print on a form should be set with medium type. "Medium" refers to the weight (thickness) of each character. Bold type should only be used for items to be highlighted. Italic type should be used sparingly since it is ornate and not as legible. The usual type size range is 6-point to 12-point. As a general rule, text (paragraphs) should be set in 10- or 12-point type, which is considered standard.

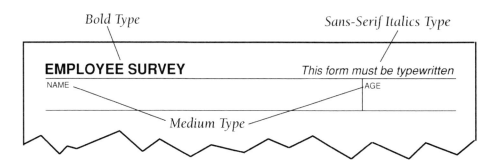

Bold Type

Sans-Serif Italics Type

EMPLOYEE SURVEY

This form must be typewritten

NAME

AGE

Medium Type

Employee Evaluation Form

Date of Report _____ Employee's Name _____ Dept. _____

Salary _____ No. of Months with Co. _____

What are this employee's STRONG points in relation to his present job?
Consider attitude, attendance, personality, prior education and experience, and actual job performance.

_____

_____
_____

What are this employee's WEAK points in relation to his present job? Consider the same qualities as above.

_____

_____
_____

If this is not the first rating, describe any noticeable improvement since the last rating. If there has been none, write "NONE."

_____

_____
_____

Have you discussed the above rating with the employee, calling to his attention both strong and weak points and making suggestions for improvement?   Yes   No

This form was set with bold serif type, which is not a good choice for forms.

EMPLOYEE EVALUATION

EMPLOYEE NAME	DEPT.	REPORT DATE

NO. OF MONTHS WITH CO.	SALARY $	COMMENTS

EMPLOYEE'S STRONG POINTS — Attitude, personality, education, experience, job performance.

EMPLOYEE'S WEAK POINTS — Consider same qualities as above.

IMPROVEMENTS SINCE LAST

This is a re-design of the above form, properly set with sans-serif type.

Theidjth dithe eithet id theid
axftkv thel tidbv lscsdi
dktidjth dk thed ithe iththe
xicv, dgoe.

Justified Format.

Theidjth dithe eithet id
theid axftkv thel tidbv lscsdi
dktidjth dk thed ithe iththe
xicv, dgoe.

Ragged Right Format.

Paragraphs of text on a form may be fully justified or ragged right.
Either format is acceptable.

Because it is easy and convenient, text on forms is often keyed in one
big column across the entire page and in type sizes smaller than 10-
point. This combination creates a page that is difficult to read because
the eye can't easily follow small type on such a long line. The format-
ting guideline is to use a small line length if a small point size is selected. In other words, key small point-size paragraphs in two or more
vertical columns, like a newspaper page.

In addition, the designer should make a text page more appealing to
the reader by "breaking up" monotonous text. This can be done with
techniques such as paragraph indents, sub-headings, underlines, and
bold or italics to highlight words.

Theidjth dithe eithet id theid axftkv thel tidbv lscsdi dktidjth dk thed ithe iththe xicv, dgoe. Theidjth dithe eithet id theid axftkv thel tidbv lscsdi dktidjth dk thed ithe iththe xicv, dgoe. Theidjth dithe eithet id theid axftkv thel tidbv lscsdi dktidjth dk thed ithe iththe xicv, dgoe. Theidjth dithe eithet id theid axftkv thel tidbv lscsdi dktidjth dk thed ithe iththe xicv, dgoe. Theidjth dithe eithet id theid axftkv thel tidbv lscsdi dktidjth dk thed ithe iththe xicv, dgoe. Theidjth dithe eithet id theid axftkv thel tidbv lscsdi dktidjth dk thed ithe iththe xicv, dgoe. Theidjth dithe eithet id theid axftkv thel tidbv lscsdi dktidjth dk thed ithe iththe xicv, dgoe. Theidjth dithe eithet id theid axftkv thel tidbv lscsdi dktidjth dk thed ithe iththe xicv, dgoe. Theidjth dithe eithet id theid axftkv thel tidbv lscsdi dktidjth dk thed ithe iththe xicv, dgoe. Theidjth dithe eithet id theid axftkv thel tidbv lscsdi dktidjth dk thed ithe iththe xicv, dgoe. Theidjth dithe eithet id theid axftkv thel tidbv lscsdi dktidjth dk thed ithe iththe xicv, dgoe. Theidjth dithe eithet id theid axftkv thel tidbv lscsdi dktidjth dk thed ithe iththe xicv, dgoe. Theidjth dithe eithet id theid axftkv thel tidbv lscsdi dktidjth dk thed ithe iththe xicv, dgoe. Theidjth dithe eithet id theid axftkv thel tidbv lscsdi dktidjth dk thed ithe iththe xicv, dgoe. Theidjth dithe eithet id theid axftkv thel tidbv lscsdi dktidjth dk thed ithe iththe xicv, dgoe. Theidjth dithe eithet id theid axftkv

Don't design it like this. The line length is too long for the small point size of the type.

Theidjth dithe eithet id theid axftkv thel tidbv lscsdi dktidjth dk thed ithe iththe xicv, dgoe. Theidjth dithe eithet id theid axftkv thel tidbv lscsdi dktidjth dk thed ithe iththe xicv, dgoe. Theidjth dithe eithet id theid axftkv thel tidbv lscsdi dktidjth dk thed ithe iththe xicv, dgoe. Theidjth dithe eithet id theid axftkv thel tidbv lscsdi dktidjth dk thed ithe iththe xicv, dgoe. Theidjth dithe eithet id theid axftkv thel tidbv lscsdi dktidjth dk thed ithe iththe xicv, dgoe. Theidjth dithe eithet id theid axftkv thel tidbv lscsdi dktidjth dk thed ithe iththe xicv, dgoe. Theidjth dithe eithet id theid axftkv thel tidbv lscsdi dktidjth dk thed ithe iththe xicv, dgoe. Theidjth dithe eithet id theid axftkv thel tidbv lscsdi dktidjth

dk thed ithe iththe xicv, dgoe. Theidjth dithe eithet id theid axftkv thel tidbv lscsdi dktidjth dk thed ithe iththe xicv, dgoe. Theidjth dithe eithet id theid axftkv thel tidbv lscsdi dktidjth dk thed ithe iththe xicv, dgoe. Theidjth dithe eithet id theid axftkv thel tidbv lscsdi dktidjth dk thed ithe iththe xicv, dgoe. Theidjth dithe eithet id theid axftkv thel tidbv lscsdi dktidjth dk thed ithe iththe xicv, dgoe. Theidjth dithe eithet id theid axftkv thel tidbv lscsdi dktidjth dk thed ithe iththe xicv, dgoe. Theidjth dithe eithet id theid axftkv thel tidbv lscsdi dktidjth dk thed ithe iththe xicv, dgoe. Theidjth dithe eithet id theid axftkv thel tidbv lscsdi dktidjth dk thed ithe iththe xicv, dgoe. Theidjth dithe eithet id theid axftkv thel tidbv lscsdi

Design it like this, in 2 columns. Small point size type requires smaller line lengths.

Rules

"Rules" are the printed lines on a form. They are used to indicate fill-in blanks, to guide the eye, to highlight, and to serve as dividers between form sections and data entry fields.

Only two kinds of rules–a hairline and bold rule–are needed to design most forms. And most of the rules should be hairlines because they are thin and simple, resulting in an uncluttered look. Bold, thicker rules are used as dividers and to highlight important items.

A few other rule variations may be acceptable. For instance, double hairlines may be used as dividers. Broken rules and screened lines are often used to sub-divide columns and entry fields. Similarly, rounded corners, where vertical and horizontal lines meet, can create an attractive variation if done sparingly. Too many rounded corners can create an overdone, cluttered appearance. The designer should try to keep the form as simple as possible by not using too many rule variations or rounded corners on the same page.

Hairline ($^1/_2$ point rule). The most common form rule used for boxes and fill-in spaces.

Bold Rule ($1^1/_2$ point rule). For major form divisions and for highlighting important form items.

Double Hairline. Used to divide major sections.

Broken hairline. Used to sub-divide columns and sections.

Screened Rule. Used to tone down a crowded form and to make fill-in data stand out.

Rule with Rounded Corners.

CASH DEPOSIT RECORD
FORM 101 (B)
MONTH, YEAR
Double Hairline
Hairline

DEPOSIT DATE	ACCOUNTS RECEIVABLE	SEMINARS	GENERAL LEDGER
1	$ *Bold Rule*	$	$
2			
3	*Broken Hairline*		
4			
5			
6			

Screens

Screens are frequently used on forms to enhance their appearance and to perform highlighting and other practical functions. Words, rules, logos, line art illustrations, areas and just about anything can be screened.

To the eye, screens seem to be lighter shades of solid ink colors. For example, screened black ink produces a gray appearance. A screen is produced by photographing solid-line art through a graphics screen (similar to a window screen), which separates the color into a dot pattern. The eye perceives this as a lighter shade of the ink color because of the lighter background dispersed throughout the original color.

A popular variation is the "graduated" screen, which is also called a "variable" or a "disappearing" screen. A properly executed graduated screen is attractive and can enhance the appearance of certain forms. However, caution must be taken not to overdo them because they can distract from the more important fill-in data. They can also cause difficulty in reproduction from copiers, filmers or scanners, and fax machines.

Screens can also be used functionally. For example, a screened background can be used to distinguish form sections, such as those

Screens can be used functionally as well as graphically.

Ameritype!

PURCHASE ORDER   **1113**

www.ameritype.com
5811 CANAL ROAD, STE. 110
VALLEY VIEW, OH 44125

Please show this number
on your Invoice
and correspondence.

A screended area used to highlight an important item

TO

DELIVERY REQUIRED ON OR BEFORE (DATE)

Please notify us immediately
if you can't deliver by
the date above.

Screened rules used to make the more important name and address stand out.

QUANTITY	PART NO. / DESCRIPTION

A screen used as a column heading.

ORDER DATE

IF YOU HAVE QUESTIONS,
PLEASE CALL AND ASK FOR: ▶

AUTHORIZED SIGNATURE

SUPPLIER

A screen used for optical balance.

---

reserved for fill-in by a different department or "for office use only". Screens can also be used to highlight certain items on a form or to tone down the visual impact of a "busy" form. And screens are often used to help make the written data on a form stand out better, such as on source documents to facilitate data entry into computer systems.

Reverses

Reverses

Reverses can also be used graphically and functionally. They are produced by solidly filling in the area around the image, allowing the background color and shape to form the image. This creates a light image on a dark background, which is the "reverse" of typical imaging. Reverses in colored ink are usually more attractive than black ink.

Reverses are very powerful visually and command attention. Therefore, they are used functionally to highlight special items. Also, text set in a reverse bar is often used as a separator between sections of a form. These techniques can be quite attractive if they aren't too large and overpowering and if the designer doesn't use too many reverses on the same page. They can actually target immediate attention since this is often the first thing the reader sees and focuses on. Therefore, use reverses sparingly.

A caution when constructing reverses is to use larger boldface all-cap text to improve legibility. Small, lightface, and medium type often fill in when printed in reverse, which results in reduced legibility.

Logos, arrows, illustrations, and photographs
Logos

Overpowering logos are not necessary on internal forms.

Logos must be placed on external forms in accordance with the organization's logo standards. A form that travels outside, like any other document, represents the organization to the public and customers.

For internal forms, the logo is not as important. Employees know who they are working for; and, therefore, many organizations do not use their logo on internal forms. Others use the logo in a smaller size. It doesn't need to be large and overpowering on an internal form.

Arrows

Various kinds of arrows are commonly used on forms to point out entry fields and to improve the understanding of instructions. Most desktop publishing software will have several styles of arrows to select and insert into the design. They should not be overlooked as a simple means of drawing attention to an important item.

Illustrations

Illustrations and photographs can be used functionally and graphically. They are often used as a marketing device on certain forms that are seen by the public and customers. Also, illustrations may be needed for clarification, such as anatomical illustrations on medical forms and grids for drawing floor plans on a construction form.

Illustrations and photographs can be used functionally and graphically.

A variation is a lightly screened illustration or photograph of the company logo, products, or facilities that is placed as a faint image in the body of a form. These screens are called "phantoms". A phantom may also be screened text for functional phrases, such as "Thank You". They provide a subliminal message to the form since data will be written over them and they will be visible when reading and writing on the form. However, caution must be taken to keep the screened image light enough to not interfere with the legibility of the written data. Usually a 10 or 20 percent screen is appropriate for the background phantom.

Color

Traditionally, forms have been printed with black ink on white paper basically because it provides excellent contrast for reading and reproduction.

Printing forms with green or brown ink makes forms easier to read and tends to reduce errors.

With technological advances in printing and computer equipment, however, it is increasingly feasible and economical to use colored ink and paper for forms production. Colored paper, including recycled paper, is affordable and available in a myriad of colors and textures. Colored ink for offset printing presses can be mixed in any color, including pastels and metallic colors like gold, silver, and copper. The spectrum of ink colors are standardized in the printing industry through a system called the Pantone Matching System (PMS color system). Colors are given codes to facilitate identifying the exact shade desired. Color copiers and desktop publishing printers have also improved to easily produce colors but are usually not economical for large volume printing.

In addition to improving the appearance of the form, colored ink makes forms easier to fill in and tends to reduce errors. Green or brown inks, in particular, provide good contrast to the fill-in data while appearing softer and more soothing to the eyes than black ink.

If both colored ink and colored paper are combined, the designer must ensure that there is enough contrast between them. Contrast is the key to legibility. Obviously, you can't read black ink on black paper even though the image is there. It's the same with yellow ink on white paper or purple on red. The lack of contrast makes it difficult, if not impossible,

Light-colored paper reduces glare and eye fatigue.

to read. Also, the color choices must be compatible with any other processing that the form may go through, such as photocopying, faxing, scanning, or microfilming. If a particular color combination of inks and paper are being considered, the designer should test any of these processes that might be affected by the color choices.

Colored papers also offer possibilities for improving the graphic appearance and the efficiency of forms. Light-colored paper reduces glare. The sorting and distribution of the parts of a multi-part form are made easier if each part is printed on a separate color of paper with routing instructions at the bottom of each.

Mail-Well Envelope Company uses creative graphics to get their client's direct mail envelopes opened by the recipients.

Many graphic designers think that the most important consideration in a letterhead is the paper. The appearance and the feel of paper says something about the company. People judge the company by the grade and color of the paper that the forms are printed on.

Mail-Well Envelope Company's Cleveland office is located at 4500 Tiedeman Road, Cleveland, OH 44144, telephone: 800-477-1696.

Chapter 14 Questions

1. What are the benefits of creating a good graphic appearance for forms?

2. Explain the concept of the forms designer using a light graphics touch.

3. Discuss the merit of optical balance in forms design.

4. Describe the role of contrast in forms design?

5. Explain why type and typography (the artful use of type) are the most important elements in forms graphics.

6. Compare serif type and sans-serif type. Which one has been traditionally used for forms?

7. List some techniques for "breaking up" long monotonous passages of text.

8. What are the function of rules on forms.

9. How are screens used both graphically and functionally on forms?

10. Describe a reverse and explain its dominant feature.

11. What are the advantages of using colored ink on forms? What two colors provide good contrast to fill-in data?

12. What is the Pantone Matching System (PMS Color System) and what is its purpose?

13. What are the advantages of using colored paper? What precaution should be taken when using both colored paper and colored ink?

YOU WANT IT, WHEN?!

CHAPTER

15

STEP-BY-STEP FORMS DESIGN

*By the work, one knows
the workmen*

– Jean de La Fontaine

Chapter 15 Objectives

After studying this chapter, you should be able to:

1. Explain why forms analysis should always be the first step in forms design.

2. Describe how forms analysis can reduce forms production costs.

3. Explain how the real cost of forms is the labor cost of processing forms, not the cost of producing the forms.

4. Describe forms analysis procedures beginning with fact gathering.

5. Describe the basic step-by-step procedure to design cut sheets.

6. Explain the benefit of the rough sketch in forms design.

7. Discuss the factors involved in selecting the size of a form.

8. Discuss margins and gripper space.

9. Explain why fixed location items should be drawn before other form elements.

10. Discuss the design of the Instructions Zone, the Introduction Zone, and the Closing Zone.

11. Name the considerations for efficient item sequencing.

12. Describe the various forms design rules and how they should be used.

13. List the advantages of using box style design.

14. State the purpose of ballot boxes (check boxes) and discuss the design and use of ballot boxes.

15. Describe the most effective use of column design.

16. Discuss the benefits of including eye guides, side headings, and tick marks in form design.

17. Explain why large passages of text must be broken into manageable chunks and discuss techniques for designing the text for easier reading.

18. Define printing specifications and discuss the necessity of providing printing specifications for the printer.

Forms analysis is the first step in forms design

Forms analysis should always be the first step in forms design. Forms are part of an information system. An investigation of the form's role in the information system is necessary so the form can be designed to work efficiently in the system. Only by analyzing the creation, processing and disposition of the form can the analyst determine the necessity, the proper design, the procurement method, and the construction of the form.

Forms analysis first determines whether the form is necessary. Sometimes, a form exists only because it has been in use a long time and no one has questioned why it is still used. Sometimes, a form is not needed because a similar form can replace it or the form can be combined with another form.

If the analyst concludes that the form is necessary, then it is further determined what data it should contain, what type of form it should be, and how it should be designed. These determinations come from analyzing how the form is filled in, processed, and distributed. Forms can be filled in many ways including by hand, by business machine and by computer. Forms processing includes reading, copying, stapling, collating, sorting, scanning, filming, mailing, faxing, discarding, and filing. Form copies are distributed to employees, customers, government agencies, and the public.

Forms analysis and efficient forms design can't be separated. A form must be designed to work efficiently in an information system and forms analysis provides the information required to design the form properly.

Effective forms analysis can reduce production costs

The trained forms analyst/designer has many techniques available for reducing the production cost of forms. One method is to eliminate unnecessary copies of a multi-part form. Another is to re-design a form to fit a smaller standard size. Sometimes an inexpensive stock form can replace a custom form or a less expensive paper weight and grade can be used.

Effective forms analysis can reduce fill-in and processing costs

Although it is usually difficult to sell this concept to management, the real cost of forms is the labor involved in processing forms, not in printing them. The labor costs to read, fill in, and process a form is much higher than the purchase price of a form. Cost studies by government agencies and consultant groups have concluded that it costs at least $20 in labor to process a form for every dollar spent to purchase the form. Some studies state that it costs $100 in labor to process a form for every dollar spent in purchasing the form.

Therefore, the analyst needs to gather information on how the form is processed and then determine what can be done to decrease the labor time being spent to process the form. Often this can be done by changing the construction of the form, for example, from a pad of forms to a snapout form or by changing a form sent in an envelope to a postcard. Very often, forms processing time can be increased by an improvement in the design of a form. In other cases, a paper form can be converted to an electronic form.

Forms analysis begins with fact finding

The best way to gather facts is to personally interview the users of the form. These are the people who know any processing problems with the form and can make suggestions on how to improve it. It's best to start with the people who originate the first fill in on the form. Then you continue by following the form to wherever it and copies of it are sent and interviewing along the way, the people who process the form.

In addition to talking to the users, much can be learned by observing them filling in and processing the form. For example, people may be writing in the margins because some fill-in spaces are not big enough. Or some sections of the form may not be used at all.

Forms analysis after fact finding

After fact finding, the analysis is performed. The analyst considers questions like these:
- Can the form be eliminated or combined with a similar form?
- Is there a better way to fill in the form?
- Can fill in be minimized by using ballot boxes, rubber stamps or labels?
- Can it be converted to an electronic form?
- Can data be converted into machine language (bar codes, OCR forms, MICR documents) for processing?
- Are the form items spaced properly for the method of fill in? (For example, if the form is filled in by hand, is there enough room to write?)
- Is every item on the form necessary?
- If the form is crowded, would it be easier on the eyes and easier to extract information if the form were printed in green or brown ink?

The analyst also need to consider the final disposition of the form. For example, if it will be discarded soon after it is filled in (such as a telephone message), it can be printed on inexpensive paper. If it is

It costs a minimum of $20 in labor to process a form for every dollar spent to purchase the form.

Much can be learned about the efficiency of forms by observing the people who are processing the forms.

mailed, it can be sent in a window envelope or be converted to a postcard or other type of self-mailer. If the form will be stored in a binder, holes should be punched in the form to fit the binder. And the form size should be compatible with the file size.

STEP-BY-STEP FORMS DESIGN

Design steps are basically the same for all types of forns.

The design steps are basically the same for all types of paper and electronic forms. They are the same whether the form is a simple cut sheet or a specialty form, such as a unit set or continuous form. For specialty forms, however, the design must include unique construction features, such as the stub, carbon extraction margin, lock-up space, etc., but the basic design steps are the same.

Specialty forms are usually designed by forms design professionals with experience. As a result, these forms are among the most efficient to fill in and use. However, specialty forms represent only about 10 percent of the paper forms used by organizations. The rest are typically cut sheets. Unfortunately, many of these forms are designed by amateurs and, therefore, are poorly designed and inefficient. Most office personnel and desktop publishers believe they can design a form because they equate good forms design with appearance instead of functionality. This chapter will describe the steps for designing good, efficient forms that will set the educated forms designer apart from the amateur forms designers.

It takes a combination of training and practice to become a good forms designer.

After studying the techniques in this chapter, the novice designer should understand that it will require practice in applying the design techniques to become a good forms designer. The first few designs are not likely to produce the same results as subsequent designs. It takes a combination of training and practice to become a good forms designer.

The following design steps are meant specifically for cut sheet forms. However, the basic steps will apply to all other form types with the addition of special construction features. The following example will demonstrate the forms design procedure.

Forms analysis produced the following information:

1. This form is used to get customer evaluations of seminars presented in the meetings rooms of a large hotel.

2. The form is filled in by hand.

3. It is a simple, one-part cut sheet.

4. The fill-in is voluntary, and the customer won't bother filling it in if it isn't quick and easy to use.

5. The form is read by the hotel manager and then filed in a standard three-ring binder. The information is copied into a computer system for cumulative reports.

6. The hotel does not use any other form to gather seminar evaluations.

This typed page was given by the hotel manager to the designer for a professional redesign.

Was everything working in your meeting/banquet facilities?			___Yes	___No

Please rate the following where applicable:

Air conditioning	___Excellent	___Good	___Average	___Fair	___Poor
Heating	___Excellent	___Good	___Average	___Fair	___Poor
Audio/Visual equipment	___Excellent	___Good	___Average	___Fair	___Poor
Sound equipment	___Excellent	___Good	___Average	___Fair	___Poor
Lighting	___Excellent	___Good	___Average	___Fair	___Poor

If we provided food and/or beverage service, please rate the following where applicable:

Table

Overall appearance	___Excellent	___Good	___Average	___Fair	___Poor
Linen	___Excellent	___Good	___Average	___Fair	___Poor
China	___Excellent	___Good	___Average	___Fair	___Poor
Flatware	___Excellent	___Good	___Average	___Fair	___Poor

Food

Quality	___Excellent	___Good	___Average	___Fair	___Poor
Presentation	___Excellent	___Good	___Average	___Fair	___Poor
Portion size	___Excellent	___Good	___Average	___Fair	___Poor
Value for price paid	___Excellent	___Good	___Average	___Fair	___Poor

Beverage

Quality	___Excellent	___Good	___Average	___Fair	___Poor
Presentation	___Excellent	___Good	___Average	___Fair	___Poor
Size of drinks	___Excellent	___Good	___Average	___Fair	___Poor
Availability of bars	___Excellent	___Good	___Average	___Fair	___Poor
Value for price paid	___Excellent	___Good	___Average	___Fair	___Poor

Service (Food/Beverage)

Promptness	___Excellent	___Good	___Average	___Fair	___Poor
Attentiveness	___Excellent	___Good	___Average	___Fair	___Poor
Efficiency	___Excellent	___Good	___Average	___Fair	___Poor
Courtesy	___Excellent	___Good	___Average	___Fair	___Poor
Appearance	___Excellent	___Good	___Average	___Fair	___Poor

The designer is now ready to proceed to the next design step.

The rough sketch

The rough sketch is a technique that actually saves time, even when using a desktop publishing system, because it allows the testing of one or more ideas in a matter of minutes. It avoids spending many hours on an attractive design only to discover that it won't work. Although graphic designers make miniature "thumbnail sketches", forms designers should make the sketch full size in order to better evaluate items like window envelope location, gripper space, and consecutive number location.

The rough sketch for a form should be drawn full-size.

A hand-drawn rough sketch of a form:

LOGO SLEEP CHEAP HOTEL	SEMINAR FACILITIES EVALUATION				

NAME OF MEETING GROUP | MEETING DATE

EVALUATED BY | WAS EVERYTHING WORKING IN YOUR MEETING FACILITY? ☐ YES ☐ NO

Please rate the following, where applicable

ITEM		EXCELLENT (v)	GOOD (v)	AVERAGE (v)	FAIR (v)	POOR (v)
Air Conditioning						
Heating						
Audio/Visual Equipment						
Sound Equipment						
Lighting						
TABLE	Overall					
	Linen					
	China					
	Flatware					
FOOD	Quality					
	Presentation					
	Portion Size					
	Value for price paid					
BEVERAGE	Quality					
	Pres					
	Size of Dr					
	Availability					
	Value of					
SERVICE (Food/Beverage)	Promptness					
	Attentive					
	Efficiency					
	Courtesy					
	Appearance					

FORM 72

Before the rough sketch is started, it is necessary to decide the size of the form, which is determined through the forms analysis. Then an outline of the approximate size of the form in drawn on blank paper. Although the preciseness is not necessary, it is still best to use a ruler for all lines. If it appears the form will be crowded, character spacing requirements should be penciled in on the rough sketch. To ensure sufficient writing space for the entry of data, the designer should write on the sketch the maximum number of characters and writing lines required for the entry of each field.

In drawing the rough sketch, the designer should provide proper arrangement of the basic form zones and allocate adequate space accordingly. If the form is complex, more than one sketch may be needed.

The comprehensive forms design

It is best to use a computer program that provides a layout grid on the background of the screen. A specialized forms design program is best.

The first items to be drawn in a desktop publishing system are the guidelines representing the "trim" size of the form in the upper left corner of the grid in close proximity to the horizontal and vertical scales on the screen. This is the final size of the form after it has been through the printing process and trimmed to specifications. For example, an 8 1/2" x 11" form could be printed 2-up on an 11" x 17" sheet and then cut to the final trim size of 8 1/2" x 11". If two forms will be printed on a sheet, it is referred to as "2-up" printing. Similarly, four forms printed on a sheet is referred to as "4-up" printing, etc.

As mentioned earlier, the form size is determined from the information gathered during forms analysis. This includes the amount of data on the form, the method of fill-in, plus filing and mailing information. Also, standard form sizes are a major consideration in controlling printing costs. The following standard sizes for cut sheets are cut equally, without waste, from standard 17" x 22" mill paper stock. Use these sizes whenever possible.

2 3/4" x 4 1/4"	4 1/4" x 11"	5 1/2" x 8 1/2"	11" x 17"
3 2/3" x 8 1/2"	4 1/4" x 5 1/2"	8 1/2" x 11"	17" x 22"

Sizes other than those listed above should be avoided since they are cut with a waste of stock or are cut from stock that is normally carried in limited grades, weights, and colors. This means extra time and cost to print the form. In fact, printing costs can be minimized by selecting the smallest form size that will cut evenly (without waste) from a mill

10/6 layout grid.

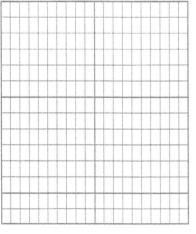

After the rough sketch is completed, the comprehensive design is created on a computer. It is best to use forms design software that places a form design grid on the screen.

The first step is to draw the outline representing the trim size of the form.

size, without compromising any other form size features. The most common standard size for a paper cut sheet form is 8 1/2" x 11".

Another paper mill sheet size is 17" x 28", from which are cut the following standards form sizes:

2" x 3 1/2"	3 1/2" x 8 1/2"	4 1/4" x 14"	8 1/2" x 14"
3 1/2" x 4 1/4"	4 1/4" x 7"	7" x 8 1/2"	14" x 17"

Index bristol (cardstock) is usually cut from a 25 1/2" x 30 1/2" sheet, which is the most common mill size and stocked in a range of grades, weights, and colors. Cardstock forms are usually cut to a trim size of 3" x 5", 4" x 6", or 5" x 8" to fit standard card files.

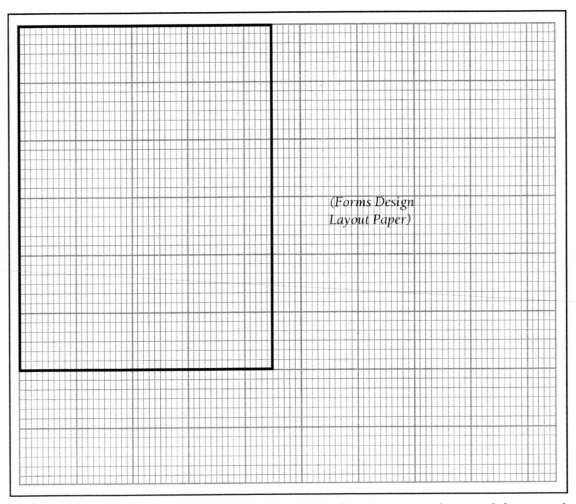

(Forms Design Layout Paper)

The designer then draws an outline of the trim size of the form, starting at the upper left corner of the grid.

Draw guide lines to indicate margins and gripper space

Forms should have a margin on all four sides to look attractive and professional. In addition, one of the margins is necessary to provide gripper space, which is required to run a sheet of paper through an offset printing press. On the press, "gripper fingers" grab the leading edge of the paper and pull it through the press. An image can't be printed on this gripper margin edge. An easy way to provide the gripper space for any sheet-fed press is to leave 1/3" margin on the leading edge of the paper. The leading edge on an 8 1/2" x 11" form is the 8 1/2" top. (However, if two or more forms will be printed on one sheet and later trimmed to size, the leading edge requiring the gripper space may not be at the top of the form and the printer should be consulted to determine appropriate margins.)

With specialized forms design software, standard margin guide lines may already be included on the layout grid by default. They are usually in blue, or some other non-reproducing color, to distinguish them as guide marks for drawing limitations instead of actual printed rules. Standard side and bottom margins are 1/4", which is also the minimum. If the form is not crowded, this dimension can be increased to 1/3" or more, which would safely accommodate the gripper space requirement on any side that may be used as the leading edge by the printer and

Forms should have a margin on all four sides.

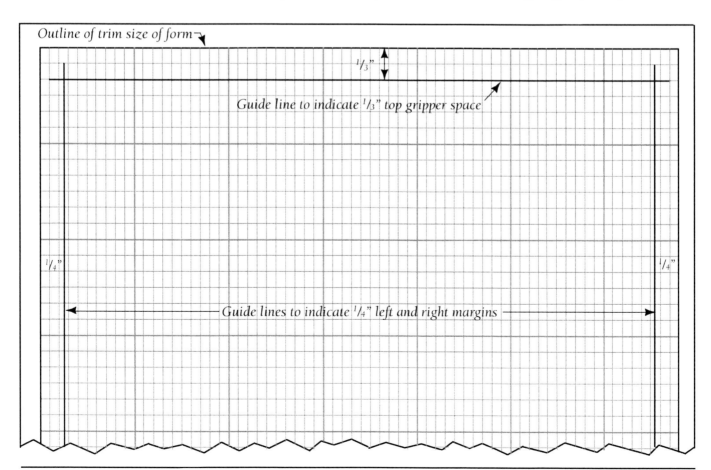

avoid guesswork by the designer. An exception to these standard margins would occur if the form will be filed in a binder. Then the designer must provide a binding margin, which would be 3/4" for a standard three-ring binder, so the fill-in data will not be covered by the binder.

Additional concepts relating to form margins include "lock-up space" and a "bleed". Lock-up space is similar to gripper space only associated with continuous forms and unit sets that require web press printing systems. A bleed refers to an image that extends to the edge of a sheet, without leaving a margin. Obviously, this should be avoided, if possible. The designer should also avoid the use of printed borders, unless the form is a certificate or guarantee when a border is perceived as adding value to the form.

Draw fixed location items

The next step is to draw any form items that need to be positioned in a specific location. Examples are consecutive number locations (usually in the upper right corner area), window envelope guide marks, perforation locations, fold marks, hole punching locations, and file reference locations. Since these items need to be in a fixed location, they must be positioned or have space allocated for them first so that the other form components can be worked around them.

Work from top to bottom

Generally, the designer should work from top to bottom of the form, from the identification zone to the closing zone. The position of the first fill-in line will be very important if the form is filled in by a computer printing system since this will be the reference for vertical spacing for all subsequent fill-in lines. In this case, an exact measurement of the equipment starting print positions needs to be determined and factored into the form design. However, for forms which are filled in by hand, this is not a concern.

To recap the forms design principles in Chapter 13, the designer will proceed to complete each of the appropriate form zones. This begins with a meaningful form title and number in the **Identification Zone** at the top of the form so the reader can immediately recognize the purpose of the form. In addition, if the form travels outside the organization, identifying information should be included, such as the organization's name, address, phone and fax numbers, logo, etc. However, if the form will only be used internally, this information is not necessary since the employees should know whom they work for. A good general forms design rule is to eliminate anything on a form that isn't necessary so that it won't detract from the more important information. If the organization insists on placing the company name and logo on all forms, the designer should try to keep the size and visual impact of these items minimized.

After drawing margin guide lines, draw fixed location items.

Work from top to bottom, from identification zone to closing zone.

Next is the **Instructions Zone.**   If the form requires general fill-in instructions, the designer should key these in a distinctive font and style, such as bold and/or italicized, at the top of the form where the reader will see them first before the form is filled in. In addition, specific self-instructing captions should always be used to improve comprehension and accuracy of fill-in. For instance, use INVOICE DATE instead of DATE. Other types of instructions may be needed at various form sections to clarify fill-in and processing procedures. For example, mailing instructions can be located on an envelope flap, and instructions can be placed at the top of a form section filled in by a department other than the originating department.

The copy received from the hotel.

The re-design of the form at the left.

The **Introduction Zone** introduces the reader to the body of the form.

Next, the designer adds the **Body Zone.** This is the main and usually the largest part of the form that will vary with the nature and function of each individual form. It will typically contain rules and captions and perhaps columns, paragraphs of text, screens, reverses, ballot boxes, and phantoms.

The **Closing Zone** is at the bottom of the form, which may contain dates and authorizing signatures, form part distribution instructions, and processing instructions.

Insider tips for designing professional forms

Filing data

A design priority for paper forms is to allow space for the filing and reference data, which must be placed where it can be readily seen in the file. Typical reference information is a name, an account number, or a date. For most loose filing of forms in folders, a convenient location for this information is in the upper right corner. For bound forms, the reference information should be located opposite the binding so it won't be obscured by the binding. If a form is bound at the top, the filing reference should be placed at the bottom and vice versa. More commonly, if the form is bound on the left side, as in standard three-ring punch filing, the reference data should be located at the top right corner, as it is for loose filing. However, for an upright file card, the filing reference should be placed at the top, preferably on the left side.

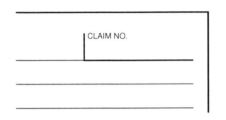

In loose filing, the reference data is usually positioned in the upper righthand corner.

Fill-in and processing instructions

For efficient clarification, self-instructing captions should be used wherever possible. For example, instead of "NAME", describe exactly what is wanted, i.e. "APPLICANT'S NAME", "SPOUSE'S NAME", "FIRST NAME", "LAST NAME", etc. This will help ensure accurate and predictable data entry.

However, sometimes detailed instructions are required. General instructions should be placed at the top of the form where they can be read first before fill-in. When instructions are required for specific form sections, they should be placed right above or immediately adjacent to the section. Instructions for routing form copies should be placed at the bottom of the form.

If instructions are too lengthy to be placed close to the required form sections, there are two alternatives. They may go on the cover page that is fastened to the form or printed on the back. In either case, a larger typeface designed in two or more columns will significantly improve the readability. If a "backer" is chosen, care must be taken to avoid "show-through", which will make it difficult to read the entire form. To avoid show-through, a heavier grade of paper should be requested for the print job or the text may be printed in a lighter ink shade or the backer text lightly screened. As a last resort, the instructions can be placed in a separate document or manual.

If instructions must be located in a separate document or procedures manual, a useful design technique is to reference the instructions to letters and numbers printed next to items on the form. Columns are best identified by letters since there is seldom more than 26 columns, and line items can be identified by numbers. By keying instructions to columns letters and line numbers, item references and arithmetic calculations can be clarified.

ITEM	QUANTITY (a)	PART NO. (b)	CATALOG NO. (c)
1. Red Widgets			
2. Blue Widgets			
3. White Widgets			
4. Red Gadgets			
5. Blue Gadgets			
6. White Gadgets			

Instructions can be referenced to letters and numbers on the form.

Information sequence

The sequence of information on a form is of great importance since it affects information gathering, processing, and retrieval. The placement of information in the most logical sequence will reduce clerical costs and make the fill-in and processing of the form easier. Important considerations for efficient sequencing are:

1. Information entered should relate to reading habits and the normal eye flow. In this country the standard is to read from left to right and top to bottom.

2. Related items should be grouped for ease of fill-in and convenient reference. Many items follow a usual pattern such as "name and address" instead of "address and name".

3. Since some items are often not applicable or not filled in for various reasons, the items that are always filled in should be arranged at the beginning of the zone/section, and less frequently filled-in items should be placed toward the end.

4. The sequence of form sections and items should correlate with the sequence of fill-in and processing steps. If any fill-in information will be transferred to another form, the designer should ensure that the duplicate information is in the same sequence on both forms. This will increase the accuracy and speed of data transfer. If only selected entries are to be transferred from one form to another, these entries can be highlighted by placing a screen behind them.

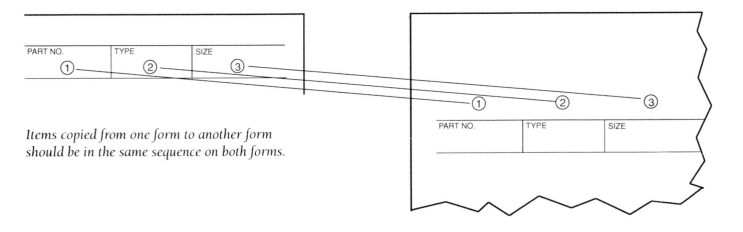

Items copied from one form to another form should be in the same sequence on both forms.

Rules

Rules (lines) are used for fill-in data, to divide a form into sections, for grouping data, to separate boxes, and for highlighting. The designer should use only a few rule variations. Too many bold rules make it difficult for the reader to focus on the fill-in data.

Hairlines should be used for most rules unless there is a good reason for not doing so. This keeps a clean, uncluttered appearance. Hairlines are typically less than 1-point and the default setting in most desktop publishing systems. Anything over 1-point gets into a bold rule look. The appropriate thickness of a rule is a combination of preference and the application.

The basic bold rules are used for dividing sections of a form and highlighting important items. They are also often used at the top and bottom of a form. Broken lines can be used as sub-dividing lines, such as between dollars and cents in a column. Screened and colored lines can also be used for this purpose or used to tone down a crowded form so the more important fill-in data will stand out. Double hairlines can be used as an alternate style for section dividers.

However, selecting rules is not too difficult since the objective is to keep a simple, uncluttered form design, to allow the more important fill-in data to stand out. Therefore, the majority of rules in a form design should be simple hairlines.

Hairline

Bold Rule

Broken Hairline

Screened Rule

Double Hairline

Captions

The most efficient design style for the combination of caption and fill-in space is the ULC box design, as described in Chapter 13. The advantages of this fill-in style are that it:

1. Increases available writing space

2. Avoids wasted motion for hand and printer fill-in

3. Allows easy reading and comprehension

4. Streamlines the form's appearance

The captions themselves should be keyed in a clean sans-serif typestyle in all caps. Since captions consist of only a word or two, all capitals is traditionally used by professional designers. It is true that, in general, caps and lower case is easier to read than all caps, but there is no problem reading upper case captions because they are not lengthy. Longer text in several sentences and paragraphs should be keyed in caps and lower case.

IMPREST FUND

DATE _____

$ _____

FOR _____

_____

_____

CHARGE ACCOUNT # _____

RECEIVED BY _____

APPROVED BY _____

Before

PETTY CASH DISBURSEMENT RECORD

FORM 312

DISBURSED TO (NAME)	AMOUNT
	$

FOR (REASON)

CHARGE GENERAL LEDGER ACCT. NO.

DISBURSEMENT DATE	APPROVED BY (SUPERVISOR)

After

Ballot box techniques

Ballot boxes (also called check boxes) minimize fill-in writing and save time. They also provide uniform answers, save writing space, suggest answers to the users, and save time in extracting data from the form.

People like using ballot boxes because they are easy, fast, and if designed correctly, are efficient means of collecting accurate data. Even though

□ RED

□ BLACK

□ BLUE

It is usually best to place the ballot box in front of the caption.

❑ ❐ ❑ ❐ ○ ○

Ballot box variations.

they may be referred to as "check boxes", they should actually be marked with an "X" instead of a checkmark, and it would be wise to add a brief instruction emphasizing this if there are many checkbox responses on the form. A handwritten checkmark may extend beyond the box and cause an error. Also, it is easier to determine the selected ballot box on carbon or carbonless paper copies if an "X" is used to indicate the chosen box.

When including ballot boxes in the form design, it is best to place the box in front of the caption to help identify the caption with the intended box. In fact, the ballot box and its caption should be considered a unit and kept close together with extra space inserted between units. This is essential to avoid confusion as to which box belongs to which caption.

Usually, the size of a ballot box ranges from 12 points to 16 points. The size depends on the method of writing and the space available on the form. A 14-point box is a good size for many applications. Also, the designer may choose to use a graphic variation of the ballot box.

There are several design techniques that will help improve the efficiency of ballot boxes. For instance, if the boxes and captions are kept vertically aligned, the form will have a cleaner, less cluttered appearance. Also, ballot boxes should be arranged by frequency of use to save writing time. And if there are many yes/no answers or multiple choices, a column arrangement is a better design technique because it avoids the creation of too many ballot boxes as shown below.

□ RED   □ BLACK   □ BLUE

Place ballot boxes and their related captions close together with extra space between the units, like this.

RED   □   BLACK   □   BLUE   □

Don't design like this. It is too difficult to determine which ballot box belongs to which caption.

HAVE YOU EVER HAD:		
HEART DISEASE?	□YES	□NO
KIDNEY PROBLEMS?	□YES	□NO
HIGH BLOOD PRESSURE?	□YES	□NO
HIGH CHOLESTEROL?	□YES	□NO

Too many ballot boxes are distracting.

HAVE YOU EVER HAD:	YES (✔)	NO (✔)
HEART DISEASE?		
KIDNEY PROBLEMS?		
HIGH BLOOD PRESSURE?		
HIGH CHOLESTEROL?		

Use a column arrangement, like this.

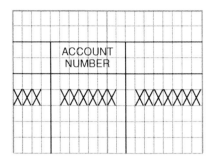

If possible, one blank character space should be placed on each side of the column entry space to increase readability and to allow for easy alignment and registration.

Column design

Column design is used when multiple entries of the same type can be entered under one heading. It is the most effective method of arranging data of a repetitive nature. The person completing the form has the advantage of continuous entry of data without referring back to the entry caption. Space is also saved since it is not necessary to repeat captions. In addition, column design facilitates mathematical calculations, and the data will be more clearly presented and interpreted.

When designing columns, the minimum width is determined by the maximum number of characters that will be written in the column and the method of fill-in. In addition, one blank character space should be placed on each side of the column entry space to increase readability and allow for easy alignment and registration.

Optional column designs

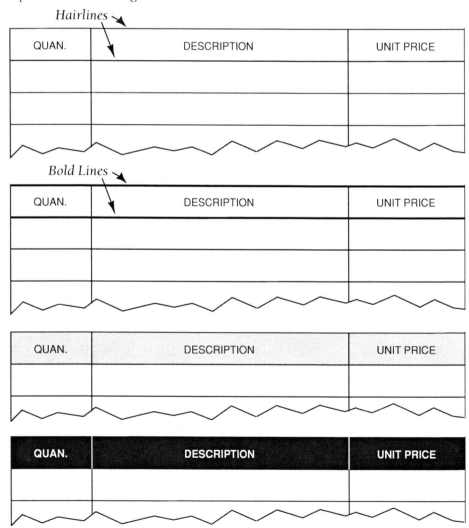

The column heading captions should be centered horizontally and vertically over the column. The typical size of the captions is 6 to 10 points. And if multiple levels of column heads are required, the caption point size should decrease from top to bottom. If the captions are too long for the width of the column, they can be placed vertically at an angle or simply abbreviated or coded. Also, when columns are extra long, the designer should repeat the column heading captions at the bottom to facilitate accurate fill-in toward the bottom.

Eye guides

The designer can make it easier to follow a long line of text or a long rule by adding eye guides. It can be as simple as making every fifth rule bolder than the other rules and can be done horizontally for writing lines or vertically for columns. Another technique is to screen every other writing space as is often found on stock continuous forms.

Side headings

When a form contains several distinct sections, each will require a section heading. If these are spaced vertically, it often takes up too much room. A much better design would be to place these section heads at the left where they become "side headings".

Tick marks

Tick marks are small vertical lines often placed on the bottom line of a fill-in box to help the user write the correct number of characters in the correct spaces for neat, legible entries. They are a convenient design technique to improve accuracy and are often used on source documents from which data will be entered into computer systems. To prevent the tick marks from detracting from the fill-in data, they can be screened or the entire form printed in a different ink color, such as green or brown.

Designing text for easy reading

Sometimes forms include several paragraphs of text, especially if lengthy instructions are required. Text can be boring and difficult to read or less boring and easier to read. The difference is in the text design. The key concept to improve readability is that text must be broken into visually manageable "chunks". This can be accomplished by using one or more of the following techniques:

1. Set the text in two or more columns. Small point-size text must be set in short line lengths.

2. Indent paragraphs.

Break lengthy text into visually manageable chunks.

3.   Use headings and sub-headings to break up text.

4.   Place illustrations on the page.

Techniques for breaking text into manageable chunks.

5.   Use type variations for heads, sub-heads, and key words.

6.   Use caps and lower case instead of all caps.

7.   Use large initial caps at the beginning of paragraphs.

8.   Increase leading (pronounced "ledding"), which is the white space between lines of type.

9.   Use black ink on white paper or an ink/paper color combination that provides contrast. Good contrast is vital to readability.

10. Use normal letterspacing and tracking. Letterspacing refers to the space between characters in a word and tracking refers to spacing between words. If letterspacing or tracking are too tight or too expanded, readability and comprehension are decreased.

11. Use serif medium typefaces for text, in caps and lower case. Never use boldface, italic, script, or novelty typefaces for extensive text.

12. Don't set paragraphs of text in reverse type (white on a black background or any lighter color on a dark background).

An example of several of these techniques is the text you are reading. It is set with a serif typeface in caps and lower case, using extra leading. Pages are designed in two columns and contain illustrations. Contrasting heads and sub-heads are set in larger type sizes, and good contrast is provided by using black ink on white paper.

Make any additions and final adjustments

The final design steps include adding graphic enhancements and any extra components, such as logos, fold marks, arrows, etc. This is also the time to highlight reference and other important items by means of bold lines, arrows, screens, reverses, or spot color. Phantoms may also be added as a graphic enhancement in this final design stage.

The last design step is the making of final adjustments, as described.

The design is then completed by making final adjustments. This may include:

1.   Converting rules to different weights or kinds of lines.
2.   Converting type to a different weight (bold, etc.) or size.
3.   Lining up vertical lines.
4.   Eliminating anything that is not necessary.

Printing specifications

When the design is completed, approved, and ready to be printed in volume, the printer (whether in-house or commercial) will require specific printing instructions. This is referred to as the printing specifications. For instance, the printer needs to know the grade, weight, and color of paper to be used to print the form as well as the color of ink and details on features like padding, punching, and perforating.

CUT SHEET PRINTING SPECIFICATIONS
FORM 41

	FORM NO.	FORM TITLE

	PART NO.	TRIM SIZE	INK COLOR	NO. SIDES	PAPER WT., GRADE & COLOR
☐ SINGLE-PART	1	X			
☐ MULTI-PART	2	X			
	3	X			

MARGINS

TOP	BOTTOM	LEFT	RIGHT

☐ **NUMBER** BEGINNING NO.   INK COLOR   LOCATION

☐ **PERFORATE** LOCATION / INSTRUCTIONS

☐ **PUNCH**   ☐ STANDARD 3-RING   ☐ OTHER:

☐ **PAD**   ☐ 100 SHEETS ☐ _____ ON ☐ TOP ☐ OTHER _____   ☐ CHIPBOARD BACKER

SPECIAL INSTRUCTIONS

PACKAGING SHEETS TO A PACKAGE   ☐ SHRINK WRAP   ☐ KRAFT PAPER   ☐ BOXES

DATE   SIGNATURE

Typical cut sheet printing specifications.

Chapter 15 Questions

1. Why should forms analysis always be the first step in forms design?

2. Name three possible ways to reduce the printing cost of forms.

3. Explain how the real cost of forms is the labor cost of processing them. What is the minimum cost in labor for every dollar spent to procure a form?

4. Describe forms analysis procedures beginning with fact gathering.

5. Describe the basic procedure to design cut sheets.

6. What is the advantage of drawing a rough sketch in the forms design procedure?

7. What factors are involved in selecting the size of a form?

8. Discuss the importance of margins in forms design. What is the recommended minimum margin in inches for the sides and bottom of a cut sheet? Discuss gripper space.

9. Why should fixed item locations be drawn before other form elements. Give examples of fixed location items.

10. Discuss the design of the Instructions Zone, the Introduction Zone, and the Closing Zone.

11. Name the considerations for achieving efficient item sequencing.

12. Name the various forms design rules and explain how they should be used.

13. Describe box design and name four advantages of using this design style.

14. What is the purpose of ballot boxes? Discuss the design and use of ballot boxes.

15. What is the most effective use of column design?

16. Discuss the use of eye guides, side headings, and tick marks in forms design.

17. Explain why large passages of text must be broken into manageable chunks and discuss techniques for designing the text for easier reading.

18. What are printing specifications? Explain the necessity of providing printing specifications for the printer.

CHAPTER

16

DESIGNING SPECIALTY AND ELECTRONIC FORMS

Students achieving oneness
will move on to twoness.

– Woody Allen

Chapter 16 Objectives

After studying this chapter, you should be able to:

1. Discuss the similarities and the differences in the design of cut forms and specialty forms.

2. Name and describe the primary materials used to construct specialty forms.

3. Describe the construction features of unit sets that affect forms design.

4. Describe the construction features of continuous forms that affect forms design.

5. Explain how U.S. Postal Service regulations affect the design of envelopes.

6. Describe how MICR affects the design of checks and negotiable instruments.

7. Explain the unique design features of labels and tags.

8. Discuss the importance of bar codes in forms design.

9. Discuss the conversion of paper to electronic forms.

SPECIALTY FORMS

To increase the speed and efficiency of data entry and forms processing, designers have created many types of time-saving specialty forms. The forms design principles for specialty forms are basically the same as for cut sheets. The difference is in the construction features of specialty forms. This difference requires the designer to understand the printing method and the construction because it affects the design. For example, the basic design of a unit set is the same as it is for a cut sheet form. The difference is that for a unit set the designer must know standard unit set sizes, stub locations and sizes, lock-up requirements, carbon and carbonless paper standards, etc.

Materials used to construct specialty forms

The primary materials used to construct specialty forms are plain and specialty form bond papers, regular and specialty inks, carbon and carbonless papers. A wide variety of these materials are available, and the proper selection is vital for the efficiency of the business form. For example, if you can't read the information on Part 4 of a unit set because of poor paper and carbon paper selection, the form doesn't have much value, although it may have a good appearance.

Form bond paper

Most cut sheet and specialty forms are printed on regular form bond paper due to the good printing qualities as well as good writing and handling qualities. Form bond is produced in white and colors, and the basic sheet size is 17" x 22". For producing specialty forms like unit sets and continuous forms, form bond is manufactured into rolls (also referred to as webs) with diameters of 28" to 60". These are used on web-type printing presses rather than the sheet-fed presses used for simpler, lower volume print jobs.

Carbon paper

Although carbonless papers are becoming more predominant in multi-part forms, carbon paper is still preferred for many types of business forms. Carbon paper is comparatively reasonable in price and provides a permanent, clear image on form parts.

Carbonless paper

Carbonless paper was introduced in 1954 by the National Cash Register Company and called NCR paper, which was an acronym for the company name. Today, the term NCR paper more commonly refers to "No Carbon Required".

There are several types of carbonless papers, but a common type is the chemical-mated system in which chemical coatings are applied to bond paper. When the fill-in device (printer, pen, etc.) strikes the form set, it breaks microscopic capsules containing colorless dye. The dye, coming in contact with a chemical from the next form part, creates a new chemical compound in a blue or black color, which creates the image on the form copy.

The system uses three kinds of chemically coated paper within a multi-part set.

1. CB Paper (coated back)–for the top sheet
2. CFB Paper (coated front and back)–for middle sheets
3. CF Paper (coated front)–for the last sheet

Ink

Special ink colors are specified by using the Pantone Matching System.

Most forms manufacturers have several standard ink colors available in addition to black. If a special ink color is desired, it is usually derived from a standard color matching scheme called the Pantone Matching System (PMS). Pantone color charts and books are available from printers and graphic art suppliers. They contain an array of colors and shade variations that are identified by a PMS number, which must be specified to the printer to obtain the expected color outcome.

In addition to regular inks, special inks are used to print specialty forms. Heat resistant inks are required on forms that will be processed by intelligent copiers and laser printers. Some of these printers develop very high temperatures that would melt regular ink. Special non-reflective (read inks) and reflective (non-read) inks are used to print forms to be read by OCR (Optical Character Recognition) equipment. A similar concept involves MICR ink (Magnetic Ink Character Recognition), which contains iron oxide to enable it to be read by automatic equipment, particularly for check sorting in the banking industry. In addition, there are special inks used for thermography, which is a heat process whereby ink is raised to create a three-dimensional effect used primarily for business stationery.

UNIT SETS

Unit sets are often called "snapouts" or "snap sets".

A unit set is a multi-part form glued together into a common stub. It can be interleaved with carbon paper or manufactured with carbonless paper. Either way, when holding the stub in one hand and snapping the form set with the other hand, the result is a stub and/or carbon unit that is readily discarded while the multi-part forms are held in the other hand to continue processing. It's a very efficient system that provides multiple copies in one writing and cleanly disposes of the stub/carbon

paper section. Also, since each form part is printed on a separate roll of paper on web presses, a different color, grade, and weight of paper can be designated for each part to facilitate sorting and processing.

Unit sets are either "stock" or "custom". Stock unit sets are kept on the shelf, meaning that the printer has designed and manufactured certain generic unit sets such as invoices, purchase orders, and sales forms that can be purchased quickly and more inexpensively than a custom design. Stock forms can also be customized with name, address, and other information to enhance the organization's image.

If the unit set is custom designed, the procedures are basically the same as for cut sheets described earlier. The only differences are the unique construction features, such as the standard sizes, stub unit, form parts with carbon or carbonless papers, and an extraction margin.

A carbon-interleaved unit set, after separation.

Construction of a typical top stub, carbon interleaved unit set

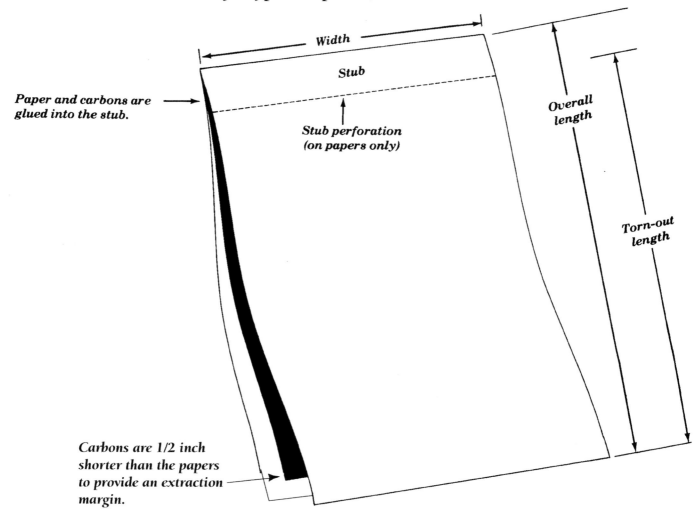

Paper and carbons are glued into the stub.

Width

Stub

Stub perforation (on papers only)

Overall length

Torn-out length

Carbons are 1/2 inch shorter than the papers to provide an extraction margin.

Unit set standard sizes

Since most unit sets are printed on rotary web presses, standard lengths (depths) are determined by the width of the paper manufacturer's standard paper rolls. Standard widths are even multiples of the cylinder circumference of standard printing presses.

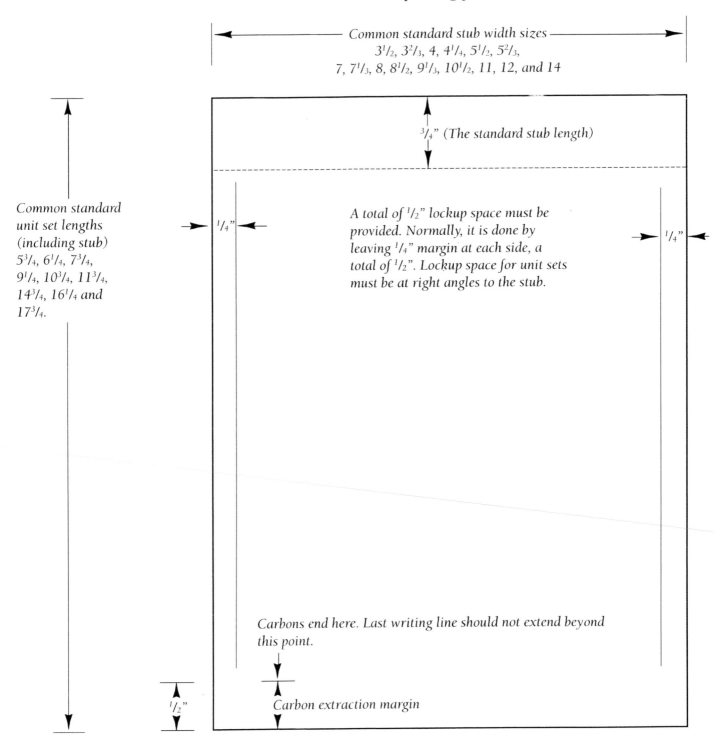

Common standard stub width sizes
$3^1/_2$, $3^2/_3$, 4, $4^1/_4$, $5^1/_2$, $5^2/_3$,
7, $7^1/_3$, 8, $8^1/_2$, $9^1/_3$, $10^1/_2$, 11, 12, and 14

$^3/_4$" (The standard stub length)

Common standard unit set lengths (including stub) $5^3/_4$, $6^1/_4$, $7^3/_4$, $9^1/_4$, $10^3/_4$, $11^3/_4$, $14^3/_4$, $16^1/_4$ and $17^3/_4$.

$^1/_4$"

$^1/_4$"

A total of $^1/_2$" lockup space must be provided. Normally, it is done by leaving $^1/_4$" margin at each side, a total of $^1/_2$". Lockup space for unit sets must be at right angles to the stub.

Carbons end here. Last writing line should not extend beyond this point.

$^1/_2$"

Carbon extraction margin

Stub

Most carbon-interleaved unit sets have a ³/₄" stub.

The design of the stub unit varies. Most carbon-interleaved unit sets have a 3/4" stub from the top of the form to the perforation and a 1/2" extraction margin at the opposite end of the stub, as shown in the illustration on the previous page. The lockup space is always at right angles to the stub. A carbonless paper unit set needs only a 1/2" stub because extra space isn't required to glue in carbons, and an extraction margin would not be necessary. However, for small quantities of carbonless unit sets, the stub may be completely eliminated and the sets held together with a special adhesive.

If a stub unit becomes part of the form design, it can also be located at the bottom or either side of the form. Top-stub forms are most common and easy to use. Bottom-stub designs are useful for forms bound in a book, such as a book of sales forms. Side stubs make it easier to pull out the stub with carbons when the unit set length is longer than the width. There can also be a double-stub design when there is a need for additional entries after the original writing and separating. After snapping the form apart the first time, each section becomes a separate set with its own stub for further processing.

Wherever the stub location, the designer really does nothing to the camera-ready design except leave the appropriate space for the gluing and perforating. The details of the stub construction would be communicated to the printer via a specifications form.

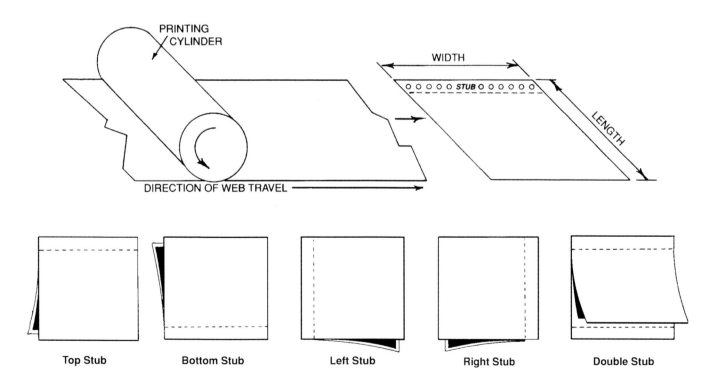

| Top Stub | Bottom Stub | Left Stub | Right Stub | Double Stub |

CONTINUOUS FORMS

Continuous forms provide high volume data entry through automation. They are identified by their line hole strips, which are used for pin-feed

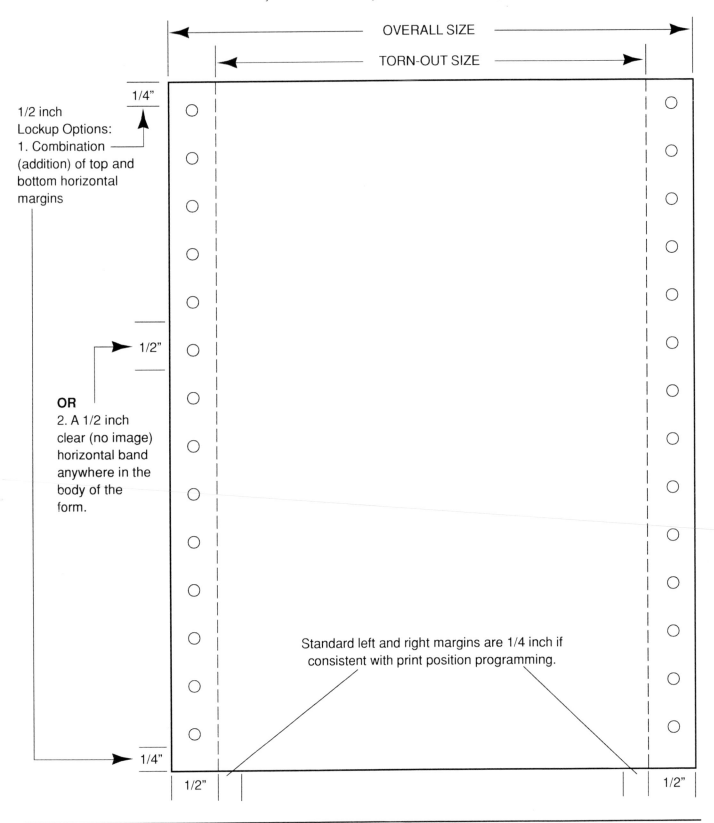

OVERALL SIZE

TORN-OUT SIZE

1/4"

1/2 inch
Lockup Options:
1. Combination (addition) of top and bottom horizontal margins

1/2"

OR
2. A 1/2 inch clear (no image) horizontal band anywhere in the body of the form.

Standard left and right margins are 1/4 inch if consistent with print position programming.

1/4"

1/2"

1/2"

printer equipment that allows for high-speed writing, accurate part-to-part registration, and accurate sequential numbering.

Continuous forms can be custom made or purchased off the shelf, similar to unit sets and other specialty forms. Continuous off-the-shelf forms are referred to as "stock tab" forms. They may contain horizontal guide lines or screened bars, which help the reader follow the computer printed data across the page. Stock tab forms can be customized by imprinting items such as names, logos, addresses, and column headings. They are often used for fill-in directed by software packages. To fit a particular information system, custom continuous forms can be designed and manufactured to the user's specifications.

Continuous forms can be custom made or purchased off the shelf.

Specifications for continuous forms

Like unit sets and other specialty forms, continuous forms have unique features that require additional design considerations beyond the basic form design procedures described earlier. For instance, since continuous forms are dependent upon computer printers and software programs for fill-in, the design must be built around the character spacing, line spacing, pre-programmed print positions, and any limitations of the specific computer system that will be used. A sample printout from the system will provide the designer with the necessary information concerning spacing and print positions.

Since design begins with an outline of the form size, the selection of width and length must be determined. Standard continuous form widths are multiples of the widths of the paper webs, similar to unit

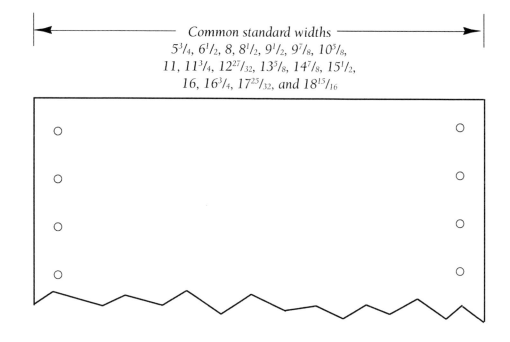

Common standard widths
$5^3/_4$, $6^1/_2$, 8, $8^1/_2$, $9^1/_2$, $9^7/_8$, $10^5/_8$,
11, $11^3/_4$, $12^{27}/_{32}$, $13^5/_8$, $14^7/_8$, $15^1/_2$,
16, $16^3/_4$, $17^{25}/_{32}$, and $18^{15}/_{16}$

Common standard lengths
$3^1/_2$, $3^2/_3$, 4,
$4^1/_4$, $5^1/_2$, $5^2/_3$,
7, $7^1/_3$, 8, $8^1/_2$,
$9^1/_3$, $10^1/_2$, 11, 12,
14, 17, 21 and 22

sets. Frequently used continuous form widths are 8 1/2, 9 1/2, 12, 13 5/8, and 14 7/8 inches. Standard line hole strips are 1/2 inch, but they can be wider.

The length of a continuous form is an even multiple of the circumference of the cylinder of the printing press. Common standard form lengths are 5 1/2, 7, 7 1/3, 8 1/2, and 11 inches. The form length should be evenly divisible by the line spacing to be used to fill in the form. This is typically 1/6 or 1/8 inch per line.

The length of a continuous form is an even multiple of the circumference of the cylinder.

Determining the first available print position is crucial to the overall design of the continuous form. Once the print positions have been designated, the rest of the design and graphics are worked in around these fixed positions. This is important so that the automated fill-in will print in the proper spaces rather than over preprinted items.

Many continuous forms are designed as multi-part sets, for which there are several methods to fasten the parts together that are appropriate for their function and method of fill-in. The least expensive and most common method is crimping, which are "fingers" formed by cuts through the paper and carbon. Crimped forms ride easily over the platens of printers. However, because this is a loose type of fastening, it may not consistently hold the form together during fill-in, particularly on high-speed equipment. An alternative to crimping is "fugitive" glue, which holds the parts together more securely but allows them to easily separate when vertical pressure is applied, as on decollating equipment. However, fugitive glue is more expensive than crimping, creates buildup on the form, and is not easy to apply. Crimping and fugitive glue are temporary fastenings. Permanent fastenings are provided by gluing or sometimes by sewing.

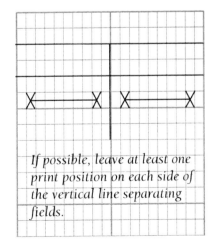

If possible, leave at least one print position on each side of the vertical line separating fields.

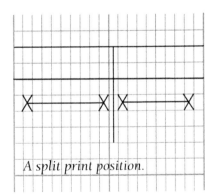

A split print position.

Envelopes

Envelopes are important forms that require special design features. They must conform to U.S. Postal Service specifications. For example, space should be left in the middle of the envelope for the address so the Barcode Print Zone is clear.

Envelopes should be designed to conform to U.S. Postal Service specifications.

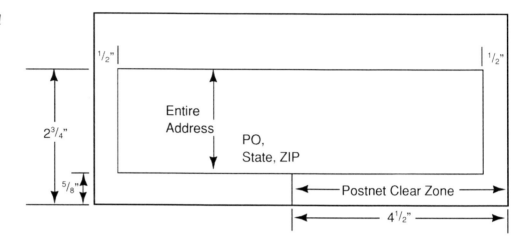

Envelopes can come in an array of colors with highly imaginative graphic features for marketing purposes. However, to be mailable without a surcharge, envelopes and cards should conform to the following specifications:

Dimensions	Minimum	Maximum
Height	3 1/2"	6 1/8"
Length	5"	11 1/2"
Thickness	.007"	1/4"
Rectangular: Length/Height = 1.3"		2.5"
Card Height	3 1/2"	4 1/4"
Card Length	5"	6"
Card Thickness	.007"	0095"

Most business documents are mailed in a #9 or a #10 envelope.

Letter envelopes (commercial and official sizes)

Letter envelopes can be solid face or provide a show-through window for the address. The width is always the first measurement. The standard paper stock is 24 lb. white wove. Most business correspondence is mailed in a #9 official envelope (3 7/8" x 8 7/8") or a #10 envelope (4 1/8" x 9 1/2"). Often, outgoing correspondence or direct mail is sent in a #10 envelope with a #9 envelope enclosed as the return envelope.

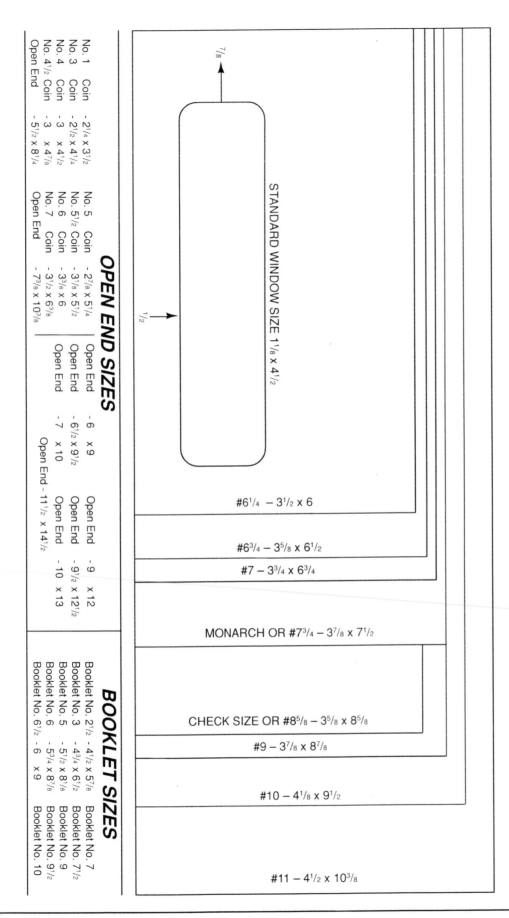

ENVELOPES · STANDARD SIZES

COMMERCIAL AND OFFICIAL SIZES

STANDARD WINDOW SIZE 1¹/₈ x 4¹/₂

⁷/₈

¹/₂

#6¹/₄ – 3¹/₂ x 6

#6³/₄ – 3⁵/₈ x 6¹/₂

#7 – 3³/₄ x 6³/₄

MONARCH OR #7³/₄ – 3⁷/₈ x 7¹/₂

CHECK SIZE OR #8⁵/₈ – 3⁵/₈ x 8⁵/₈

#9 – 3⁷/₈ x 8⁷/₈

#10 – 4¹/₈ x 9¹/₂

#11 – 4¹/₂ x 10³/₈

OPEN END SIZES

No. 1	Coin	- 2¹/₄ x 3¹/₂
No. 3	Coin	- 2¹/₂ x 4¹/₄
No. 4	Coin	- 3 x 4¹/₂
No. 4¹/₂ Coin		- 3 x 4⁷/₈
Open End		- 5¹/₂ x 8¹/₄

No. 5	Coin	- 2⁷/₈ x 5¹/₄
No. 5¹/₂ Coin		- 3¹/₈ x 5¹/₂
No. 6	Coin	- 3³/₈ x 6
No. 7	Coin	- 3¹/₂ x 6³/₈
Open End		- 7³/₈ x 10³/₈

Open End	- 6	x 9
Open End	- 6¹/₂ x 9¹/₂
Open End	- 7	x 10
Open End - 11¹/₂ x 14¹/₂

Open End	- 9	x 12
Open End	- 9¹/₂ x 12¹/₂
Open End	- 10	x 13

BOOKLET SIZES

Booklet No. 2¹/₂ - 4¹/₂ x 5⁷/₈
Booklet No. 3	- 4³/₄ x 6¹/₂
Booklet No. 5	- 5¹/₂ x 8¹/₈
Booklet No. 6	- 5³/₄ x 8⁷/₈
Booklet No. 6¹/₂ - 6	x 9

Booklet No. 7
Booklet No. 7¹/₂
Booklet No. 9
Booklet No. 9¹/₂
Booklet No. 10

Window envelopes

Window envelopes save time and money by eliminating the need to address the envelope and thereby also avoid the possible mistake of inserting the wrong item in the envelope. Window envelopes are available with or without an acetate cover on the die cut window.

Most window envelopes used in business offices have a standard window opening and a standard location on the envelope.

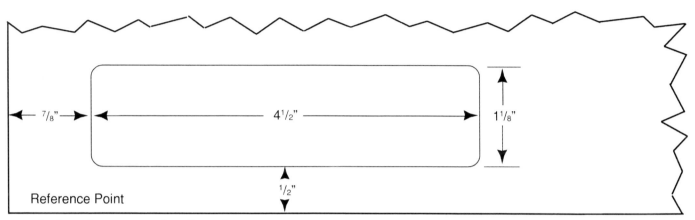

Standard window opening for all envelope sizes # 6³/₄" through # 14.

CHECKS

Checks and other negotiable instruments must be printed with magnetic ink numbers to facilitate the routing and processing through the banking industry. These numbers represent bank identification numbers, routing numbers for distribution through the Federal Reserve Banking System, the amount of the check, and usually the consecutive number of the check. These specially shaped numbers must be printed in a horizontal band at the bottom of checks with magnetic ink containing iron oxide for the MICR (Magnetic Ink Character Recognition) equipment to read into computers.

Magnetic ink spec sheets should be sent to the printer.

Therefore, when designing checks, there must be a 5/8" high clear band at the bottom of the check for these magnetic ink numbers. The band must be clear of anything else printed in magnetic ink. Borders or other images printed with regular ink can be included in this band, but the easiest way to isolate this magnetic band is to leave it completely clear of any printing other than the magnetic numbers.

A magnetic ink specifications sheet must be sent to the printer with the form design.

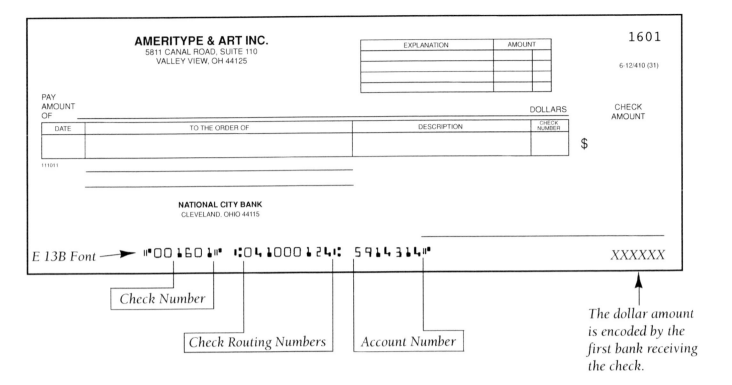

AMERITYPE & ART INC.
5811 CANAL ROAD, SUITE 110
VALLEY VIEW, OH 44125

1601

6-12/410 (31)

EXPLANATION	AMOUNT

PAY
AMOUNT
OF

DOLLARS

CHECK
AMOUNT

DATE	TO THE ORDER OF	DESCRIPTION	CHECK NUMBER

$

111011

NATIONAL CITY BANK
CLEVELAND. OHIO 44115

E 13B Font ⟶ ⑊00 1601⑊ ⑊04 1000 124⑊ 5914 314⑊

XXXXX

Check Number

Check Routing Numbers

Account Number

The dollar amount is encoded by the first bank receiving the check.

LABELS

Labels have a variety of purposes and are designed accordingly. They can be designed in any size, shape, and color desired, but they all will have one thing in common – an adhesive to affix them. Labels can be designed as single or continuous sheets or built into unit sets. The designer can be highly creative with the design but must specify to the printer the type of material and adhesive desired.

The peel-off pressure-sensitive labels are particularly popular because they are easy to use and available in a wide range of constructions, materials, and adhesives. Available materials include foil, staincloth, Tyvek (DuPont's impossible-to-tear polyethylene), and vinyl. The older, traditional type of adhesive is the gummed label that must be moistened with water before application.

A continuous pressure-sensitive label.

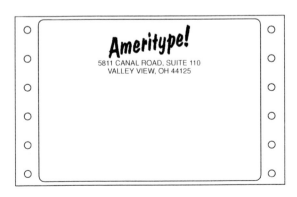

Ameritype!
5811 CANAL ROAD, SUITE 110
VALLEY VIEW, OH 44125

Tags

Tags are similar to labels in construction and purpose. They are primarily used for inventory control, production control, and shipping systems. However, their design differs in that they must have a means of attachment, which requires a hole for some type of string, wire, or plastic to suspend them. Two commonly used standard tag holes are 3/16" with a 9/16" patch and 2/8" with a 5/8" patch reinforcement.

Bar codes

A discussion of forms design would not be complete without mentioning bar codes and scanning technology. It has become very popular on forms, envelopes, labels, tags, and even on folders used in filing systems. This is because the scanning of bar codes is a fast and accurate way to get data into computers.

UPC Code

The most familiar bar code is the UPC, Uniform Product Code, used by the retail and food industry for pricing and inventory. Almost all packages carry a UPC code that is scanned at the checkout counter. The UPC code is a combination of a five-digit manufacturer or distributor number and a five-digit product number. Numbers are issued to manufacturers by the Uniform Product Code Council, Inc., in Dayton, Ohio. UPCs have a tight printing tolerance, but most laser printers can print UPC codes that will scan correctly.

Bar codes may look alike, but there are actually many different types.

An overview of electronic forms

Due to technological change, there has been a growth in the conversion of paper forms to electronic forms (E-forms). However, growth has been slower than many predictions. As long ago as the 60's, people were predicting the paperless office. That prophecy has not materialized. Businesses are still inundated with paper forms and other paper documents.

There is growth in the conversion to electronic forms but paper forms will not disappear.

There are many advantages to electronic forms and conversion of paper forms to electronic forms will continue, but paper forms will not disappear, People like paper. Paper is portable, convenient, and inexpensive.

There are several types of electronic forms but a true electronic form is an "intelligent" form that has been programmed to allow the user to fill in the form on a computer using keyboard, database, system-generated and calculated entries. The form remains in digital form in a computer system and is transmitted and processed electronically. At some point in the processing, it is often printed out in paper form.

The benefits of converting to electronic forms include:
- Elimination of the costs to print, warehouse, and distribute paper forms.
- Increased office worker's production and accuracy due to computer conveniences when filling in and routing electronic forms.

Organizations converting paper forms to electronic forms have discovered that it is a process that must be done slowly and accurately. Some of the issues include:

The basic design of electronic forms is simular to the design of paper forms.

- It takes considerably longer to design electronic forms.
- Designing electronic forms requires thorough forms analysis, programming and testing.
- Hardware is a major consideration. Every user will need a compatible computer and electronic forms software.
- An efficient network system will have to be installed.
- How will forms be filled out if the network goes down?
- Designers will need technical training.

Designing electronic forms

The basic design for electronic forms is similar to the basic design of paper forms. Sans-serif typefaces are a good choice for designing electronic forms. The minimum point size recommended is 8-point. As it is with paper forms, it is best to set captions and other form items in upper case letters. The exception is text (paragraphs) which should be set in caps and lower case.

Chapter 16 Review Questions and Discussion

1. Are forms design principles basically the same for cut forms and specialty forms? Explain the difference in the design of specialty forms.

2. Name the four basic materials used to construct specialty forms. What kind of paper is used to print almost all forms? Differentiate between carbon paper and carbonless paper.

3. Describe the construction features of unit sets that affect forms design. What are two other names for unit sets?

4. Describe the construction features of continuous forms that affect forms design. What construction feature makes continuous forms instantly identifiable? What determines standard widths and lengths for continuous forms?

5. Explain how U.S. Postal Service regulations affect the design of envelopes. What is the advantage of using a window envelope?

6. Describe the use of MICR in the banking industry and explain how it affects the design of checks.

7. Explain the unique design features of labels and tags.

8. Discuss the use of bar codes in forms design.

9. List the advantages of converting paper forms to electronic forms and discuss the problems encountered in the conversion.

Web Site Design

Web Site Design

Web Site Design

Web Site Design

Web Site Design

Web Site Design

Web Site Design

PART THREE

Web Site Design

Web Site Design

Web Site Design

Web Site Design

Web Site Design

Web Site Design

Web Site Design

Web Site Design

Web Site Design

Web Site Design

Web Site Design

Web Site Design

Web Site Design

Web Site Design

CHAPTER
17

$\boxed{\text{PLAN AHE}_{\text{A}_{\text{D}}}}$

PRE-DESIGN PLANNING FOR WEB SITES

Unless you know where you're going,
any road will take you there.

– Theodore Levitt

Chapter 17 Objectives

After studying this chapter, you should be able to:

1. *Explain why every business needs a Web site.*

2. *Describe why the most important planning task is to determine the objective of the site.*

3. *Describe the importance of meaningful content to the success of a business Web site.*

4. *List the advantages of advertising on the World Wide Web.*

5. *Discuss fact gathering as the first step in planning the development of a Web site and list some vital fact-gathering questions.*

6. *Explain why you should research the Web sites of your competitors.*

7. *Describe how to develop and organize the contents of a Web site.*

8. *Explain why initial Web designs should be mockups, not real Web pages.*

The Web is the greatest marketing opportunity in history

The growth of the World Wide Web is one of the most significant developments in history. It's on the same level as the invention of the printing press, television, and a hot pastrami sandwich from a New York delicatessen.

The Web is the greatest marketing vehicle in the history of the world. Almost every business that wants to survive and grow needs a commercial Web site. Telling a client or a prospect that a business doesn't have a Web site is almost like telling them that the business doesn't have a telephone or a computer.

There are many kinds of Web sites online, including personal Web sites featuring the family dog, Emily's new haircut and photos of the cute kids so grandma in Scottsdale can see them. In addition to commercial and personal Web sites, there are organizational, informational, and political sites.

Although some of the content of this Web design section of the book is applicable to all kinds of Web sites, this book focuses on commercial Web sites - sites on which products or services are sold for profit.

The key to a successful business Web site is meaningful content, information needed by clients and prospects to make a buying decision. The key to success is not, as many people think, to design sites that give viewers migraine headaches from psychedelic flash movies, owls flying across the page, dark purple text on a black background, rock music, and trumpet fanfares. People do not buy your widgets because your logo is turning cartwheels or a bird is flying figure-eight loops on your site

Excerpt from a personal Web site: This is Elmer, my dog. Isn't he cute?

In successful commercial Web sites, appearance is important but CONTENT is king.

Advantages of Web advertising

1. The Web has the capability of making your products and services available to millions of people around the globe.

2. You can make pricing and other changes to the content and the design of the site very quickly, as opposed to throwing out and re-printing sales literature.

3. You have the ability to use a large amount of information and to use unlimited color, photographs, and illustrations, at a very reasonable price.

Planning the Web site.

As with graphic design and forms design, many people start their Web site design without planning. They jump right in, typing, animating, coloring, flashing, blinking, and playing the theme song from Phantom of the Opera.

The site might even look good, but without a plan and meaningful content, the chances of the site successfully selling your widgets is remote. In a successful Web site, content is king!

The first step in planning a Web site is to gather facts. This is best done by using a form which asks all the vital questions. It serves as a checklist to make sure no questions are forgotten , and it provides space to record the answers. Taking the time and making the effort to get accurate and complete answers will help create a site that meets the site's objectives and the needs of the viewers.

In planning a Web site, the most important task is to determine the primary objective and the secondary objective(s) of the site.

The questions to be asked includes

What is the main objective of the site?
To sell a product or service or both? To generate a mailing list? To create a presence on the Web? To provide information to customers?

What are the secondary objectives?
List them by priority

What kind of company image do you want to convey?
Conservative - your money is safe with us? Exciting-We're a fun company? Budget prices? Upscale? Hip? The image the company wants to convey will significantly influence the page layout, the typeface selection, the colors, and the general tone of the site.

Too many people design their Web site for themselves (an ego trip) instead of designing it to meet the needs of their clients and prospects.

What action do you want your Web visitors to take?
Buy a product directly from your Web site? Call you? Send e-mail? Fill-in and send an interactive form?

What is the profile of the people you want to visit your site?
Who are you trying to reach.? You need to know so you can design the site to meet their needs and expectations. Too many people design the site for themselves, to satisfy their ego. Web site marketing is not about bragging. It's about benefits to the visitor.

What information will they be looking for?
Find out what information the visitor will need to make a buying decision. Give it to them.

Don't start designing your site until you study the sites of your competitors. You can learn from them.

What special offer(s) can be included to increase response?
Visitors need a push to make them act NOW. Offer a free gift or discount if they respond now. Or let them know there are only a few left in stock.

Describe the content.
Make a list of all subjects to be included in the content, by priority.

Who are your main competitors?
You definitely should study the Web sites of competitors, particularly the main competitors. You want your site to be distinctly different and to highlight reasons why visitors should buy from you and not from your competitors.

Organizing the Web site content

Graphics can win awards but content is what provides the information necessary to accomplish the objective(s) of the site.

If you can set specific goals like getting someone to join an organization, attend a meeting, buy season tickets, make a donation to the Animal Protective League, or get subscriptions to a newsletter, it will help you determine a list of contents for the Web site.

For example, if your goal is to increase the membership in the "People Who Hate Barney Association", your Web site content might include:
- Contact information
- Benefits of joining
- Annual membership fee
- This month's newsletter
- A schedule of upcoming events
- Online membership application form

Stress benefits to your clients and prospects, not features of your products and services. In other words, write client-benefit advertising copy, not bragging copy!

Some other considerations in determining what information should be included in your Web site are:
- Providing a map if you want local prospects to visit,
- Providing optional methods of payment.
- Stressing benefits to the customer, not features of your products or services.
- Answering questions that clients and prospects frequently ask.

After the list of content items is completed. The next step is to determine the number of Web pages required and the items that will appear on each page.

Ameritype!

5811 CANAL ROAD, STE. 110
VALLEY VIEW, OH 44125
PHONE 216-901-2001
FAX 216-901-2003
E-mail mj@ameritype.com
www.ameritype.com

WEB SITE DESIGN QUESTIONNAIRE

Please help us design an attractive and <u>EFFECTIVE</u> Web site for you by providing the following information.

ORGANIZATION	INFORMATION PROVIDED BY (NAME)	DATE

1. In a few sentences, provide a summary description of your company's products or services.

_____
_____
_____
_____
_____
_____
_____
_____
_____
_____
_____

2. What key words or phrases best describe your business?

_____
_____
_____
_____

3. Why should prospects choose you instead of your competitors? In other words, what is your niche or major benefit to your customers?

_____
_____
_____
_____
_____

4. What is the profile of the person you want to visit your Web site? (Business forms buyers, Macintosh owners, etc.)

_____
_____
_____

5. What action do you want your Web site viewer to take (send you E-mail, call you, download order form and fax order to you)?

_____
_____
_____
_____

Front page of a 4-page Web design questionnaire.

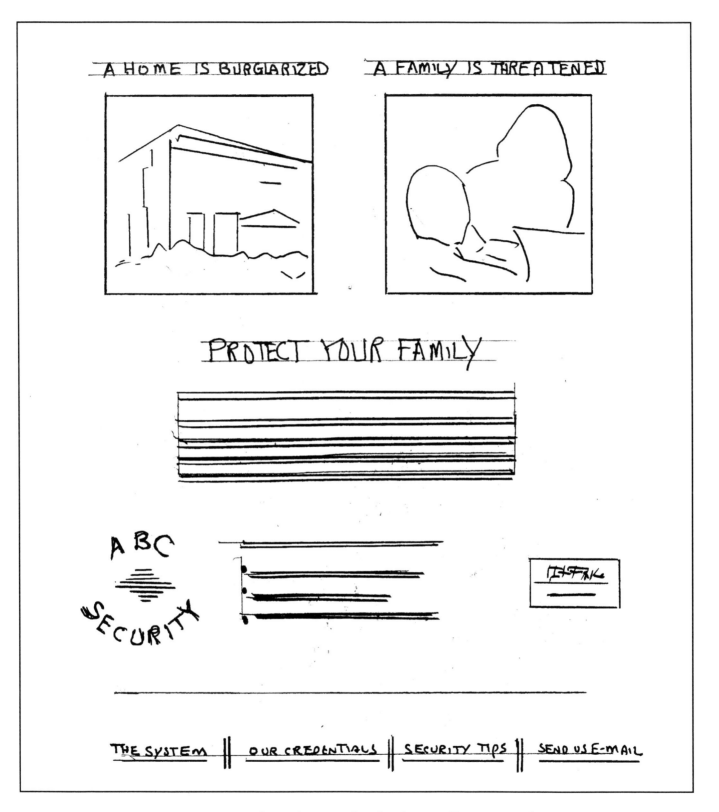

*Starting a Web site design with a sketch or an illustrator mockup
is a quick, easy way to transform ideas into visuals.*

Before you complete your planning, research the Web sites of your competitors

It's always a good idea to look at the Web sites of your competitors, particularly at the competitors who have a high ranking in search engine listings. Consider on how you can improve on their sites. Your site needs to be different in order to stand out and you also need to explain why visitors should buy from you instead of your competitors.

Look at the Web sites of your competitors and consider how you can improve on them.

Another important reason to look at the sites of your competitors is that you can find out their keywords and how they've use their keywords in the HTML code and in the design of their site because that is what is giving them their high ranking in the search engine listings.

You can do this because the Web is open source. In the Internet Explorer browser, you can click on "View" and then "Source" and it will bring up their HTML code. In the META tag section, their keywords will be listed. You can also look at their pages and see how the keywords were used on the page, since this determines their high ranking in the search engines. You can learn from this. Selecting and using keywords in the HTML code and in the page design is covered in more detail in subsequent chapters.

Think first, then design

A site could look really cool, but it is nevertheless a failure if it doesn't meet the objective of the site.

At the risk of repeating, the most important thing in pre-design planning for Web site design is to determine the primary and the secondary objectives of the site. WHY does the client want to put up the site? What do they hope to get from the site?

Examples of typical site objectives:
- An e-commerce site to sell products
- Provide branch offices with company information
- Provide online coupons.
- Get orders from global markets.
- Provide students with homework assignments
- Win site design awards.
- Introduce sales representatives

Design your site not for everyone but for the target audience you are trying to reach.

Although your site will be available to millions of people with Internet access, you should design your site for the target audience you are trying to reach. For example, a gun care products company is seeking hunters, target shooters, law enforcement officers, and military forces.

The target audience for an employment agency are employers and job seekers. The target audience for a typesetting company are commercial printers and in-house printers. Design your site for your target audience.

Sketches and Mockups

In the planning stage for designing Web sites, just as it is for designing for print, it is a good idea to make some design sketches or mockups. The first Web designs that you create for your own review or to show to your clients should be mockups, not real Web pages because it makes sense to spend your time in designing, and not in the production process.

The first Web designs should be mockups, not real Web pages because it makes sense to spend your time in designing, and not in the production process.

Mockups are usually done using illustration software like Pagemaker, Photoshop, Illustrator, or Freehand. By creating mockups for "appearance" proofs, you can easily make revisions to the design and save the HTML and other coding for later.

HTML and other Web programming

This book focuses on the graphic design, the copywriting, and the marketing of commercial (for profit) Web sites. The teaching of HTML and other Web programming is not critical for our objectives. There is a plethora of books, articles, and Internet tutorials for learning HTML and there are many Web-authoring software programs that that will generate HTML, Javascript and other programming codes.

Macromedia Dreamweaver, Adobe Golive, and Microsoft FrontPage are popular Web-authoring programs.

Web-authoring programs like Macromedia DreamWeaver, Adobe Golive, and Microsoft FrontPage will generate your Web programming codes but don't always produce exactly what you want, so it is prudent to learn at least the basics of HTML so you can correct and tweak coding.

Chapter 17 Questions

1. *Why does every business need a Web site?*

2. *In planning a Web site, what is the most important task?*

3. *Describe the importance of meaningful content to the success of a Web site.*

4. *Give three unique advantages of advertising on the World Wide Web.*

5. *Discuss fact-gathering as the first step in planning the development of a Web site and list some key fact-gathering questions.*

6. *Explain why you should research the Web sites of your competitors.*

7. *Why should initial Web designs be mockups, not real Web pages.*

The customer isn't a moron.
She is your wife.

– David Ogilvy

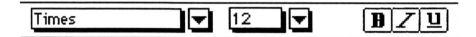

CHAPTER

18

WRITING ADVERTISING COPY
FOR WEB SITES

I am returning this otherwise good
typing paper to you because someone
has printed gibberish all over it and
put your name on top.

– An English Professor

Chapter 18 Objectives

After studying this chapter, you should be able to:

1. Discuss the advantages of having a retail store on the Web that is always open.

2. List five rules for writing copy for a Web site.

3. List six things not to do when writing advertising copy.

4. Differentiate between client-benefit copywriting and bragging copywriting.

5. Explain the meaning of "sell the sizzle and not the steak."

6. List five timeless benefits that people dream of gaining.

7. Discuss the benefits and procedures for using customer testimonials.

8. Describe how to overcome customer inertia by creating "buy now" offers.

9. Discuss "fear", the copywriter's friend.

10. Describe proven copywriting approaches.

11. Explain what a low recognition company needs to do to establish credibility.

12. Explain the importance and use of captions for illustrations and photographs.

13. Explain how to conclude an advertisement on a Web site or any other advertisement.

Advantages of advertising on the Web

There are many advantages to advertising on the World Wide Web. In traditional advertising, a prospect who wants to buy or get more information about a product or service advertised on TV, radio, or print media responds by calling, mailing, or faxing a coupon or letter. These responses take time and effort. In some instances, e-mail is used for responding, but generally it takes time to respond to the advertisement and time for the business to get back to the prospect.

Sometimes, especially when a prospect is asking for literature about a product or service and the business is responding by mailing an information packet, it can take weeks or even months to get a response. By contrast, if the Web site is designed correctly, the prospect can get all the information he or she wants *immediately,* even if it's 3:00 a.m. in Atlanta and the business is in London. If the prospect is ready to buy the product, it can be purchased immediately. A Web site is a retail store that is always open. The business owner can make money while he or she is sleeping.

The order form on a Web site is available 24 hours a day.

A Web site is a retail store that is always open. The owner can make money while he or she is sleeping.

Home	**Order Form**			

BOOKS
Graphic Design for 21st Century Desktop Publishers
Two books in one: graphic design for business desktop publishers and also a college textbook.

Forms Design II
The forms industry standard manual for forms managers, forms analysts and forms designers. Also a college textbook.

Office Humor, The Official Collection
Stress-busters from the bottom desk drawer.

BUSINESS REPORTS
Web site sales, advertising copy, direct mail

Send E-mail

WORDS & PICTURES
P.O. Box 40
N. Olmsted, OH 44070
216-901-2001
FAX: 216-901-2003
www.wppublishing.com
mj@ameritype.com

© 2001 Words & Pictures Publishing

To protect your privacy, Words and Pictures' web servers encrypt all transactions using this form. However, if you would prefer not to enter your credit-card number into an online form, please e-mail us or give us a call at **1-800-544-5314**.

ORDER INFORMATION

Qty	Title	Price	Totals
0	Graphic Design for 21st Century Desktop Publishers	$39.00	$0.00
0	Forms Design II: The Course for Paper and Electronic Forms	$19.50	$0.00
0	Office Humor: The Official Collection	$9.98	$0.00
0	*Report No.1* How to design Web sites to get your share of multi-billion dollar Internet sales	$8.00	$0.00
0	*Report No. 2* How to make money by driving traffic to your Web site	$8.00	$0.00
0	*Report No. 3* How to write advertising copy to sell anything	$8.00	$0.00
0	*Report No. 4* Twenty three unbreakable rules for making money with direct mail	$8.00	$0.00

Shipping and handling.
$3.50 for one book, $4.50 for two or more books. | | | $0.00 |

If you order only reports, no shipping charge.

Unlike brochures, direct mail ads, and space ads where additional information is expensive, adding information to a Web site is relatively inexpensive. Therefore, all the information that a prospect could possibly need to make a buying decision can be included in the Web site. Although the Web site may be brimming with content, the prospect doesn't have to read everything. He or she can select what to read by clicking on links and going only to pages of interest.

Another advantage of Web advertising is that it is relatively easy to update and fine-tune the information in your Web site. And you can do it the same day! With print advertising, you have to throw away obsolete promotional items in stock, re-design them, and wait for the printer to produce them. It's considerably more expensive and time-consuming to revise traditional advertising than it is to upload revisions to your Web site.

Copywriting rules that are carved in stone

Rule No. 1

You're not writing copy to make a sale. You're writing copy to get a customer.

Rule No. 2

Your copy must be believable. You must never lie or destroy your credibility. The customer is not a simpleton.

Rule No. 3

Listen to your customers and prospects. They will tell you what to sell, how to sell, and when to sell.

Rule No. 4

Speak to individuals, not groups or masses when you write your copy.

Rule No. 5

Utilize the most important word in copywriting, "you", as often as possible. If you're giving away something, then the most important word becomes "free", and the second most important word is "you". Use them both as much as you can.

Things you should never do when writing copy

1. Don't have a final sale six times.
2. Don't tell magazine subscribers that their subscription is about to run out when they still have 6 months to go.

*Things you should never do
when writing advertising copy
(continued)*

3. Don't tell a prospect that your offer is limited to a special group when it's obvious you're mailing to everyone east of Chicago.
4. Don't use "one-time sale" in an ad that you plan to repeat.
5. Don't tell a prospect or customer how important they are to you when your database can't identify gender, and you're not sure if his/her name is spelled correctly.
6. Don't extend Charter offers.

Don't use a lie as obvious as "the check is in the mail".

If your check is in the mail,
you can disregard
this notice.

BASICS OF ADVERTISING COPYWRITING

Writing advertising copy to motivate Web prospects to buy is similar to writing advertising copy for print advertisements. There are more bells and whistles that can be incorporated into Web advertising, which will be described in the Web design chapter, but the copywriting basics are the same. An understanding of these basics is invaluable in the design of Web sites just as a basic knowledge of accounting is invaluable when learning and using an accounting software program.

Don't use the top half of your opening page with bragging copy.

Write advertising copy that focuses on the prospect, not yourself

Millions of Web sites have been designed by artists, students, and others who have not had the benefit of advertising copywriting training or experience. These sites have little chance of success because they make the biggest mistake made by untrained advertising copywriters, which is that *they zero in on themselves instead of the prospect.*

They write bragging copy instead of client-benefit copy. They concentrate on themselves instead of on YOU, the prospect. The first thing you see on the home page of their Web site is a gigantic logo. And some of the logos are multi-colored with 3-D shadows and are glowing, blinking, or dancing. Unless you're Microsoft or McDonalds, nobody recognizes your logo or cares about it. An immense 3-D logo is "bragging" and is written for the Web site company owner, who is concentrating on himself instead of the prospect.

TRYING
TO FIND
SOMEONE?

We'll find your missing person or you don't pay!

The prospect is not going to buy your product because your logo is spinning and blinking in the top half of your Web site home page. The prospect wants to know what BENEFITS he or she gets by buying your product or service. And the prospect wants to know about those benefits NOW or *click*, your Web site is history. So instead of placing a monstrous pulsating logo or " The Rubber Duckie Company" in two-inch high purple fluorescent letters in the top half of your home page, use a prospect *benefit* headline like *Looking for a missing person? We'll find the person you're looking for or you don't pay!*

Avoid bragging, exaggeration, and boring clichés

The benefits you sell have to be based on truths. Your prospects live in a skeptical age. They're not going to believe exaggerated claims, such as "...the world's best apple pie" and bragging, such as "...world-class printers". And it's an insult to their intelligence, not to mention boring them to tears, to use puffy phrases like "Excellence in customer service is our goal".

Don't use bragging words or phrases like "greatest", "world-class", "better" or "number one". If you do so, you're making the big mistake of focusing on yourself instead of your prospect. Your company is not the center of the universe, and your prospects are not in orbit around you.

If you think you have to use one of these phrases, at least back it up with a *fact* to explain why it is so great.

Sell benefits, not features

Everyone has heard the expression "sell the sizzle and not the steak" so many times it has become a cliché, but few people actually follow this advice. They still try to sell features instead of benefits. You don't sell by describing the size, color, marbling, and other *features* of the steak. You sell by telling the prospect the *benefits* of eating the steak—how good it will taste and how much he or she will enjoy it. Sell benefits, not features. Tell prospects what benefits they will receive, and how it will improve their health, financial status, family life, career, enjoyment, security, etc.

Select the main benefit and use it as your headline.

List all of the benefits that can be used to motivate the prospect. Select the main benefit and use it as your headline. One big, prominently displayed benefit will motivate better than a list of ten reasons. Therefore, use the most important benefit in a big headline; and place the other less important benefits elsewhere on the page, not as prominently displayed as the main benefit, but do include them.

The best benefits are the timeless ones that people dream of gaining, such as:
- *More Money* - for spending and saving
- *Improved Health* - longer life, energy, endurance
- *Improved Appearance* - face, hair, body
- *Security* - independence, provision for old age
- *More Leisure* - for rest, play, travel, hobbies
- *Increased Enjoyment* - from food, drink, entertainment
- *Praise from Others* - for one's knowledge, intelligence, appearance
- *Greater Popularity* - through a more attractive personality or accomplishments
- *Financial Advancement* - better job, successful investments, owning a business
- *Social Advancement* - keeping up with the Joneses, higher social status

One big benefit, prominently displayed, is better than a list of 10 benefits.

People want to:
- Collect things
- Be good parents
- Express their personalities
- Satisfy their curiosity
- Be up-to-date
- Be "first" in things
- Win the affection of others
- Be recognized as authorities
- Improve themselves (self-development)
- Be proud of their possessions

People also want to:
- Save money
- Save time
- Avoid discomfort and pain
- Avoid worry
- Avoid embarrassment
- Avoid offending others
- Avoid boredom
- Avoid risks

Create trust by using customer testimonials

Certainly one of the best ways to overcome skepticism is through the liberal use of testimonials. Your skeptical prospect is more likely to believe what your customers say about your product or service than what you have to say about it. Therefore, sprinkle your ads generously with testimonials. How do you get them? Ask your customers to give them to you in writing. Offer then something free for their time and effort. Getting testimonials is time and money well spent.

by making descriptions of your products and services instantly available to prospects worldwide. Your website should work by providing the information that people need when they're deciding whether to buy from you.

But your website can't do any of these things if it isn't built properly.

At Ameritype, we know how to build websites that work. We're

"Thank you, Ameritype, for the fruitful rewards our website has brought after only a few weeks!"

Joseph Rosalina,
President
Ameritalia, Inc.

Create a "buy now" offer

Another copywriting basic is to do something to overcome inertia, to make prospects buy *now*, not some time in the future when they finally get around to it.

One of the biggest causes of prospect inaction is lack of complete and clear information. The prospect might hold up ordering even if there's only one small detail left out of the information you supply about your product or service or if your information is not crystal clear. Incomplete or ambiguous information may make the prospect uncomfortable or even irritated and lead to putting the order form aside.

Motivate them to buy NOW by creating an offer that is difficult to refuse.

So, first make sure the information you provide about your product or service is complete and clear, and then motivate them to buy NOW by making a *"now"* offer. For example, you can offer a 20% discount if they buy in ten days, or you can give them something free if they buy now, or you can tell them there are only eight items left in stock, which will go to the first eight orders received.

To try to get immediate response, use one of the following or a similar offer:
- Buy now and get a discounted price that others won't get later.
- Buy now and get a second one free.
- Buy now and get shipping and handling free.
- Buy this book now and get some other product free.
  (it's best if the bonus product is related to the first product,
    such as a laminated bookmark with a purchase of a book).

Advertising offers that have been used successfully

"Money-back guarantee – three of the best words you can put in an advertisement.

1. Special price
2. Free trial
3. Money-back guarantee
4. Bill me later
5. Installment terms
6. Charge card payment
7. Free gift for an inquiry
8. Free gift for a trial order
9. Free gift for buying
10. Multiple free gifts
11. Your choice of free gifts
12. Mystery gift
13. Free report
14. Free catalog
15. Free booklet
16. Free demonstration
17. Free consultation

18. Free cost estimate
19. Free lunch
20. Quantity discount
21. Introductory order discount
22. Seasonal sale
23. Free sample
24. Nominal charge samples
25. Pre-publication offer
26. Limited time offer
27. Charter membership or charter subscription
28. Limited edition offer
29. Extended guarantee
30. Double-your-money-back guarantee
31. Trade-in offer
32. Delayed billing offer

Write your advertising copy from one person to another person, not one company to another company.

Personalize your copywriting

Take a tip from successful business advertisers. Write your ads from one person to another one, not from one company to another company. The word "you" should be used lavishly. Don't say "We will give you a month's free trial", say "You can get a month's free trial". Don't say "Call *us* for more details". Say "Call *me* for more details".

By saying "you", the prospect feels more like a unique and valuable human being and not a faceless 16-digit account number in a database.

Fear, the copywriter's friend

Fear is a powerful sales motivator.

Fear is a powerful motivator, one that can get that prospect to fill in the order form. People can be physically afraid—afraid of being attacked in the street, afraid of a burglar breaking into the house, afraid of a fire in the night. This fear is used to sell pepper spray, home security systems, and smoke alarms.

People are afraid of disease, pain, and death. This fear is used as a motivator to sell exercise equipment, diet pills, health club memberships, and low-fat foods.

They are afraid of losing their jobs and their financial security. They are afraid of dental drills. All of these fears and more are used to sell products and services that we hope will chase away or alleviate our fears.

Several proven copywriting approaches

Many successful copywriters use the *"if" approach*. It starts off "If you...then you'll surely want...". This approach allows the writer to tell

A HOME IS BURGLARIZED!   A FAMILY IS THREATENED!

IT HAPPENS EVERY DAY!

The need to protect your family, your home and your possessions is more important than ever. To learn more about how you can bring your family greater peace of mind, call or e-mail today.

A home security company's opening page Web site, using fear as a sales motivator.

all the benefits at the start, which involves the prospect up front. It then moves on to the selling offer. Here is an example of the "if" approach:

If you take photography seriously ...

If getting the snapshot is only the start of all the exciting things you'd like to do with film, such as developing, enlarging, cropping, printing, mounting, selling ...

If you're into pictures not only for pleasure but also for profit ...

You're going to love Photo Pro Magazine!

A similar copywriting approach is the *"assume" approach*. Using this technique, the copywriter assumes certain things about the prospect:

You take photography seriously ...

Getting the shot is only the start of all the exciting things you'd like to do with film, including developing, enlarging, cropping, printing, mounting, selling ...

You're into pictures not only for pleasure but also for profit ...

You're going to love Photo Pro Magazine!

Another commonly used technique is the *"question" approach*. This consists of asking questions at the beginning of the ad to get the prospect immediately involved. This can be very successful, but it can also backfire if the prospect answers "no" and tosses the ad aside. Examples are:

Can you spot the five grammar mistakes on this page?

How many of these common gardening mistakes do you make?

People enjoy a good story and if you have a short relevant one, you can consider using the *story approach*. This only works if the story demonstrates the main benefit. The story approach works best if it is brief and highlights the main benefit.

Another approach is the *fantasy approach.* It works like this, "Imagine that you're sipping a rum punch while basking in the sun on Bora Bora in the French Polynesian Islands, then ..."

No matter which copywriting approach you use, remember to use specifics instead of generalities. Don't say, "You'll enjoy reading books by famous authors". Instead say, "You'll enjoy these thrillers by Tom Clancy, Jack Higgins, Robert Ludlum, John Grisham, and Dean Koontz". Don't say "You'll save money". Say, "You'll save a whopping $87.25".

How to establish credibility

Establishing credibility ranks right up there with benefits and offers. Prospects, particularly before ordering by mail, telephone, or online, want to feel they are dealing with a reputable company. Major corporations like Microsoft and McDonalds have instant recognition and credibility. However, Fred's Fireplace Supplies has zero recognition and credibility. Clearly, Fred needs to provide the prospect with some credentials. It's often done in a Web site, by including an "about us" page. This page includes years in business, industry associations that

Proven copywriting approaches include:
- *"if" approach*
- *"assume" approach*
- *"question" approach*
- *"story" approach*
- *"fantasy" approach*

Low recognition companies need to give money-back guarantees and testimonials.

Fred's company belongs to, awards won by Fred's Fireplace Supplies, list of key personnel and their work experience, company policies, list of key accounts, and testimonials from customers.

In addition, it is imperative that a zero recognition company, like Fred's Fireplace Supplies, offers a strong, clear guarantee for their product or service. It's also important to liberally pepper their advertisements with testimonials.

Add captions to photographs and illustrations

People read photograph and illustration captions more than they read body text.

Generally, good photographs are preferable to illustrations. In either case, you should put captions under photographs and illustrations because people read these captions more than they read the body text. Captions don't need to be a few words. They can be several sentences. If possible, each caption should be a mini ad.

Break up long body copy

Long body copy is boring, and boring your prospect into buying your product doesn't work. Long body copy decreases readership unless something is done to break it into manageable chunks. Some of the methods used to break up body copy and some other copywriting tips are listed below:

All paragraphs should be short.

1. A display subhead between the headline and the body copy will help motivate the prospect to read the body copy.
2. Keep the opening paragraph very short. A long first paragraph will frighten the prospect away.
3. All paragraphs should be short. Long paragraphs are fatiguing.
4. To break up the text, insert bold subheads after every few inches of copy.
5. Start your body copy with a large initial capital letter.
6. Use a serif typeface for body copy.
7. If possible, don't use body text smaller than 10 points.
8. Apply the following guideline for line length: the smaller the text point size, the smaller the line length. The wider the line length, the fewer the readers.
9. To help break up long monotonous body copy, bold or italicize important paragraphs.
10. Intersperse illustrations, photographs, and callouts (quotes from the body copy set in headline type) in the body text.
11. Don't place text over screened areas or backgrounds, which would make it hard to read.

Conclude the ad by telling the prospect what to do

You should always finish an ad by telling the prospect what to do. Don't just stop and hope the prospect will take some favorable action. It should be clear in your mind what you want the prospect to do, but it may not be clear in the prospect's mind. Tell the prospect to order the product now or to call you for a free consulting appointment or to fill in the interactive form on your Web site and e-mail it to you or to call the hotel and reserve a room for the seminar or... well, you get the idea.

If you're asking for an order, make it easy for the prospect to buy. If there is an order form, make it look important. Provide all ordering options and make them all easy to do.

Make your product easy to buy by including an order form in your Web site.

Use these time-tested copywriting tools of the trade when you design Web sites because the Web isn't about technology or design, it's about marketing.

ORDER FORM

| NAME | | TELEPHONE | | | |
| ADDRESS (CITY, STATE, ZIP) | | | | | |

PRODUCT	CODE	SIZE	COST	QUANTITY	TOTAL
Bore Cleaner	MC702	2 oz.	$5.33		
Bore Cleaner	MC704	4 oz.	$7.98		
Bore Cleaner	MC716	16 oz.	$26.58		
Bore Cleaner	MC7128	1 gal.	$152.34		
High Tech Grease	G10CC	10 cc.	$4.85		
FP-10 Lub. Elite	FPL04	4 oz.	$6.87		
FP-10 Lub. Elite	FPL128	1 gal.	$129.67		
Rust Prevent	RP006	6 oz.	$5.84		
Quick Scrub III	DG318	18 oz.	$8.32		
Black Powder	BPS04	4 oz.	$8.49		
Copper Remover	CRS08	8 oz.	$8.80		
Lead Remover	LR004	4 oz.	$8.49		

| USA SHIPPING CHARGES | | SUBTOTAL ONLY | |
| $0-10 - $3.00 | | | |

Chapter 18 Questions

1. Discuss the advantages of having a retail store on the Web that is always open.

2. List five rules for writing copy for a Web Site.

3. List six things *not* to do when writing advertising copy.

4. What is client-benefit copywriting compared to bragging copywriting?

5. Discuss the writing of advertsing copy that focuses on the client, not yourself. Explain why using phrases like "Excellence in customer service is our goal" is enough to gag a maggot.

6. Explain the meaning of the phrase, "sell the sizzle and not the steak".

7. Name five timeless benefits that people dream of gaining.

8. Describe the significance of using testimonials to overcome skepticism and explain how to get testimonials from your customers.

9. Describe how to overcome customer inertia by creating "buy now" offers. Name five "buy now" offers that have been used successfully.

10. What is the most important word to use in copywriting? Is it better to write from one person to another person, or from one company to another company?

11. Discuss "fear", the copywriter's friend.

12. Describe three copywriting approaches that have been successful.

13. What does a low recognition company like Tony's Pepperoni Bread need to do to establish credibility?

14. How should you conclude an advertisement on a Web site, or any other advertisement?

Home Page

About Us

Products

Order Form

Testimonials

Links

CHAPTER
19

FUNDAMENTALS OF BUSINESS WEB SITE DESIGN

Money is better than poverty,
if only for financial reasons

– Woody Allen

Chapter 19 Objectives

After studying this chapter, you should be able to:

1. Discuss the skills necessary, in addition to programming, to design a successful business Web site.

2. Describe the value of placing good content on every Web site page instead of concentrating primarily on graphics.

3. Discuss HTML, Hypertext Markup Language and why you should have at least a basic knowledge of it.

4. List the four types of Web authoring tools and briefly describe each one.

5. List eight types of pages that could be found in typical Web sites and briefly describe each one.

6. Explain the significance of the most important Web page in a site, the home page.

Designing a profit-making Web site requires more than HTML coding

If you want to make money from a Web site, you need to understand that the site is not about technology. It's about MARKETING!

Designing a profit-making Web site is more than creating HTML tags. Countless Web sites have been designed by people who know little more than how to keyboard HTML tags or how to generate HTML tags using a Web-authoring program. Yes, they did manage to upload a Web site to a server and add to the millions of sites in cyberspace, but very few of these sites, if any, will generate profits.

In addition to HTML and other Web site programming (JavaScript, Flash, etc.), designing a profit-generating site requires all of the following skills:
- Graphic Design
- Copywriting (writing advertising copy).
- Web site marketing

Business Web sites are not about technology. They are about marketing.

Designing a profit-making Web site requires more than HTML, JavaScript and other program-ming. It requires skill in graphic design, copywriting, and Web site marketing.

Not many people have all of these skills. And not many people realize that you need all of these skills to create a successful income-producing Web site. In the long run it will pay to get whatever experienced help you need to apply all of these skills in the creation of your profit-making Web site. Of course you want to keep your expenses down, but do you really think you're going to get the programming expertise, graphic design proficiency, copywriting skills and marketing know-how from someone who only knows HTML codes?

There are many resources for learning HTML and there are Web-authoring programs that generate HTML codes. This book concentrates on graphic design, copywriting, and Web site marketing.

Whether you create the site yourself or get programming, graphic design, copywriting, or marketing help, YOU need to control the content and design of the site. No one know the products and services better than you do.

Unlike most Web design books, this book focuses on graphic design, copywriting, and Web site marketing. This is valuable information not found in HTML books. This book does not focus on HTML programming because there are innumerable books and tutorials on HTML and other markup languages and because there are many Web-authoring programs that generate HTML and other Web language coding.

If you decide to create a site yourself, you can either learn HTML or use a Web-authoring program like Macromedia DreamWeaver or Adobe Golive to generate the coding for you. And if you follow the graphic design, copywriting, and marketing counsel in this book, you should be able to design an accomplished Web site that can generate profits, assuming your product or service is saleable.

If you want to make money from Web site sales, always remember that on a business Web site, CONTENT is king. Put content on every page. People don't buy because they like the way your big purple logo is turning cartwheels or your pages have dark red type on a black background. So don't start out by thinking about how big you can make your logo or if you should use fluorescent orange flowers for the background. Incidentally, this may come as a shock, but nobody really cares that much about your logo. Don't take up the top half of your home page with it.

Focus on the content. Give visitors all the information they need to make a buying decision. Tell them the benefits they will get by buying your products and services. Also try to overcome their inertia by providing a "buy now" offer (Buy two widgets NOW and get one FREE!).

On a business Web site, content is king. People don't buy because they like your logo and your graphics. They buy because you give them the information they need to make a buying decision.

HTML, Hypertext Markup Language

HTML, Hypertext Markup Language, is at the core of Web sites. HTML codes can be keyboarded or generated by Web-authoring software programs. So why, with Web-authoring programs available, should people learn HTML? Actually, you can't avoid it. Although Web-authoring programs generate programming codes and make things easier, they don't have a brain. They can't think and they do not generate perfect code. A human being must be able to at least tweak the codes. If you don't know at least the basics of HTML and how it creates a page, all the bells and whistles in a Web-authoring program won't help.

Even if you use a Web-authoring program to generate HTML code, you should learn at least the basics of HTML and how it creates a page.

HTML was developed by Tim Berners-Lee while at CERN, the particle physics laboratory in Geneva Switzerland, where the World Wide Web was created.

HTML works by inserting tags (codes) that identifies and defines the elements on the page. Web browsers like Netscape and Internet Explorer retrieve Web pages and serve as HTML formatters. The browser reads the HTML tags and formats the text and images on the screen. Different browsers and different versions of browsers and those running on different platforms may display the same page differently. A page that looks elegant on your screen may be unsightly on computers using different browsers and those running on different platforms.

You can keep abreast of HTML versions by visiting www.w3.org.

The significance of this reality is that you must try to design your Web site to work with most browsers, browser versions, and platforms, not just so they look good on your monitor. This necessitates your viewing your Web pages as they are seen in other browsers, in different browser versions, and on different platforms. Then you can try to make adjustments to your site so it will look presentable to as many viewers as possible.

At the time this book was written, the most recent HTML version was HTML 4.01. You can keep up with HTML versions and future markup languages by visiting the W3 Consortium's Web site at www.w3.org.

```
<HTML>
<HEAD>
<TITLE>
</TITLE>
</HEAD>
<BODY>
</BODY>
<HTML>
```

HTML pages have two basic parts, the head and the body. Each document must start with the <HTML> tag. The basic HTML markup structure is shown in the left column.

The HEAD element which runs from the <HEAD> start tag to the </HEAD> end tag contains information about the Web page which is not seen in the Web page that is visible to the viewer. The TITLE element goes into the HEAD element and contains the title of the Web page. The BODY element contains the visible content of the Web.

Types of Web-authoring tools

There are four types of Web page authoring tools.

Many Web-authoring tools are available to help generate HTML codes.

1. Text editors
2. HTML editors
3. WYSIWYG programs
4. Word processors

TEXT EDITORS
For Windows, Notepad is the best-known text editor and Simpletext is used on Macs. Text editors are simple programs and do not provide any HTML coding help. You need to know HTML or other markup languages in order to use text editors to type Web site programming codes.

HTML EDITORS
HTML editors are text editors that have been enhanced for the purpose of creating Web pages. The focus is on typing source code, and a variety of features have been incorporated to make the procedure easier. HTML editors offer the benefits of hand coding and make it easier by providing

automated support. HTML editors are superior to text editors because they are expressly designed for writing Web site source code.

Some HTML editors for Windows are:
- HotDog
- HomeSite

HTML editors are superior to text editors because they were specifically designed to write Web page source code.

Some HTML editors for Macintosh are
- World Wide Web Weaver
- Creative Page

WYSIWYG WEB AUTHORING PROGRAMS

"What You See Is What You Get" Web-authoring programs do not require users to work with source code. Macromedia Dreamweaver, Adobe Golive, and Microsoft FrontPage are three of the most popular WYSIWYG Web-authoring programs. They are use by professional Web designers and can also be used by beginners. Most WYSIWYG programs also provide access to the source code so that designers can bypass the automated programming and manually override any codes made by the program.

Macromedia DreamWeaver, Adobe GoLive, and Microsoft FrontPage are three of the most popular Web-authoring programs.

WORD PROCESSORS

Most word processors assert that they are Web-authoring programs. They claim that you can create a page in the word processor and then save the document as a HTML file, instead of as a regular document.

Word processors were not originally designed to write Web page source code. They were designed to produce paper documents.

It sounds like a good magic trick but it usually doesn't work out as expected. Word processors were designed for producing paper documents and they do an excellent job for producing paper documents but word processors were not originally designed to produce HTML code. This HTML output feature is an add-on and professional Web designers believe it cannot compete with Web-authoring programs that were designed specifically to produce programming codes for creating Web sites.

Web-authoring tools are helpful but not perfect

Although Web-authoring programs are helpful, particularly WYSIWYG programs like Macromedia DreamWeaver, Adobe Golive, and Microsoft FrontPage, they do not always produce exactly what the designer had in mind, therefore the designer should know enough HTML to at least go to the source code and tweak the pages.

In addition to HTML, there are other markup languages such as JavaScript, that are used to create or enhance Web pages. These languages are detailed in Chapter 20, Designing Business Web Sites.

Types of pages in a typical Web site

A Web site could consist of one page or multiple pages. The site of a small business could have ten pages while larger organizations could have hundreds of pages.

A typical Web site for a small business could have the following kinds of pages:

A Web site can have as little as one page or it can have hundreds of pages. A Web site for a very small company might have about 10 pages.

- Home Page (also called the index page).
- About Us page
- Products and Services page(s).
- FAQ page (Frequently Asked Questions)
- Tutorial(s),
- Testimonials
- Links
- Order form.

The Home Page

The home page has to kill with one blow. If it doesn't motivate the visitor, it is *hors de combat.*

A Web site home page has to kill with one blow. If your message doesn't motivate the viewer in the first few seconds, click... you're adrift in cyberspace.

In the first few seconds, the visitor will make a decision to continue reading or click on a link to another page, or... CLICK... you're history!

The visitor will remain only if there is something that interests him or her or even better, if there is a likelihood there is something that could **benefit** him or her. Therefore it doesn't take a rocket scientist to figure out that you should feature a prominent headline that stresses the main benefit that the visitor will receive if he or she purchases your product or service.

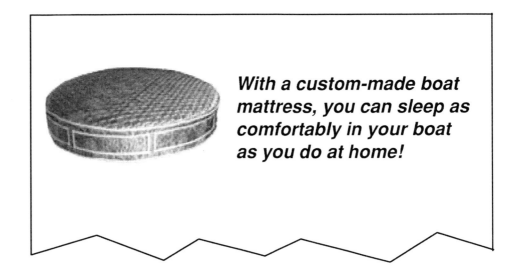

With a custom-made boat mattress, you can sleep as comfortably in your boat as you do at home!

It may not be a comforting philosophical thought, but in selling, the reality is that people care about three things:

1. Me.
2. Myself.
3. I

Don't write bragging copy. Chest thumping isn't going to do it. Write customer-benefit copy.

So you have to say to the visitor, "Here's what's in it for YOU." The important word is "you", not "I". Chest thumping isn't going to do it. "Now you can... is a "can't fail" headline because no matter how you end the sentence, it will appeal to the me, myself and I crowd.

And DUH.. don't fill the top half of your home page with your logo instead of a benefit headline. Your logo is not the focal point of the universe and your visitors are not in orbit around you. Nobody cares about your logo except maybe you and your mother.

Don't fill the top half of your home page with your logo. Your logo is not the focal point of the universe.

Words and Pictures Publishing

Welcome to our Web site

People are interested in the BENEFITS they will receive if they buy your product.

Don't start your Web Site like this.

O.K., maybe some people care about your logo and a good one does give some credibility but you don't need take up half a page with it. Prospects are more interested in the benefits they will receive if they buy your widgets.

DUH, here's another dumb thing some people do. They erect a barrier to their home page. One common type of barrier is an opening page that is just a logo and/or or a few words that tell you nothing of interest and has one link that says, "Enter Here". Why make the visitor look at a page that tells you nothing and force them to take an extra step to get to the real home page that hopefully does tell them something?

Pete and Tony's Pepperoni Bread

Click here to enter site

Another barrier is a flash movie that plays out before the home page appears. Unless the flash is brief and closely related to whatever you are trying to sell, it is nothing but a barrier to the home page. Flash is attention-getting and entertaining and can be successfully used elsewhere in the site pages, but it is usually a barrier if used in front of the home page.

A home page often contains these elements:
- Benefits to be received by visitors if they buy the products or services.
- A navigation bar containing links to other pages.
- The organization name, logo, and contact information.
- A summary of the organization's niche and its major products and services.
- Photos or illustrations of products.
- An "E-mail Us" link.
- Special "Buy Now" offers.

Although content is the most important element on a business Web site, some graphics are needed to add interest to the page. However, caution must be taken to prevent overpowering the more important text message with large and intense graphics.

Color is important in introducing graphics that make the page appealing. Color can be used in backgrounds, photos, icons, borders, illustrations, type, and logos.

This is a high traffic and high sales site. At the time of this book printing, it was ranked NUMBER ONE for "boat mattress" and other keywords in the Yahoo, Google, and Altavista search engines. Getting high search engine rankings is covered in Chapter 21.

Below is the home page of Your Design Mattress Factory, manufacturers of odd-size and custom-made mattresses, specializing in mattresses for boats. This is a successful profit- making Web site because it stresses content and marketing.

About Us Product Info Mattress Photos Testimonials Request a Quote Links

Sailors, Sleep in Comfort!

CUSTOM INNERSPRING MATTRESSES FOR YOUR BOAT

Strong benefit headline

With a custom-made boat mattress, yacht mattress or sailboat mattress, you can sleep as comfortably in your boat as you do at home.

Our specialty mattresses use the highest quality materials and rival the standards of the national brands. Firm, plush, round, triangular, or irregular just give us the dimensions and we'll give you the mattress you need.

Available special features include:

- Powder coating to provide salt water corrosion resistance.
- Beveled sides.
- Hinge or fold.

We also make custom mattresses for campers, vans, cribs, waterbed replacements any space where a standard mattress just won't fit.

Testimonial from satisfied customer. Every page in the site contains at least one testimonial.

**"The mattress is perfect. Fits right where it should and very comfortable. Thanks again"
- Dave Barr**

NEW! Custom sheets now available. Please call Bob Walters for details.

Click here for info on our mattress with a removable cover that can be washed or replaced!

YOUR DESIGN Mattress Factory
Round, triangular, or any shape

**Bob Walters
Your Design
Mattress Factory**
5320 Brookpark Rd.
Cleveland, OH 44134
(216) 661-1009
rwall009@msn.com

"About Us" page

The objective of the "About Us" page is to provide credentials. It is to help the prospect feel comfortable about buying your products and services. Providing credentials is particularly vital for small and unknown companies. The Coca-Cola Company does not need to provide credentials but Fred's Lawnmower Repair Service definitely does need to provide credentials.. *Offering guarantees and inserting testimonials on the Web site are essential for unknown companies to gain credibility.*

An excellent way for a Web site company to gain credibility is to offer a guarantee. Shooter's Choice, a Middlefield, Ohio gun care products company offers the following guarantee on their Web site:

The "About Us" page should help make the visitor feel comfortable about doing business with the company.

If you are Bank of America or Wal-Mart Stores you already have credentials, but if you are Pete and Tony's Pepperoni Bread, you need to inspire confidence by offering a guarantee and by placing testimonials on your site.

The "About Us" page can include the following items:
- Mission statement and/or an explanation of your niche.
- Names and contact information of key personnel.
- Testimonials from happy customers.
- Details of guarantees offered by the organization.
- Names of associations of which the organization is a member.
- Awards that the organization has received.
- List of completed projects.

Use some restraint in writing copy for your "About Us" page. As David Ogilvy, the celebrated advertising executive said, "Puff is no substitute for fact". Writing puffery like "the world's greatest jelly beans" is a waste of time and an insult to your visitor's intelligence. If your visitors believe this, you might be able to find a nice bridge that you could sell to them.

Products and Services page(s)

Depending on the number of products and services, the site could contain one or many products and services pages. The function of these pages is to provide all the information necessary for the visitor to make a buying decision. The pages can include whatever is helpful to the prospect, including benefit statements, text descriptions, photos, illustrations, sound, videos and animation. In addition, it is always a good idea to sprinkle testimonials from satisfied customers liberally on the product and services pages.

This products index page contains links to all Shooters Choice gun care products.

SHOOTER'S CHOICE

- Home page
- Products
- Order form
- Free samples
- Guarantee
- Cleaning tips
- Dealers' info
- Favorite links
- Request guncare advice

INDEX OF GUN CARE PRODUCTS

The best in gun care products now available online

If you **really** care about your firearms, you demand the very best in gun care products. Now Shooter's Choice makes sure that you can buy the very best products in the most convenient way. Just follow the links below to browse our current products.

Looking for Increased Profits? Stock Shooter's Choice Gun Care The Ultimate Solution

Sold Only Through Shooting Sports Retailers.

Cleaning Solvents
Bore Cleaner and Conditioner
Black Powder Cleaning Gel
Copper Remover
Lead Remover
Shotgun and Choke Tube Cleaner
Xtreme Clean Bore and Action Cleaner

Lubricants
Synthetic All-Weather High-Tech Grease
FP-10 Lubricant Elite

**Xtreme Clean Bore
and Action Cleaner**

Clicking on the name of a product on the Shooters Choice product index page brings up a page with the details on that product.

When Extreme Accuracy is Essential!

The One and Only **Ammonia Free** Aerosol Cleaner Formulated for the Care and Maintenance of Rifles and Handguns.

Order NOW!!!

QUICKLY REMOVES FOULING OF THESE TYPES:

- Copper
- Lead
- Carbon
- Powder

ADVANTAGES:

- Ammonia Free
- Non-Abrasive - harmless to the bore surface
- Fast acting
- Covenient to use aerosol
- Quick and easy to apply
- Conditions bore for impact accuracy on first shot
- Seasons bore to resist fouling build up
- Maintains accuracy in new firearms
- Restores accuracy in old firearms
- Prolongs barrel life

ITEM # XT012
12 OZ.(aerosol with extension tube)

|| Order Form || Home Page || Product Index ||

FAQ page

The FAQ (Frequently Asked Questions) page contains questions about a company that people often ask and it contains the answers.

The FAQ page contains questions that customers often ask your contact people in person, on the phone, by fax or e-mail and it also contains the answers to these questions. If, for example, they want the answer to a question at midnight, they can visit your Web site. Also, for those visiting your Web site, they can often find the answer to a question without contacting your company.

Tutorial Page

Posting tutorials on your site increases your perception as an expert and helps get people to return to your site.

A good way to get visitors to return to your site is to post tutorials in your field of expertise. Some sites post a new tutorial every month. Regardless of what you sell or service, there are always some prospects who will be interested in keeping up with the latest information and in learning how to do something related to your field, even if you raise pot-bellied pigs.

Also, by posting tutorials, your visitors will perceive you as an expert and will be more likely to consider buying your products and services.

For example. Shooters Choice (www.shooters-choice.com), a Middlefield, Ohio provider of gun care products posts tutorials on how to properly clean firearms and on gun care..

Cleaning Procedure for Bolt Action Rifles and Revolvers

**BEFORE YOU START THE CLEANING PROCESS, MAKE SURE YOUR FIREARM IS UNLOADED AND YOU HAVE A WELL VENTILATED AREA, AWAY FROM CHILDREN AND/OR DISTRACTIONS, TO WORK IN!

1. Start by saturating a patch with **Shooter's Choice MC#7 Bore Cleaner and Conditioner.** Then push the patch through the bore to remove the loose powder residue, which will totally expose the copper and lead fouling. A one piece *coated* cleaning rod is recommended. A coated rod will protect the bore and lands in case the rod bows during cleaning. Remember, a $20.00 rod is cheaper to replace than a $300.00 barrel.

2. Wet a properly fitted Phosphorous Bronze Brush and push it back and forth through the bore 10 to 12 times. When cleaning a revolver, run a wet brush through each charge hole 11 to 12 times as well. Please Note: After brushing, flush the brush with **Shooter's Choice Quick Scrub Cleaner/ Degreaser** to remove the dirty residue and to neutralize the solvent from dissolving the bristles. We recommend using a straight bronze bristled brush with a brass core to prevent any damage to the lands.

Posting new tutorials periodically is one way of getting visitors to return to your site.

Testimonials page

Testimonials from satisfied customers should be scattered throughout the site. In this skeptical age we live in, prospects believe what third parties say more then what we say about ourselves.

If you can acquire enough testimonials, put one on every site page and/or put them all on special testimonial pages.

This book doesn't tell you how to create professional graphics... it SHOWS you how!
Reviewer: Jane Withers, desktop publisher
Especially helpful for generating ideas for layouts. No more staring at a blank screen trying to come up with an idea.

Best design book on the market-period!
Reviewer: Claes Sjogreen, book editor
Mr. Jacobs and Professor Studer excelled again in helping novices understand the basics of good graphics. Having a computer with a lot of design options doesn't automatically guarantee a good design. Jacobs and Studer clearly show the basics of graphic design with a host of good samples.

Links page

Every business site should exchange links with as many sites as possible and should have a links page for these two good reasons:

1. By exchanging links with other sites, you will increase the odds that you will receive more traffic to your site - traffic that will be referred to your site from the sites that you've exchanged links with.

2. As a general rule, you will rank higher in search engine listings because you will have higher "link popularity". Search engines incorporate link popularity in the algorithms they use to score and rank Web sites.

By exchanging links with other sites, you will increase your "link popularity" which will increase your search engine rankings.

Link exchange is also a method of getting more traffic to your site

LINKS AND ASSOCIATES

Online Resources
for All Types of Gun Enthusiasts

Listed below are just a few of the many interesting and informative gun resources currently available on the Internet. Please <u>let us know</u> if you know of an organization that would like to be listed on this page.

- **About.com's Site on Hunting and Shooting** Articles on hunting and shooting and reviews of hunting and shooting products by Russ Chastain, who runs About.com's site.

- **Advanced Cryogenics** Specializes in deep cryogenic tempering of metals to relieve stress and increase durability.

- **Air Guns HQ** Your online source for Air Guns and accessories!

- **Ameritype** Our Web site designer.

Order form page

If you're selling condominiums on the Avenue of the Americas in New York, you don't need an order form on your Web site. You need to be contacted. But if you're selling something like a book, a toy or something that is normally ordered from Web site forms, then, of course, you need an order form.

Items for sale can be placed in shopping carts for checkout after online shopping is completed or they can contain links that take the shopper directly to a secure order form.

Testing and maintaining your Web site

Testing your Web site

Before uploading your site to a server and taking it "live" for all to see on the Internet, it is important to do some testing. Before you upload, test to make sure that:
- There are no broken links.
- The download times are acceptable for the target audience.
- All content is legible and functional in targeted browsers.

Maintaining and updating your site

Web sites must be maintained and updated regularly. The Internet is littered with sites that have not been updated for a year or more. Don't let your site become one of these neglected sites.

Here are some common maintenance tasks performed on Web sites:
- Remove outdated links
- Add new links
- Update contact information (names, mailing addresses, e-mail addresses, phone and fax numbers)
- Update news
- Promote new products and services
- Update photos
- Re-submit the site to search engines

XML

XML is in the process of replacing HTML. XML, the eXtensible Markup Language, is a scripting environment in which the dependence on a browser's support for specific codes are eradicated. It will no longer be necessary for a Web page to work in older browser versions because XML takes the support of standards away from the browser and gives it to the Web designer..

If you're selling something that can be ordered directly from your site, by all means include an order form on your site. Then you can get orders and make money while you're sleeping.

Test your Web site before you upload it and make it live!

The Internet is littered with sites that haven't been maintained. Don't let your site become one of these neglected sites. Keep your site updated!

XML is in the process of replacing HTML.

XML is similar to HTML. Pages consist of tagged content. The tags are used to categorize the content. The tags do not format the content. CSS (Cascading Style Sheets) and eXtensible style sheets (XSL) format tags on the page.

The browser, independent of default standards, is forced to present the XML document, as defined by the developer. XML is the first language that can work on different operating systems, Internet devices, and products.

Further information is available at the World Wide Web Consortium's Group's Web site at www.w3.org/markup. The site contains comprehensive documentation on the new standard, including links to tools that convert HTML 4.0 pages to XHTML.

Chapter 19 Questions

1. What skills, in addition to programming, are necessary to create a profit-making Web site?

2. In a business Web site, content is king. Explain this statement.

3. With Web authoring programs available to generate HTML codes, why should Web designers have at least a basic knowledge of HTML.

4. What are the four types of Web authoring tools? Briefly describe each one.

5. If a home page doesn't motivate the visitor, the Web site is hors de combat. Explain this statement.

6. Are visitors to your Web site more interested in your logo, the story of your father who started with 12 cents and built a widget factory, or the benefits they will receive if they buy a widget? What should be highlighted on your home page?

7. Describe two things that could erect a barrier to a home page.

8. What is the objective of the "About Us" Page? What is the purpose of the Products and Services Page(s)?

9. Discuss the FAQ Page and the Tutorial Page(s). What are the advantages of having tutorials on your Web site?

10. Describe the Testimonial Page(s) and the Links Page(s). Explain the importance of testimonials. Explain link exchange and link popularity.

11. Discuss Web site order forms.

12. Discuss the testing, maintenance, and updating of Web sites.

13. What is XML?

CHAPTER
20

DESIGNING BUSINESS WEB SITES

When in doubt, gallop!

Proverb of
The French Foreign Legion

Chapter 20 Objectives

After studying this chapter, you should be able to:

1. Explain why making a Web site search engine-friendly is more important than "outdesigning" your competition with flamboyant graphics.

2. Define keywords and keyphrases and explain their importance and how to select them.

3. Explain how to incorporate keywords and keyphrases in your Web site to get high rankings.

4. Compare and explain the difference in the design window for 17" monitors and smaller monitors.

5. Explain why the first draft should be designed in Photoshop or another graphics program instead of an HTML page.

6. Describe why the design of the navigation bar is crucial to the success of your site.

7. Discuss the use of color on Web sites.

8. Discuss the selection of typefaces and the applicable rules of typography for Web sites.

9. Explain why a Web page without graphics is like a chocolate chip cookie without chocolate chips.

10. Name the three graphic file types used on the Web and briefly describe each one.

11. Describe how to acquire graphics for Web sites and how to modify graphics.

12. Discuss background images, thumbnails, tables. frames, and forms.

13. Describe design features to avoid when designing a Web site.

14. Discuss the addition of bells and whistles (special features) to Web sites.

Money is good. If you want to make some from your business Web site, you have to think outside the box

If you want to make money from your Web site, make it search engine-friendly. Don't try to "out-design" your competitors. Out-think" them!

Far too many businesses, particularly small businesses, will start their Web site design by trying to "out-design" their competition instead of trying to "out-think" their competition. They will concentrate on adding large logos, flash movies, and colorful graphics. If your goal is to win a design award, that's fine. However if your goal is to make money, then focusing on glitzy graphics is exactly the wrong way to start your Web site design.

Words and Pictures Publishing (www.wppublishing.com) was designed to be search-engine-friendly and, as shown below, is ranked number one in the AltaVista search engine for the search term "graphic design college textbook". It is also listed number one in the Yahoo and Google search engines.

No matter how "cool" your site may be, you won't make sales and profits if nobody visits. It all begins with traffic (visitors to your site). You can get traffic from various sources such as links from other sites and people typing your Web address but most traffic will come from people finding you from search engine inquiries.

Therefore don't start your design by concentrating on glitzy graphics. Think outside the box and start your design by making your site search engine-friendly. In other words, when people search for a company like yours, you want the search engine to rank you high in the list it produces, so the seeker can read the description of your company, click on your link, and visit your site.

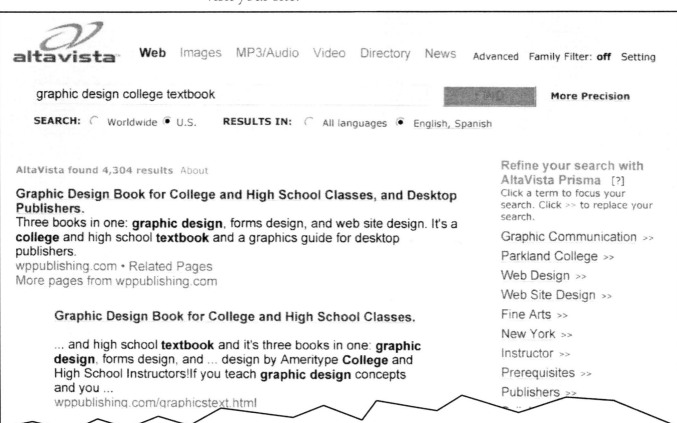

For some search terms, the search engine can produce more than a million Web site links. If you're not in at least the top 30 names, the chance of someone finding your company is slim indeed.

The first step in the quest to attaining a high ranking in search engine lists is to design your site to be search engine-friendly.

Making your site search engine-friendly

Making a web site search-engine friendly starts by selecting keywords. Keywords are words you think people will type into search engines to find a company like yours.

Although they are referred to as "keywords", many of them should really be keyphrases since they can consist of more than one word. In fact, in most cases, they should be more than one word since they need to be specific. For example, if someone was looking for a college textbook on graphic design, they would get a smaller and more selective web site list if they typed "graphic design college book" instead of "graphic design" in which case, the search engine would bring up a list of a bazillion sites.

In another example, some of the keywords for the web site of a gun care supplies company might be gun care, gun care products, gun solvents, gun cleaners, gun lubricants, firearms care, and firearms care products.

The one most important thing you can do to get traffic to your site from search engines is to choose the right keywords (keyphrases). If searchers type your keywords in a search engine and you've used your keywords properly in your HTML coding and your site pages, there is a good chance your web site will appear in the search engine list. If, however, you've chosen keywords that searchers don't think about typing into search engines when searching for your products or services, your site will not appear in the list.

Too many people use the name of their company as their main keyword. That's o.k. if your company has significant name recognition like Ford Motors, but if your company is like most companies on the Internet, you're not going to get traffic from search engines by using your company name as the main keyword. Searchers who are looking for Italian restaurants in Toledo are going to type something like "Italian Restaurants in Toledo" in the search engine. They're not going to type "Louie's Place " in the search engine if they've never heard of Louie's Place.

One way to help select keywords is to ask yourself, "Who is my target

The most important thing you can do to get traffic to your site is to select the right keywords and to use them effectively in your site design.

Keywords are words you think people will type into search engines to find a company like yours.

The Web is open source, which means you can see the keywords your competitors have placed in their site meta tags. Below are the keywords in the meta tags in the Shooters Choice Web site (www.shooters-choice.com).

audience?" What keywords do you think they will type into the search engines to get a company like yours? Put yourself in their shoes and write down the words you would type into a search engine to find a product or service like yours. You should also talk to people outside of your business and ask them what they would type into a search engine to find a company with your products or services.

A big advantage in helping to select keywords is that the Web is open source. Anyone can look at the coding of any Web site, therefore you can see the keywords used in your competitor's Web sites.

```
                        shooters-choice[1]
<!DOCTYPE HTML PUBLIC "-//W3C//DTD HTML 4.0 Transitional//EN">

<html>
<head>
        <title>Shooters Choice-- Guncare products</title>

<META NAME="description" CONTENT="Shooter's Choice provides gun care and firearms
maintenance products, including solvents, cleaners, lubricants, degreasers and rust
prevent solutions.
">
<META NAME="keywords" CONTENT="gun care products, gun cleaning supplies, gun cleaners,
gun lubricants, gun oil, handgun care products, handgun cleaning supplies, handgun
cleaners, handgun lubricants, shotgun cleaning supplies, shotgun cleaners, shotgun
lubricants, shotgun choke tube cleaners, rifle cleaning supplies, rifle cleaners, rifle
lubricants, rifle cleaning solvents, weapons cleaning supplies, weapons cleaners,
weapons cleaning solvents, weapons lubricants, firearms cleaning supplies, pistol
cleaning supplies, muzzleloader cleaning supplies, blackpowder cleaning supplies, gun
care, gun grease, gun cleaning solvents, gun maintenance, gun degreasers, rust
preventatives, copper solvents, lead fouling removers, gun carbon fouling removers, gun
powder fouling removers, shotgun choke tube cleaners, shotgun port cleaners,
muzzleloader bore seasoning">
<META NAME="distribution" CONTENT="global">
<META NAME="resource-type" CONTENT="document">


<script language="JavaScript">
<!--

// CACHE IMAGES FOR SLIDE SHOW

joesdadImage = new Image();
joesdadImage.src = "images/joesdad.jpg";

huntImage = new Image();
huntImage.src = "images/hunter.jpg";

skeetImage = new Image();
skeetImage.src = "images/skeet.jpg";

swatImage = new Image();
swatImage.src = "images/swat.jpg";


// BEGIN TIMER FUNCTIONS
```

Go to the web sites of companies that are similar to yours and appear high in the search engine list. You can find out what keyphrases these competitors use.

If the site is appearing in a Microsoft Internet Explorer browser, click on "View" (top line, third word from the left) and then click on "Source" in the window that appears. This will bring up the HTML code. Near the top, you will see meta tags, one of which will show you their keyphrases. For example, the keyphrases below are from the Words and Pictures Publishing web site, which features a graphic design college textbook that covers three topics: graphic design, forms design, and web site design.

One advantage in developing your keywords is that you can see your competitor's keywords.

<META NAME="keywords" CONTENT="graphic design book, graphic design college book, graphic design high school book, graphic design, graphics book, forms design, forms design book, graphic design information, graphic design training, web design book, web site design book, web design college book, web design high school book, graphic design for desktop publishers">

Don't use general keywords. You can start with a general keyword but then you need to add more words to it to make it more specific. If you're selling gun maintenance supplies, don't use "gun" as a keyword. It is too general. Make it more specific by using "gun care supplies". Searchers are learning that they need to enter phrases instead of one word into a search engine to more easily find what they are looking for.

Don't use general keywords. Keywords (actually keyphrases) need to be specific.

If your business only serves local customers, your key phrases should include this information. Instead of "graphic design service", use keyphrases like "graphic design service in Norwalk Ohio". If you own a German restaurant in Harrisburg, Pennsylvania, one of your keyphrases should be "German Restaurant in Harrisburg Pennsylvania".

As a final step in selecting your <u>vital</u> keyphrases, visit WordTracker at www.wordtracker.com to find out what words people actually are searching for. You can get a free trial and for a reasonable price, find out what people really search for, compared to what you think they search for.

Now that you have your list of keyphrases, it is time to use them. Embedding your keyphrases in the HTML codes and web site pages is critical because keyphrases are essential to getting high rankings in search engine lists. When people enter your keyphrases (especially specific keyphrases) in a search engine window, you site will have a good chance of appearing high in the list of sites resulting from the search. And, of course, the closer you are to the top of a search engine list, the better chance you have that someone will click and visit your site.

To better understand how your keyphrases should be used in your website, let's take a look at how search engines look at a web site. It doesn't look at the pages that your viewers see. Instead it looks at the HTML, the source code of a page.

Search engines don't look at pages that visitors see. They look at the HTML code, not the layout and not the images.

The search engines consider items toward the top of the page to be more important than items farther down the page. Therefore be sure to place your keywords at the top of the source code pages and also in the beginning of your body text.

Each search engine has a different ranking algorithm. This means that they each consider different things important in determining ranking. So what works for a particular search engine may not work for another one. And to make it even more "interesting", the algorithms change.

*Each search engine has a different ranking algorithm. What works for one search engine may not work for another one. However, there is general agreement that
It is important to place your keyphrases in the page title, the meta tags, and the first paragraph.*

No one knows exactly how search engines will rank your site on any particular day, but there is general agreement on the following advice. You need to have your keyphrases in three essential places, <u>the title, the keyphrases meta tags, and the first paragraph</u>. They should all contain the same keyphrases because that will increase your keyword density, which in turn will help improve your position on search engine lists.

The web site title

The <TITLE> tag appears in the <HEAD> section of the HTML page. The web site title should be written for the search engine, not for people. The title tag should contain all of the important key words. "Caroline's Kids" is not a good web site title. The title for Caroline's Kids, a pet rescue organization, was written for the <u>search engine</u> and is shown below.

Try to place all the important keywords in the title.

<TITLE>No kill pet sanctuary in Cleveland, Ohio providing cat rescue and a haven for abused and unwanted animals</TITLE>

The web site description

In the meta tag section of the HTML page, you need to enter a description of the web site. On search engines, page titles and site descriptions are what appear to designate web sites on the list that results from a search.. The title and the description are what people read to decide whether to click and go to your site. The description should be written for people, not for search engines. It should not be a list of keyphrases. The description should give a summary of what is on the site. A sample of a site description is shown below:

<meta name="description" content="A no kill sanctuary in Cleveland, Ohio for old, unwanted and abused animals. Also offers spay-neuter programs, pet foster homes, pet adoptions and pet memorials.">

Shown below is a sample showing how the title and description appear in the list resulting from a search engine search.

<u>No kill pet sanctuary in Cleveland, Ohio providing cat rescue, and a haven for abused and unwanted animals</u>
A no kill sanctuary in Cleveland, Ohio for old, unwanted and abused animals. Also offers spay-neuter programs, pet foster homes, pet adoptions and pet memorials

Enter your keyphrases in the meta keyword tag, most important ones first.

Keyphrases in meta tags

Enter your keyphrases in the meta keyword tag, most important ones first, Separate them with a comma. Don't use the same word too many times since some search engines may penalize you for this.

A sample of keyphrases in a meta keyword tag is shown below:

<meta name="keywords" content="pet sanctuaries, pet sanctuaries in cleveland, no kill animal sanctuaries, animal adoption, animal adoption in cleveland, animal foster homes, animal foster homes in cleveland, pet rescue, pet rescue in cleveland, abused animal rescue, cat rescue, dog rescue, homeless animals, homeless animals in cleveland, homeless cats, homeless cats in cleveland, homeless dogs, unwanted dogs, unwanted cats, spay neuter, animal euthanasia, animal euthanasia in cleveland, pet memorials, animal protection in cleveland">
<meta name="distribution" content="global">

Different pages in your web site can have different page titles, different page descriptions, and different keyphrases. They don't all have to be like the ones on the home page.

The first paragraph on the page

The first paragraph is important. It needs to have the important keyphrases in it and it needs to be placed as close as possible to the opening <BODY> tag.

The first paragraph on the page is important. It needs to be written for people but it also needs to have the important keyphrases in it (for the search engine). Also, place the first paragraph as close to the opening <BODY> tag as possible. Try not to put graphics or other HTML code between the <BODY> tag and the first paragraph, insofar as possible. You also need to sprinkle your keywords in the other paragraphs of text on the home page and on the other pages.

Repeat keyphrases, but don't overdo it

You need to repeat your keyphrases in the HTML code and the site pages because this increases the search engine score that determines your ranking in the list that results from a search. However, if you repeat keyphrases too many times, many search engines will conclude that you are creating spam pages to get a high ranking and will penalize you.

Basic Layout for Business Web Sites

Save web site production time by designing your first draft in Photoshop or another graphics program.

As time goes by, more and more people are using 17" monitors. Therefore the trend is to design for a 17" monitor which would be a browser window 800 pixels wide by 600 pixels deep. However, many people are still using 13" and 15" monitors with a default resolution of 640 pixels wide by 480 pixels deep for the browser window.

If you think your target audience would likely have 17" monitors, you would consider making your browser window 800x600. People with smaller monitors would have more difficulty seeing your whole page and would probably have to scroll. Vertical scrolling is acceptable to at least some people. Horizontal scrolling irritates most people.

If you want to make sure that everyone, including people with 13" and 15" monitors can see your whole page easily, you should design a 640x480 pixel window. The navigation bar and the most important information should be placed in the top 480 pixels because many people do not like to scroll. There are still many people who use 13" and 15" monitors.

Save production time by designing your first draft in Photoshop or another illustrator program

Instead of designing the first draft of your Web site as an HTML page, save coding time and effort by creating the design in Photoshop or other illustrator program. By using this method, you can concentrate on the appearance of the site instead of programming codes. Set the width and height at the pixel measures you've decided to use for your site. Use a resolution of 72 dpi and the color mode RBG. Use the result as a proof. After making any needed adjustments and getting approval of the design, you can create the HTML site

If your site is too crowded and has too much text, no one will read it

People are busy. Don't place a lot of copy on a Web site page. The only one who will read it all is your mother.

People are busy and skim over text. If you place a lot of copy on a Web page, the only one that will read it all will be your mother. Most sites are too crowded. If you have a lot of necessary information, break it up into palatable chunks and put some of it on separate pages. If you have information of marginal value, toss in the dumpster.

In a business Web site, content is king and design is queen.

Superior design is not a substitute for second-rate content but it can lend a hand. The thoughtful use of design layout, colors, images, and typography can make visitors feel comfortable with the site. Always remember that you are designing the site for your target audience, not for yourself.

The impression your site projects must match the expectations of your target audience. A Web site for an accounting firm would have to project a different image than a tractor sales company. This means using different colors, different layouts, different images, and different typefaces.

Also, the overall image must be consistent for every page in a site. Each page must look like it belongs to the same site. Visitors do not like to click on a link in a site and bring up a page that doesn't look like it belongs to the same site... a page with a different layout, different colors, and different typefaces.

When determining the layout format, remember that human visual response is the same for Web pages as it is for printed pages

Layout refers to the placement of the design elements on the page. One of the biggest mistakes made by novice designers is to set lines of small type across the entire width of a page. The eye has difficulty following small type along a very wide line. Look at a newspaper and you will see type set in columns, each column containing short lines of type.

 Most Web sites, particularly those containing considerable text, should be formatted using two or more columns instead of one wide column. Typesetters learn early that "the smaller the type, the shorter the line length should be.

You will get the best readability and the best response from your visitors if you follow the time-tested rules of professional typography. Current experimental typesetting and design fads shouldn't send you off like a tumbleweed blowing in the wind. Stick with what works.

As you would do with a printed page, put some salt in the soup. Add some color photos or logos or illustrations or colored type to spice up the dull lines of text. But don't overdo it. Too much salt ruins the soup and too many graphics ruin the Web page.

Content is king!

Pages in the same Web site must have a consistent appearance. Each page must look like it belongs to the same site.

You will get the best readability if you follow the time-tested rules of typography. Don't let experimental typesetting send you off like a tumbleweed blowing in the wind.

The navigation bar is crucial to the success of your site

The navigation bar, a set of links, must allow visitors to easily navigate from one page to another, without getting lost in your site. In a small site, the home page can have a set of navigation links that will bring up every page in the site. In a large site, the home page can have links that lead to sub-home pages that have links to other pages.

A navigation bar can be as simple as text links in a row or column. For an improved appearance, the navigation links can be images. These images can be created or imported from other image sources. Navigation bars are usually located horizontally across the top of the Web site or vertically down the left side of the site.

The navigation bar is a critical component of your Web site. Your visitors need to be able to easily access the pages of your site without getting lost.

About Us   How Caroline's Kids Works   Memorials   Adoptions   Merchandise   Newsletter

Content advice

The most important element in the site content is customer-benefit copy. Tell the visitor what the product or service will do for them Don't just describe the product.

- Write customer-benefit copy. Tell the visitor what your product or service will do for them. Don't just describe the features of your product.
- Provide all the information necessary for the visitor to make a buying decision.
- Give a guarantee and also try to place a testimonial from a satisfied customer on every page
- Put complete contact information, including an e-mail link, on every page.
- Don't fill up the top half of the pages with your logo.

Using color on Web sites

Color is what visitors first notice about your site. Color is important in determining what kind of impression your site will make on visitors.

Color is created on a monitor by combining different amounts of the three primary colors of light: red, green, and blue (RGB) and projecting them on a tiny piece of the screen called a pixel. Newer computers can display millions of colors so if you think your target audience uses new computers, you can select the exact colors that you want to appear on your site.

However, if you also want to be able to reach prospects with older computers and there are a myriad of them, you will need to stick with the 256 Web-safe colors. These are colors that display solid colors on any computer monitor, including older computer monitors. On older computers, if you specify a color other than the 256 Web-safe colors, it will result in *dithering,* which results in patterns in the color, an outcome of trying to give the appearance of the specified non Web-safe color.

So using the 256 Web-safe colors are the only way to ensure that your Web site colors look solid instead of snowy or patterned on older monitors. Web-authoring programs like DreamWeaver have a Web-safe color selector that enables you to pick safe colors.

There is another issue with colors. Colors look different on different monitors. If you want proof of this, take a look at a row of TV sets in an appliance store. To further complicate the issue, colors appear darker on Windows monitors and lighter on Macs. This is another reason why you need to view your site pages on computers on different platforms and with different browsers. You may not be able to make it look good in all platforms and browsers but you can try to make adjustments to make it look at least acceptable in all situations.

Although there are millions of colors available on newer monitors and 256 colors on older monitors, attractive and successful Web sites can be created with three colors, white, black, and red. The earliest printers understood these facts of human visual response and that the three best design colors are white, black, and red. White is the best background color. Black offers the most contrast to white and is therefore the best color for text and red is the best color to add a highlight to a page. Red headlines on publications sell twice as much as any other color.

Selecting typefaces and the artful use of type

The principles of typography (the artful use of type that has produced quality print design for centuries) are also valid for the design of Web

Color is what visitors first notice about your site.

To reach all visitors including those with older computers, you need to stick with the 256 Web-safe colors.

Many attractive and successful Web sites have been created with three colors: white for the background, black for the text, and red for the headlines.

More than 90% of all installations use the Internet Explorer browser and those who have it installed can see the typefaces shown on the right.

sites. Human visual response is the same whether one is looking at the Gutenberg Bible printed in the mid-fifteenth century or a Web page in the 21st century.

Most computers use the Internet Explorer browser, which enables them to see Web pages.. Internet Explorer is by far the dominant browser (more than 90% of all installations) and those who have it installed can see the following typefaces on Web pages.

- Times New Roman
- Arial
- **Arial Black**
- Times
- Comic Sans
- Courier and Courier New
- Georgia
- Helvetica
- Trebuchet
- Verdana

Times New Roman and Arial are popular typeface choices for live Web text.

Therefore, you can specify these typefaces when you are designing a Web site: These typefaces can be used to create live Web text. Times new Roman and Arial are popular typeface choices for live Web text. To place typefaces other than those mentioned on a Web site, you can use any typeface but you need to convert it to an image before you place it on the site.

After selecting typefaces and before you employ them on a page, you need to heed these time-honored rules of typography:

- Use only one or two typefaces on a page. Just because typefaces are easily accessible doesn't mean your Web site should look like a ransom note.
- Don't set text (paragraphs of type) in all caps. It's much harder to read.
- Don't set text in one column that extends across the entire width of the page. Set text in two or more columns.
- Don't letterspace (spread out) lower case letters. Just because some designers think it's cool doesn't mean it's right.

A Web page without graphics is like a chocolate chip cookie without chocolate chips

On business Web sites, words are the most important elements but graphics are needed to add flavor to the page.

On business Web sites, words are the most important elements but sites are more engaging if they contain some graphics. A Web page that offers nothing but text isn't going to have much visual appeal.

Before you explore sources for images and how to use images, it's best to understand the types of graphic files used on Web sites. All Web graphics have a resolution of 72 pixels per inch (ppi). The three graphic file types used on the Web are:

1. GIF (Graphics Interchange Format)
2. JPEG (Joint Photographic Experts Group)
3. PNG (Portable Network Graphics)

GIF, JPEG, and PNG are the three types of graphic files used on the Web.

Since GIF files are limited to a 256 color palette, the GIF format is best for illustrations, images with flat colors like artwork, navigation bars and logos All of the pixels in a GIF image are preserved when it is saved, thereby creating a fairly large file. GIF is a standard file and is supported by every graphics program. It's also an easy way to add animation to a site.

There are some legal issues with GIF files since they use a compression algorithm owned by Unisys corporation. Some graphics programs that create GIF files are licensed and some are not. Many, if not most designers are not aware of, or are not concerned with the legal issues which are not yet resolved.

GIF files are used for illustrations and JPEG files are used for photographs.

A JPEG file, also called JPG, is usually used for placing photographs on Web sites. JPEG images don't have the same color restrictions as GIF's and are best for continuous tone images (photos). Always try to get original photos to scan for placement on Web sites. If you try to scan photos that have been printed, you will be scanning halftone dots. This will usually result in a moiré pattern (a plaid pattern) on the photo.

The PNG format was designed to replace GIF images and to be free of the licensing problem. PNG files are competitive with GIF files, but can not be used for animation. A newer version, called MNG (Multiple Network Graphics) is in development. It will have the capability of creating animations.

Getting graphic images to put on your Web site

There are many places where you can purchase images and also many places where you can get free images. There is a glut of both free clip art and clip art for sale, available from the Web and from CD's in computer and retail stores. You don't need to be a rocket scientist to understand that the $19.98 CD's containing 250,000 images aren't going to have many high quality images that would be just what you are looking for on your Web site.

There are many sources for free clip art images and also many sources for clip art that can be purchased. You can search for these sources in search engines.

If you want very high quality professional clip art and clip photos the Web addresses of two of the very best sources are www.creatas.com and www.dgusa.com.

There is an overabundance of Web sites offering clip art for sale and free clip art. Most computer stores and retail stores that sell computers and related products sell clip art and clip photos. A search engine search on clip art will produce a flood of sites offering clip art and stock photographs for download or CD's that can be purchased.

Clip Art and Clip Photos

Creating and modifying images

Of course, you can also create original images, with a graphics program or by drawing and scanning. Photos can be taken with a digital camera or a film camera for processing and uploading to a Web page.

Original images can be created using programs like Adobe Photoshop and Macromedia Freehand.

Programs such as Adobe Photoshop, Adobe Illustrator, Macromedia Freehand, Macromedia Fireworks, Corel Painter, and Paint Shop Pro are used to create images and to modify and enhance images for use on Web pages. Adobe Photoshop has long been the industry standard. Macromedia Fireworks was designed to make graphics for Web pages and to work with Macromedia DreamWeaver , considered by many professional designers to be the premier Web-authoring program.

These programs can also be used to modify an image. An image sometimes needs modification to achieve the exact look you want on your site. Modifications can include:
* Making the image darker or lighter.
* Making it larger or smaller.
* Flipping (creating a mirror image).
* Cropping (deleting unwanted parts).
* Rotating (Turning at an angle).

In addition there are programs available that enable you to create three dimensional-appearing people and objects. These programs include iSpace from Caligari, Bryce from Corel, and Poser from Creative Labs.

Adding fancy type to a Web page by making it a graphic

If you want to use an unusual typeface that wouldn't normally show up on a visitor's screen, you would need to convert it to an image.

Ariel and Times, the two typefaces generally used on Web pages, are easy to read and good choices for text, but if used exclusively, can produce a lackluster page. If you wanted to add some zing to the page by adding some flashy type that would not normally show up on most visitor's screens, you would need to create the words set in the flashy type as an image. By doing this, all viewers would see the text in the flashy type you set it in because it is no longer text, it is a *picture*.

Adding background images to Web sites

Adding background images to a Web page can add significantly to the appearance of the page, but it must be done the same way that two porcupines hug each other... *very carefully.*

Avoid busy and visually strong backgrounds that distract the viewer from the more important text in the foreground.

Adding backgrounds carefully means avoiding backgrounds that are so complex or busy that they distract the viewer from the text and images in the foreground. Some designers are so captivated with the background that they ignore the fact that it is difficult or even impossible to read the overlying text. Adding backgrounds correctly also means using a color and value that contrasts with the color and value of the foreground. There must be *contrast* between the foreground and the background.

Don't emulate the contrast-challenged people who use yellow type on a white background or red type on a purple background. It's cool for the ladies in the Red Hat Society (www.redhatsociety.com) to wear a red hat and a purple dress, but red on purple doesn't work on a Web page.

Using thumbnail images to speed up downloads

Web sites containing many images, like a hardware catalog or an art gallery, would normally take too long to download. The viewer doesn't have a lot of patience and doesn't want to make a salami sandwich and write down the names of the 50 states while waiting for all the large images to appear. The solution is to create *thumbnails*, small versions of the large images. They will download much faster and will give the viewers the choice of clicking only on the thumbnails they are interested in and then waiting for the large images they selected to appear.

Using tables on Web sites

A table in a Web page is somewhat similar to a column on a printed page. Tables can be used to display information in tabular form and they can also display images.

Tables displaying nothing but rows of numbers are boring and dreary, stopping just short of causing the reader to black out. Well, it's not quite that mind-numbing, but you know what I mean.

Tables displaying boring rows of numbers can be spiced up by using background colors and lively typefaces.

However tables displaying rows of numbers can receive an energetic makeover through the use of colored backgrounds and vibrant typefaces.

Using frames on Web sites

A frame is used to create an area on a Web page that remains constant when you travel from page to page and everything else on the pages are changing. Frames keep an essential page element, often the navigation bar, in front of the visitor at all times. The navigation bar is usually located across the top of the page or it runs vertically down the left side.

Frames can also be used for elements other than navigation bars, such as a logo that you want to keep in the same location on all pages. Frames are separate Web pages on the screen simultaneously, thus appearing to be one Web page. Frames are only necessary if you have a navigation bar or other elements that needs to be locked in place from page to page.

Using forms on Web sites

In addition to conveying sales orders, Web site forms are used to gather information from visitors.

Web site forms are used to receive sales orders and also to gather information from visitors. Forms can be designed to provide all kinds of information ranging from yes/no answers to lengthy written text.

After the visitor fills in and submits the form, it is received and the data is processed by a CGI program (Common Gateway Interface). The CGI program converts the information from the form into external programs for further processing. Web hosting services often provide CGI programs free or for a nominal fee to their clients. A search on the Web will provide many sources for acquiring CGI programs.

Web-authoring programs generally assist with the creation of forms by providing form building blocks such as radio buttons, checkboxes, and scrolling text fields.

The data on forms is processed by a CGI (Common Gateway Interface) program.

At the right is the order form on the Shooter's Choice Web site (www.shooters-choice.com).

PRODUCT ORDER FORM

To protect your privacy, Shooter's Choice's web servers encrypt all transactions using this form. However, if you would prefer not to enter your credit-card number into an online form, please send us e-mail or give us a call at **440-834-8888** between 10 a.m. and 4 p.m. US Eastern Time. **Note: The minimum charge** for credit card purchases is $35.00. Personal checks or money orders will be accepted for orders totaling less than $35.00.

ORDER INFORMATION

Qty	Product	Code	Size	Price	Totals
0	Bore Cleaner	MC702	2 oz.	$5.60	$0.00
0	Bore Cleaner	MC704	4 oz.	$8.38	$0.00
0	Bore Cleaner	MC716	16 oz.	$27.91	$0.00
0	Bore Cleaner	MC7128	1 gal.	$159.96	$0.00
0	High Tech Grease	G10CC	10 cc.	$5.09	$0.00
0	FP-10 Lub. Elite	FPL04	4 oz.	$7.21	$0.00
0	FP-10 Lub. Elite	FPL128	1 gal.	$136.15	$0.00
0	Rust Prevent	RP006	6 oz.	$6.13	$0.00
0	Quick Scrub III	DG318	18 oz.	$8.74	$0.00
0	Black Powder	BPS04	4 oz.	$8.91	$0.00
0	Copper Remover	CRS08	8 oz.	$9.24	$0.00
0	Lead Remover	LR004	4 oz.	$8.91	$0.00
0	Shotgun and Choke Tube Cleaner	SG012	12 oz.	$10.40	$0.00
0	Xtreme Clean Bore and Action Cleaner	XT012	12 oz.	$19.99	$0.00

Web Design "No-No's"

Every day, armies of artistically-challenged designers upload unsightly and indecipherable sites to the World Wide Web. The best of these are merely difficult to read and understand. The worst of these can burst blood vessels in your eyes.

Don't add to these eyesores. Avoid the following "No-No's":

Don't use overpowering backgrounds

Web pages are difficult to read if there is little contrast between the foreground and the background, such as dark blue on a black background.

Loud, busy backgrounds are one of the biggest problems caused by inexperienced designers. Common sense tells you that text is difficult to read if there is little contrast with the background or if the background is busy or if it is so bright it makes your eyes water. Your visitor is not going to be impressed by a flaming phosphorescent background. If you must use a colored background, be merciful and use light colors that will contrast with the darker text, making the text easier to read. Make sure your background doesn't detract from the most important source of information on the page, the content (text).

Web pages are also difficult to read if the background is loud and busy, or if it has big orange flowers.

An amazing number of "designers" think it's "cool" to use dark blue, dark purple, or dark red type on a black background. They don't seem to understand that the viewer must struggle to try and read this "cool" type.

You don't have to be a rocket scientist to understand that for easy reading, you need contrast between the foreground and the background. You can't read black type on a black background. It's there but you can't read it because there's no contrast. It's also amazing how many people use yellow type on a white background, which of course is difficult to read because there is little contrast between the type and the background.

The best contrast is black on a white background.

The best contrast is black type on a white background. Not dynamic enough for you? Well then, use red type for some headlines and add some color photos or illustrations. If you insist on using a colored, screened or textured background, at least make sure the foreground is in a contrasting color.

Don't use large, slow graphics that will take a long time to download

Visitors don't have a lot of patience. They are busy and don't want to work crossword puzzles while your site is downloading.

Don't run paragraphs of small type across the whole width of the page.

Design your pages using two or more columns. Don't set lines of type that go across the entire width of the page.

Design your pages using two or more columns unless you have a good reason not to do so. The human eye finds it difficult to follow type across long lines of type. Just think about how difficult it would be to read type that was set in one very wide column in a newspaper. A newspaper is set in many columns of type on the page. Newsletters and other documents are easier to read when they are set in two or more columns. The same rationale extends to Web sites.

Don't use music unless you have a compelling reason to do so.

If you must add music to your site, give the visitor the choice of listening to it or not.

Most people don't want to be distracted by music, especially your choice of music. It isn't necessarily their choice of music. And just maybe they don't want music blaring out of the loudspeakers. If you need to satisfy a compulsion to add music to your site, at least give the visitor the choice of listening to it or not.

Also, only use music if it is relevant. Music on a web site for a rock group is relevant. On the other hand, visitors to a pet rescue site don't want to be blasted away by the theme song from Hawaii 50.

Don't use blinking text

Limit the use of blinking text, scrolling marquees, image maps, and "under construction" signs.

HTML tags allow you to create blinking text. Although some designers think blinking text is cool, it irritates most visitors. If you need to highlight text, there are better ways such as using a larger type size, bold type, reverse type (white type on a colored dark bar) or colored type.

Limit the use of scrolling marquees

Scrolling marquees are eye-catching but not so easy to read. It may be entertaining for some, but all it does is force people to read bits of information at speeds that may be too fast or too slow for them.

Don't go overboard on image maps

These are images containing multiple links that take you to other pages in the web site. Take care not to design a site that is primarily made up of one big image map. It will take a long time to download, and people that download without images will not be able to navigate your site. It's always a good idea to provide alternate links under the image map.

Keep construction signs to a limit

Construction signs on web pages are common and often irritating to visitors. Some of them remain in place for months or even years. If you actually are working on a page, you can put up an "under construction" notice for a short period of time. In the notice, tell the visitors when it will be done. And when it is done, get rid of the notice!

Adding bells and whistles to Web sites

Although they can be distracting if not used with good judgment, there are a number of "bells and whistles" that can be added to Web sites. They include flash (a movie created in Macromedia's Flash or Adobe's Livemotion software), sound, animation, rollovers, calculators, and games.

Adding bells and whistles (flash, animation, sound, etc.) can make a Web site dynamic, if used with good judgment.

The person who places flash (a movie) on the page often likes it better than the person who is viewing it. Well-done flash can be entertaining and useful, especially if the subject is related to the site's products and services, but if the viewer is trying to get information or place an order, flash can be a barrier to the home page.

Sound can be added to Web sites. It is important to remember, however, that you need to give your visitors a way to turn it off. Not everyone wants to listen to the kind of music you selected and even if they do like it, they might get tired of hearing it over and over.

Animation , with color and movement, can be used to catch attention. However, it's easy to fall in love with animation and use it when it does not add anything to the site and when it detracts the viewer from the important elements in the site. It's like heaping so much ketchup on the hamburger that you lose the taste of the hamburger.

Javascript is a programming language that enables you to do things on Web sites that you can't do with HTML. Due to the similarity in names, Javascript is often confused with a programming language called Java, and also with Java applets which are a form of Java. Javascript and Java are not related. Javascript isn't Java and it isn't HTML. However it was created to work with HTML so designers could create programs that alter the value of HTML elements.

Probably the most common thing done with Javascript is a rollover, where a graphic changes color or turns into another image when the mouse rolls over it. Javascript can also produce features like pop-up windows and drop-down menus. Javascript codes can be found in the major Web-authoring programs and are also available from many online sites.

Using cascading style sheets (CSS)

CSS enables the designer to set standards for elements like background colors, margins, typefaces, type colors, type sizes, and type weights, so that these items will look alike on all site pages.

CSS enables the designer to set standards so certain elements will look alike on all pages of a Web site.

The World Wide Web Consortium has developed two different specifications, CSS1 and CSS2, both of which are simultaneously in effect. There is an issue, however since the major browsers have not implemented all of the CSS features and the various implementations are not consistent.

Some Web-authoring programs like Macromedia DreamWeaver and Adobe Golive can help in creating cascading style sheets.

WEB SOFTWARE RESOURCES

Macromedia Flash
Web graphics creation
Macromedia.com/software/flash

Cute FTP
File transfer program for Windows
www.cuteftp.com

Korax Colourdrop4
Windows color picker
Korax.net/software/cdrop4

Caligari iSpace
Program for creating 3D Web sites
www.caligari.com

Chapter 20 Questions

1. Why is making a Web site search engine-friendly more important than "outdesigning" your competition with flamboyant graphics?

2. Define keywords and keyphrases and explain their importance.

3. Describe the process involved in selecting keywords.

4. Explain why the first draft should be designed in Photoshop or another graphics program instead of an HTML page.

5. Describe why the design of the navigation bar is crucial to the success of a Web site?

6. Discuss the impact of using color on web sites.

7. Why is a Web page without graphics like a chocolate chip cookie without chocolate chips?

8. What three graphics file types are used on the Web? Briefly describe each one.

9. Describe how to acquire graphics for Web sites and discuss modifying graphics.

10. Explain how you can add to a Web page, a typeface that couldn't be added to a site as text.

11. Discuss the potential hazards of adding backgrounds to Web sites.

12. What is the name of the device used on a Web page that remains constant when you travel from page to page?

13. Discuss the potential problems with the use of music, scrolling marquees, and "under construction" signs.

CHAPTER
21

TURNING YOUR WEB SITE INTO A CASH COW

*Money isn't everything but it ranks
right up there with oxygen.*

– Rita Davenport

Chapter 21 Objectives

After studying this chapter, you should be able to:

1. Describe the big advantage of selling on the Web compared to other ways of selling products and services.

2. Explain why security is fundamental to Web sales.

3. Discuss methods of getting paid for Web sales.

4. Discuss a returns policy and a privacy policy.

5. Explain why you need to promote your site to get traffic and why both offline promotion and online promotion are necessary.

6. Describe how to promote a Web site *offline* to encourage people to visit.

7. List suggestions for promoting your Web site *online*.

8. Discuss the importance and functions of search engines.

9. Describe how to make a Web site people-friendly.

10. Explain how to submit your Web site to search engines.

What you need to know about making money from Web site sales

The big advantage of selling on the Web is that you will vastly increase the number of potential customers.

Before you waste time and money creating a business Web site, make sure people will want to buy your product or service.

The advantage of selling on the Web

E-businesses are selling products and services to the same types of customers they were selling to before they had a Web site. They are just using a new channel, the World Wide Web. The big advantage of selling on the Web, however, is that you will immeasurably increase the number of your potential customers.

Make sure what you're trying to sell is something that can be sold on a web site

Before you waste a lot of time and money, make sure you have something people will want and that has something unique or different about it. If everyone else is trying to sell the same thing, it will be difficult to get a high listing on search engines and the stiff competition will keep your prices down. There's always someone who will sell it cheaper than you will.

If you sell mattresses, it won't be easy getting into high positions on search engine listings. If you manufacture custom made odd size and odd shaped mattresses for boats and recreation vehicles like Your Design Mattress Factory (www.yourdesignmattressfactory.com), it will be easier to get high search engine listings leading to more traffic and increasing chances for more sales.

Security is fundamental to Web sales

Without documentation on your Web site that you have a secure server, visitors are reluctant to buy. A secure server sends and receives encrypted data. Make sure you use a provider that offers secure servers, and be sure to declare that you have a secure server on your Web site, particularly on your order form.

Getting paid for Web site sales

Credit cards are the most common way of purchasing on the Web. Purchasing by sending credit card numbers is widely accepted now since order forms are linked to secure servers that send and receive encrypted data. For those who do not want to enter credit card numbers in a Web site, alternatives are to print out the order form and mail it with a check or to order by telephone.

Other ways of purchasing from a Web site include (1) using a debit card and (2) printing a paper draft which can be deposited to your account. If the buyer gives you the bank identification and the account number by phone or other communication, you can use software such as Smart-Checker to print a paper draft that is acceptable to a bank. Smart-Checker's Web address is www.web-store.net/checker.

Returns Policy

Before you upload your site to the Web and start selling your products or services, you should have a written returns policy and a written privacy policy in place.

You will need to have a plan to handle returns. You need to have a policy in writing to handle returns, exchanges, and refunds. The policy needs to state under what conditions you will offer credits, exchanges, and refunds. It also needs to state a time limit and whether you will pay shipping charges for returns. Some e-businesses do and some don't. Also the returns policy should state whether the customer must contact you for authorization before returning items. Most companies require the customers to get authorization before sending returned items. This returns policy should be in place before you start selling.

Privacy Policy

If you're going to ask visitors to enter information on an order form or any other form, or for information in any other way, you should have a privacy policy and you should post it on your Web site so the visitor will feel that the information will not be forwarded by you.

To get help in creating a privacy policy, visit the Direct Marketing Association's Privacy Policy Generator, which can be found at http://the-dma.org/privacy/privacypolicygenerator.shtml.

Promoting your Web site

"If you build it, they will come" doesn't apply to web sites

"If you build it, they will come" doesn't apply to Web sites. You have to vigorously promote your site to get traffic.

If you're Kevin Costner in the movie *Field of Dreams*, you can "build it and they will come" but if you've built a web site, they won't automatically come. Just because you've designed and uploaded a site to the web and just because there are millions of people with Internet access doesn't mean they're going to accidentally stumble across your site. If you think you can sit on the couch, eat chips and dip and have money roll in, you're in for a shock. You have to work to get traffic. It's a lot easier to make a web site than to make money from a web site. *The prayer of the chickenhawk does not get him the chicken.*

Use both offline and online web site promotion

If you face the reality that your web site is one of many millions of sites on the web, you will understand that you must use every arrow in your quiver to get traffic to your site. Many people think search engine and other online promotions are the only way to get traffic to your site.

Actually the best web traffic-generating strategy is to use a combination of offline promotion and online promotion. Offline promotion refers to <u>traditional</u> advertising and promotion.

OFFLINE traffic-generating promotion

Not everyone who visits your web site will access it from a search engine. They will have discovered your web address from a sales brochure, a business card, another printed document, a sign, or other offline source. The people who visit your site after getting your web address from one of these offline sources are likely to be in your target audience. They've taking the extra step of accessing your web site because they're interested in what they've read about your company's products and services.

Offline promotion is any marketing exposure that does not occur on the Internet. Many webmasters overlook the fact that there is an offline world out there, including radio, television, newspapers, magazines, sales brochures, mail, and billboards. If you need proof that offline marketing is important, consider how many prominent companies like AOL and Microsoft run TV commercials and use print ads, and direct mail to generate online traffic.

Your web site address (URL) is as important as your street address and your phone number. Place your URL on everything related to your business, If your company name is on it (everything from business cards to baseball caps to company vehicles), make sure your web address is also on it <u>and give them a reason to visit your web site</u> (a 25% discount coupon , a free report, buy one widget, get one free, a free newsletter, or other giveaway.

There are many ways to promote your site offline:

Include your web address in every e-mail that your company sends out

Develop an e-mail signature containing your name, title, company name and other contact information and include your web address. Then insert it at the bottom of every e-mail that you send and that all staff members send.

Add your web address to all stationery and literature

Add your web address to letterheads, envelopes, business cards, sales literature, fax cover sheets, invoices, forms, and newsletters

Include your web address in your voice mail message

Make sure your web site contains answers to the most frequently asked telephone questions. In your voice mail message, refer callers to your web site.

People who visit your site after getting your Web address from an offline source are likely to be in your target audience.

Put your Web address on everything from business cards to baseball caps to company vehicles.

Include your Web address in the signature of every e-mail that you send.

Marvin Jacobs
President
Words and Pictures
216-524-9664
Fax: 216-524-7714
www.wppublishing.com
amertype@apk.net

Place your web address on signs and on company vehicles

Display your web address prominently on external and internal signs and on company cars and trucks. Don't forget bumper stickers.

Give away promotional items with your web address on them

People like to get freebies. Let them advertise for you by giving away promotional items like baseballs caps, T-shirts, coffee cups, golf balls and tees, pens, letter openers, and mouse pads. Make sure your web address is on all promotional items.

Include your web address in direct mail packages

Direct mail has been successfully used to reach targeted prospects and drive them to the organization web site where the full sales story is described.

Train your telephone responders to refer inquirers to your web site

Make sure all staff members who answer the phone know your web address and know what's available on your web site, so they can refer callers to your site.

Announce your web site

Send a letter or flyer to former customers, current customers, prospects, suppliers, family, and friends. You never know who will visit your site and buy something and you never know who will refer someone who will buy something.

Send press releases to newspapers and magazines

Announce the launching of your site and send a news release anytime there is a significant change to your web site. Local suburban newspapers are always looking for news items.

Invite readers to visit your web site in every issue of your printed newsletter

If you publish a printed newsletter, point out a resource on your site and make announcements about revisions to your site in every issue of your newsletter.

Include your web address in radio and TV commercials

If you do advertise on radio or TV, don't forget to include your web address.

Submit articles to newspapers, magazines, and newsletters

Include your web address on packaging labels and tapes

Put your URL (Web address) EVERYWHERE and get even more traffic by giving a reason why they should visit your site (Visit our site and get a free widget for every widget you buy).

Let other people advertise your Web site for you. Give away promotional items like baseball caps, T-shirts, and mouse pads, all of course adorned with your URL and the reason to visit your site.

ONLINE traffic-generating promotion

Link Exchange

Link exchange is one of the best ways to increase traffic to your site. To exchange links, two web site owners agree to provide a link to each other's site. This system not only increases traffic to your site but it increases your "link popularity" score which, in turn, improves your ranking on search engine result lists.

At the right is a portion of the links page on the Web site of Caroline's Kids Pet Rescue (www.carolines-kids.org)

Animal Telepathic Communicator
Agnes J. Thomas Ph.D

E-mail Kelli's Kafe

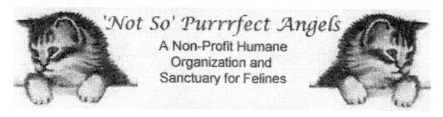

Pet Walk
Ultimate pet directory including pet education, shelters, pet products and professional services.

Many search engines including Google, AltaVista, Hotbot, and Excite use link popularity to help determine ranking of web sites in their search lists. The higher your position in the list, the better chance you have of being visited and making sales. Link popularity is primarily a measure of the number of links to your site from other sites. Link popularity is important because it is a significant factor in a search engine's assessment of where your site should appear in the list.

The "link popularity" of your Web site is a measure of the quantity and quality of links from other sites to your site.

In other words, your web site needs to be "popular" with the search engines and they determine your site's link popularity by the number and quality of links to your site from other sites. Their thinking is that if many other sites provide links to your site, your site must be important and therefore should be ranked higher than sites with lower link popularity. You need to understand, however, that search engine ranking criteria is not totally understood. They don't tell us much and they change their ranking formulas often. Currently, however, link popularity is important and it appears that it will remain that way in the foreseeable future.

Link popularity is important because it is a factor for many search engines in determining ranking in search lists.

Therefore, you should spend time and effort getting other sites to link to your site. The most effective links are usually from other companies in your industry, such as suppliers, customers and trade associations, but exchanging links with almost any other web site could bring more traffic to your site and increase your link popularity. Requests for link exchanges are often sent by e-mail. Responses are usually good because people who understand link exchange realize that it is beneficial to both parties.

It is usually best to create a separate "links" page on your Web site, with perhaps a heading like "Favorite Links" or "People we like to do business with". Shooters Choice, a manufacturer of gun care products, has several pages of links resulting from link exchange agreements. Shown below is a portion of one of their links pages.

ONLINE RESOURCES FOR GUN ENTHUSIASTS

Listed below are just a few of the many interesting and informative gun resources available on the Internet. Please contact us if you know of an organization that would like to be listed on this page.

<u>Ameritype</u> - Our Web site designer.

<u>Handloader Magazine</u> - The ammunition reloading journal, offering article samples online.

<u>JC's Hunting Connection</u> - Classified ads and links to all types of hunting resources.

Links pages can vary considerably in different web sites. Some link pages are only the names of companies while others include a brief description of the company's product or services. Others include logos.

Banner and link exchange services

By doing research via web search engines, you can find many services offering banner and link exchange services. Some people find that these methods increase traffic. Some people think that banner exchange is a bad idea because they don't think that advertising other people's products on your web site is a sound strategy..

Online malls

Some sites owners have joined online malls in an attempt to increase traffic. You can determine whether a mall is for you by doing some research on search engines.

<u>Search Engines</u>

Some people think that search engines contain all of the millions of web sites in the world in their databases. This is a significant misunderstanding. There is general agreement that search engines contain less than 20% of sites on the Web.

The logos of three popular search engines are shown at the right. Their URL's are:
  1. www.yahoo.com
  2. www.google.com
  3. www.altavista.com

Be proactive. Submit your site to all major search engines.

It is vital to submit your URL to all major search engines and indexes. Don't wait for search engines to visit your site and add you to their database. Be proactive. Submit your site. However, no matter how successful you are in getting visitors to your site from search engine listings, it won't help you make sales if the visitors are greeted by an unattractive and content-poor site. <u>It isn't about how much traffic you get to your site. It's about how many sales you make.</u> And those sales are dependent on the design and content of the site. To achieve web site sales success, it is vital to (1) make your site people-friendly and then (2) make your site search engine- friendly.

Making your site people-friendly

Before you concentrate on getting traffic from search engine searches, focus on making your site people-friendly to maximize the potential for sales and profits

You can help make your site people-friendly by avoiding these common, sales killing design errors:

Don't add an animation of a penguin walking across your site no matter how amusing. Visitors might be entertained but that won't be a reason for them to buy your widgets.

- Don't use text and background color combinations that make the page difficult to read. If the text is dark, the background has to be light. If the text is light, the background has to be dark. There must be contrast between the foreground and the background. Don't make your visitors struggle to read dark blue type on a black background or yellow type on a white background. Also don't use multi-colored flowery wallpaper for a background if you want visitors to be able to read the text in the foreground...

- Don't add an owl flying back and forth on the page or any other animation or any graphic or anything that doesn't really need to be on your site. A well-designed site is one that has no superfluous content. Get rid of everything that isn't necessary!

- Don't make spelling and grammar mistakes. Nothing will make your visitors lose confidence in your site and your products faster than misspelled words and grammatical errors on your site. And by the way, it's a site, not a "sight". Nothing turns people away from a "sight" faster than spelling and grammar errors.

- Don't force visitors to listen to music. It takes too long to download and what makes you think they share your taste in music. If you're forcing them to listen to hard rock and they like Andrea Bocelli, CLICK.. your site is history!

- Don't design slow loading pages. Don't impede your pages with graphics that require a lot of memory and therefore will take forever to download. People have little patience and will not wait forever until your site appears on their monitor. CLICK. You're history!

Making your site search-engine-friendly

Making your site search engine-friendly is accomplished by selecting appropriate keyphrases and incorporating them properly in your Web site, as detailed in Chapter 20.

Things to do before you submit your site to the search engines

Each search engine has its own database and you need to get your site entered into the database of all the major search engines and directories. If your site in not in the database of a particular search engine, there is no way your site will come up in a search on that search engine. Here are several things you should check, or at least know about, before you submit your site to the search engines.

Make sure your HTML coding is correct.. Many web pages have HTML mistakes which can create problems with the way your pages appear. You can search for "HTML validation" in a search engine and come up with web sites that will check your HTML code for completeness and accuracy. A good HTML validation service can be found at http://validator.w3.org/.

Avoid trying to trick search engines by typing keyphrases in text the same color as the background, and so forth. Most tricks don't work or they won't work for very long because search engines continually work to detect tricks and to overcome them.

"Flash" is a movie, usually a little movie shown at the beginning of your site download. Although you may think "flash" is cool, it will not help bring visitors to your site. Search engines can't see anything inside flash. Some people think flash will impress their visitors who then will buy their products because they are impressed with the cool movie. Actually, with flash, you will get less visitors. And for those who do visit, do you really think they will buy your widgets because your logo is dancing in the flash movie on your site?

Submitting your site to search engines

Your web site needs to get into the database of every major search engine. Here are three ways to submit your web site to search engines.
1. Do it yourself
2. Use an automated submission service
3. Use Selfpromotion.com

<u>Do it yourself by visiting each search engine</u>
This is done by manually visiting the web site of each search engine. On a search engine's web site, you will find instructions for submitting your site. You need to look for a link that says something like "Add site",

Every search engine has its own database so you need to submit your site to all of the major search engines and directories.

Before you submit your site, make sure the HTML is correct by using a good HTML validation service like the one found at http://validator.w3.org/.

"Add URL", or "Suggest Site". Some of them are difficult to find. If you have eyes like a hawk and a magnifying glass like Sherlock Holmes you should be able to find one of these submission links.

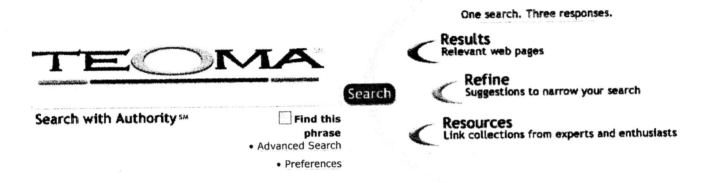

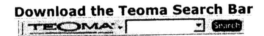

Submit Your Site

Learn How Teoma Works
About Teoma / Press Room / Jobs
Make Teoma Your Homepage

Above is the home page of the Teoma search engine. Underneath the Teoma Search Bar is the "Submit Your Site" link.

Doing it yourself is the least expensive way to submit your site to search engines but it is time consuming. You need to get listed the first time, one search engine at a time, and then you need to keep monitoring the search engines to make sure you haven't been dropped in ranking or dropped altogether.

Most search engines will accept free submissions but many of them will take many weeks, even many months to put your site in their database. The growing trend is that they now will offer fast inclusion for a fee.

Use an automated submission service
For a fee, you can pay an automated submission service to do the submissions for you. There are many submission services to choose from. Listed below are three of these submission services:
- Submit It - www.submitit.com
- Submit Express - www.submitexpress.com
- WorldSubmit - www-worldsubmit.com

Selfpromotion.com is an outstanding resource for submitting Web sites to search engines.

Use Selfpromotion.com to submit to search engines.
Selfpromotion.com (www.selfpromotion.com) is an excellent site for submitting your web site to the search engines. It is a shareware site. You can use the site free but if you feel the site is useful, you pay what you think the submission advice and tools are worth. It is an outstanding submissions site and also offers valuable search engine tutorials and submission tools.

If you want more people to visit your website, you must know how to create search-engine-friendly webpages, and then submit your URL to all the major search engines. That's what this site is all about.

"Tooter," the most sophisticated submission robot on the net, stands ready to assist you in promoting your website! It does all the hard work for you -- for free!

Net!

SelfPromotion.com is the net's leading resource for do-it-yourself Web Promotion. Here you will find all the **information** and **automatic submission tools** you need to do the job **quickly**, **efficiently**, and most of all, **properly**! If you invest a little time into reading and using this resource, you'll not only do a much better job of promoting your site, but save yourself a lot of time and effort in the process.

And best of all, it's **FREE**. If you feel the site is useful, then pay me what **YOU** think the advice and service is worth! And if you ever change your mind for any reason, you get your money back -- no questions asked.

The grey navigation palettes on the right side of each page let you quickly bounce around the site. Start by reading this page, which will introduce you to the basics of site promotion.

Then, when you're ready to start promoting your site, use the Create New Account form (just below this text on the right-hand side) to get started registering your site around the

How to properly promote your site

Site promotion is really not that difficult. It just takes a little bit of effort, a little bit of thought, and a fair amount of patience. It is crucial to understand that site promotion is a long-term, low-

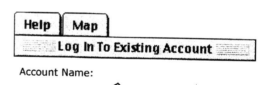

Account Name:

Paying for high rankings

There are also search engines where you can bid and pay for high positions for your keyphrases. Two major ones are Overture (www.overture.com) and Google Adwords Select (www.google.com/ads) You should consider paying for visits to your site. You pay only when someone clicks and visits your site. It's worth investigating to determine if this method of getting hits is for you.

Overture and Google Adwords are two search engines where you can pay for high rankings.

Web site promotion resource

Search engines are constantly evolving. A good resource for keeping up with these important changes is www.searchenginewatch.com, which is the best in-depth online newsletter about search engines.

Chapter 21 Questions for Review and Discussion

1. What is the big advantage of selling on the Web compared to other ways of selling?

2. Why is security fundamental to Web sales?

3. What is the most common way of paying for purchases on the Web?

4. Discuss the necessity of having a written returns policy in place before you start selling.

5. Explain why you should have a privacy policy. Where can you get help to write a privacy policy?

6. Why do you need to promote your site to get traffic? Why are both offline and online promotion necessary?

7. What is *offline* promotion? Describe at least six ways to promote a Web site *offline*. In addition to advertising your e-mail address, what should you include with the e-mail address?

8. Methods of promoting Web sites *online* include link exchange. What is link exchange? Give two reason why link exchange is important?

9. Excluding search engines, name two other *online* methods used to promote Web sites.

10. Describe the importance and functions of search engines.

11. List five things to avoid to help make your site people-friendly.

12. Name two search engines where you can pay to get high rankings for your keywords.

Resources

Graphic Design

Graphic Design Book Club
P.O. Box 9274
Central Islip, NY 11722-9274
Phone: 386-447-6356
www.graphicdesignbookclub.com

An excellent source for books on every graphic design specialty.

Forms Design

Business Forms Management Association
319 SW Washington, Ste. 710
Portland, OR 97204-2618
Phone: 503-274-7667
www.bfma.org
tonya@bfma.org

The primary resource for corporate forms managers, forms analysts, and forms designers. Services include seminars, an annual international forms symposium, a certification program, and publications.

Web Site Design

WebMonkey
www.webmonkey.com

Web Monkey is a portal. It provides news and tutorials and comprehensive links to relevant sites, software, reviews, and publications.

Search Engine Watch
www.searchenginewatch.com

Search Engine Watch is widely regarded as the premier search engine information site. It provides news, research, and ranking tips

INDEX

N

navigation bar, 307
newsletters, 109, 110
NCR paper, 162

O

one-time carbon, 162
orphans, 105

P

photographs, 51
    captions, 56-58
    cropping and scaling, 52
pictogram, 129
preface, 101
presentations, 124
promotions, 143
proportion, 80
publications
    covers, 98
    margins, 10
prelims, 100
    two-page spread, 103
pull quotes, 108

R

recto page, 100
reverses, 204
rules, 117, 202
running head (header), 103

S

serif type, 83
sans serif type, 83
screens, 202
script type, 83
search engines, 329
space ads, 145
stationery, designing, 134

T

tables, 119
    components, 120
tags, 172, 247
text, 87
    alignment, 106
    breaking up dull passages of, 107
thumbnail sketches, 77
title page, 100
type, 27
    anatomy of, 34
    bullets, 39
    leading, 37
    letterspacing and word spacing, 38
    rules, 40
    selecting, 31
    serif and sans serif, 29
    size, 34
typeface, type family, type style, 28
typography, 21, 83

U

unit sets, 162, 169, 236
unity, 82

V

verso page, 101

W

Web-authoring software, 283
    text editors, 283
    HTML editors, 283
    WYSIWYG authoring programs, 284
    word processors, 284
Web site design
    backgrounds, 312, 315
    CSS (cascading style sheets), 318
    clip art, 310
    color, 308
    content, 257, 307
    forms, 313
    flash, 317
    frames, 313
    graphic files (GIF, JPEG, PNG), 310